Critical Criminolog

Editorial Group

John Clarke, Mike Fitzgerald, Victoria Greenwood, Jock Young.

Contributing Editors: Rosa dol Olmo (University of Caracas), Tamar Pitch (University of Perugia), Herman Schwendinger (State University of New York), Annika Snare (University of Oslo), Boaventura de Sousa Santos (University of Coimbra, Portugal), Ian Taylor (University of Sheffield), Anthony Platt (Institute for the Study of Labour and Economic Crisis, San Francisco).

This new series aims to publish work within the radical criminology perspective. It is international in its scope, providing a rallying point for work in this rapidly growing field. The substantive areas covered are the sociology of crime, deviance, social problems, law and sexual deviance. It includes work in ethnography, historical criminology and the practice of social work and law as it relates to radical criminology. The series is two-tiered, publishing both monographs of interest to scholars in the field and more popular books suitable for students and practitioners. One of its aims is to publish the work of radical organisations in the area, particularly that of the National Deviancy Conference, the European Group for the Study of Deviance and Control, the Crime and Social Justice Collective and La Questione Criminale.

Titles in the Critical Criminology series

Vagrancy, Alcoholism and Social Control

Peter Archard

First published 1979 by
THE MACMILLAN PRESS LTD
London and Basingstoke
Associated companies in Delhi Dublin
Hong Kong Johannesburg Lagos Melbourne
New York Singapore and Tokyo

Printed in Great Britain by
Lowe & Brydone Printers Limited
Thetford, Norfolk

British Library Cataloguing in Publication Data

Archard, Peter
  Vagrancy, alcoholism and social control. – (Critical
  criminology).
  1. Alcoholics – Great Britain   2. Homelessness
  – Great Britain   3. Social control
  I. Title   II. Series
  362.2′92   HV5446

  ISBN 0–333–23190–2
  ISBN 0–333–23191–0   Pbk

To everyone who helped in the making of this study, but especially to Andy, Jim and Johnnie for accepting me into the company of their drinking school.

Contents

List of Figures and Tables

Figures

Tables

Acknowledgements

My efforts to complete this research enterprise would not have come to fruition without the help I received from numerous sources and individuals. The staff and Management Committee of the Alcoholics Recovery Project, for whom I worked in a research capacity, provided me with the support that comes from allowing me the freedom to work at my own pace and in the directions I felt to be most productive. In particular I would like to thank Tim Cook, past Director of the Alcoholics Recovery Project, who helped with the supervision of this work. Dougie Warke was of immense assistance in deciphering the views and activities of homeless alcoholics written up in my extensive fieldwork notes, which he diligently read and commented on. Without the financial assistance of the City Parochial Trust this work would, of course, not have even got off the ground.

I derived considerable enthusiasm for the perspective applied to the skid row phenomenon by participating in several meetings of the National Deviancy Conference. The Conference has continuously stressed the need to study the intersection of deviancy and social control, thereby taking the heat off the deviant or criminal as someone atomised and untouched by the 'stage army of the good'.

Noel Parry, Head of the Department of Sociology at North London Polytechnic, encouraged me throughout. His valuable supervision, comments and suggestions helped guide me through all the stages of preparing this work.

In the initial stages of formulating a research proposal David Triesman, past Research Sociologist at the Addiction Research Unit, Institute of Psychiatry, University of London, commented on some of the ideas I explored as potentially fruitful lines of research action. Colin Roberts, also past Research Sociologist at the Addiction

Research Unit, helped me to understand the day-to-day activity of doing participant observation by exchanging experiences with him while he was engaged in fieldwork with drug addicts.

Liz Chappell lived with this study as long as she has known me. Living with alcoholics on skid row meant spending many irregular hours away from home. I often returned home tired, dirty and somewhat drunk. At every stage, but particularly during fieldwork, Liz helped me to attain my objectives by organising my time and giving me the necessary emotional support.

Sylvia Ghosh, Pat Hawks and Gwen Ambrose typed my copious field notes. Derek and Judy Beard, together with the secretarial staff of the Department of Sociology, North East London Polytechnic, were involved in typing preliminary and final drafts. To see one's material set out neatly in type I found gave me particular joy. I am indebted for their prompt and accurate work.

Finally, and most of all, I wish to thank all those individuals on skid row with whom I came into contact during my research investigations. Their assistance in providing the data on which my findings are based cannot be measured.

April 1978   PETER ARCHARD

Introduction

Over seven years have passed since I first embarked on this study. At the outset it was envisaged that I should undertake a piece of research that would look only at the life style of homeless alcoholics. In the event the terms of reference were considerably widened to include society's reaction to the skid row man. The decision to broaden the scope of this work was based on the premise that without looking at how society seeks to contain or change skid row and its inhabitants our understanding of homeless alcoholics would be severely limited.

From a sociological perspective the study of the British skid row scene as a social phenomenon has for the most part remained unexplored. Most accounts of down-and-outs have remained at a purely journalistic level. In addition several demographic surveys, usually conducted by either government departments or the medical profession, have offered us statistical profiles of skid row inmates resident in one or other of the institutions homeless men use.

In this study an attempt is made to go beyond traditional approaches to understanding one section of the s•id row population – namely the skid row alcoholic. The reader will soon appreciate that any notion of the derelict alcoholic as someone suffering from some kind of individual or social pathology is absent from these pages. The spotlight has been taken off the alcoholic as if he stood in isolation from society's endeavours to bring him into line. Instead, attention is focused on the social relationships that have unfolded among alcoholics and between alcoholics and their guardians.

Firstly, then, the analysis extends beyond any one single typical skid row institution, such as a common lodging house or reception centre. The homeless derelict inebriate leads a nomadic life within our urban centres; he is continuously on the move, stopping only temporarily in institutions located on a closed circuit which he rarely moves out of. His definition of these institutions and life in them informs our understanding of how he confronts his homelessness, poverty and alcoholism.

Secondly, this report incorporates a new dimension in the sociological analysis of skid row. It pays as much attention to society's reaction to the problem of homelessness and alcoholism as it does to the problem itself. Insofar as society's response is examined, three levels of that response are spelled out: the interpersonal, in which professionals comment on their work with homeless men; the institutional, in which the basic ideologies and objectives of skid row establishments are articulated; and the political, in which contemporary social policy is outlined.

Chapter 1 describes the skid row institutional complex in terms of three dominant strategies devised to control the derelict alcoholic: moral reform, penal correction and socio-medical rehabilitation.

Chapter 2 brings into focus some prevalent views of skid row alcoholics as perceived by research experts, by personnel handling homeless men and by alcoholics themselves.

The strategies homeless men have developed to survive the strictures of poverty, homelessness and alcohol dependence are spelled out in detail in Chapters 3 and 4. In both these chapters the starting point for the analysis are accounts of life on skid row as told by alcoholics.

In Chapter 5 the interaction of habitual drunken offenders and law-enforcement agencies is explored at length. How the skid row drunk, on the one hand, and police officers, magistrates, and prison personnel, on the other, view their respective roles and the situation that bring them together forms the basis of this chapter.

Chapter 6 also counterposes two points of view: in this instance that of alcoholics and social workers in the context of a particular rehabilitation structure. As examples of interaction in two rehabilitation settings, a street-level contact facility and a rehabilitation hostel are defined by alcoholics and social workers.

Chapter 7 widens this account of skid row alcoholism and social control by locating the previous chapters within an analysis of the general direction social policy is pursuing as a result of the contemporary redefinition of the problem.

Chapter 8 provides an explanatory sociological framework; the notions of subculture, deviant identity and social control are used as three interlocking concepts serving to bring together the material presented in the preceding chapters.

Finally, Chapter 9 gives a critical account of the perspective and method used to research the skid row phenomenon. Too often the substantive product of research work is published without the author making explicit what theoretical perspective guided his investigations. Neither are the research techniques explained in any detail. Bringing a fresh research approach to the problem of vagrancy and alcoholism resulted in many enquiries from students, practitioners, research workers and criminologists as to how I conducted my investigations. Methodological and theoretical issues are often anathema to the British empiricist mind; but in trying to answer queries as to the method, theoretical issues are impossible to avoid. This in turn led me to ask why I had chosen a specific perspective in deviancy theory and, by way of a postscript, why and how that perspective itself came under attack, thus posing problems as to the adequacy of my sociological account of skid row alcoholism.

1
Skid Row in Great Britain

Society's response to the homeless alcoholic

The specific concepts by which social problems are identified are not
value-free terms. Instead they are anchored in and reflect particular
ways of thinking and acting towards social problems. Matza[1] clearly
demonstrated the significance for our understanding of social problems when he analysed the shifts in our conceptual understanding of
disreputable poverty. He pointed out that, historically, the same
objective fact of disreputable poverty has been identified by a
succession of concepts that serve to pinpoint the moral and social
dimensions of the phenomenon. Insofar as skid row is a highly visible
sector of disreputable poverty,[2] it is significant that those persons
who make use of the institutions on skid row have also been
successively identified by a variety of concepts. Terms such as
vagrants and tramps, the residuum, down-and-outs and single
homeless persons all have been or are still used to identify a specific
type of poverty; and the focus on a particular sector of single
homeless persons distinguished by repeated public drunkenness,
arrest and imprisonment is sharpened when labels such as public
inebriate, habitual drunken offender, and skid row or homeless
alcoholic are involved. All these terms, in some sense, reflect the
interests of groups concerned either with the punishment, treatment
or rehabilitation of these men. Moreover they serve as a useful point
of departure by which an analysis of the ideas and institutions serving
skid row men may be offered.

What is skid row?

Skid row is a generic American term[3] used in three distinct but
interrelated ways. Firstly, the term refers to a geographical area

located in the centre of large cities and towns where certain institutions serving single men are concentrated. Secondly, skid row is identified by the social and economic characteristics of the men who use the institutions. Thirdly, it is held to represent a particular culture – that is, a style of life which clearly separates men from the mainstream of activities and responsibilities associated with the family, work, politics and leisure. Clearly, if the geographical concentration of skid row is used as the only basis for defining the phenomenon, then American researchers have some justification for claiming that the problem is exclusive to the United States. Thus, Wallace introduces his study by stating:

> Skid Row is a phenomenon peculiar to the United States. It is that run-down area in almost every American city where the homeless men can and do live. It is that collection of saloons, pawn shops, cheap restaurants, second-hand shops, barber colleges, all-night movies, missions, flop-houses, and dilapidated hotels which cater specifically to the needs of the down-and-outer, the bum, the alcoholic, the drifter.[4]

But by emphasising the geographical concentration of the institutions *on* skid row Wallace has not only claimed, incorrectly, that the phenomenon is unique to his own country but has failed to include in his list institutions that are physically removed from skid row areas but are frequently used by the derelict alcoholic, namely prisons and mental hospital alcoholism units.

The institutions, the men and the life style, as this study demonstrates, do exist in most of Britain's larger towns and cities although certainly not as extensively as across the Atlantic. The major difference is that in Britain skid row is not ecologically concentrated – the institutions associated with the culture are spread intermittently or are located in small pockets within working class and commercial districts. Thus, in referring to London, Edwards *et al.* are able to write:

> Certain localities are . . . frequented by broken-down inebriates. The areas by the Elephant and Castle and Waterloo in South London remain among the chief haunts of these men, while in the East End, the Stepney and Aldgate districts have their 'Skid Row'. Filthy and dishevelled, with faces often blackened by the smoke of

the fires which are lit in derelict houses or on bombed sites, the Skid Row alcoholic is not difficult to recognise.[5]

Matza[6] has correctly pointed out that there is not necessarily an exact relationship between the ecological concentration and the cultural manifestation of a social problem. He argues that although ecological segregation facilitates the development of a peculiar world, it does not constitute a necessary prerequisite for that development. Thus, although the institutions of skid row in Britain are relatively dispersed geographically speaking, they are nevertheless connected for their inhabitants by a continuous psychological and sociological territory. Police cells, courts and prisons, common lodging houses and government reception centres, soup kitchens and missions, mental hospitals and rehabilitation hostels, pubs and cheap cafés, parks and open spaces, derelict buildings and commuter railway stations make up the institutions and facilities that skid row men rarely leave. As one man in a rehabilitation hostel put it to a skid row director: 'The point is not to pull the man out of skid row; it's to get skid row out of the man.'

Similarly, in Allsop's *Hard Travellin'*, an American skid row wino recounts:

> You say 'Let's go to Tucson, Arizona, let's go to New York to look at the World Fair, let's go up to Seattle' – but you take your troubles with you from state to state. It's a life of a thousand jails and a thousand flophouses. All the time you got your own skid row right there inside your head.[7]

Both these quotations reflect the psychological and sociological ties men have to skid row rather than identifying it as a physical locale. The institutions in Britain that single homeless men use may thus appropriately be labelled skid row, since it is the common 'phenomenological' world they inhabit which justifies use of the term on this side of the Atlantic. Moreover the historical roots of vagrancy in the United States and the institutions that arose to meet the problem can be directly linked to the way vagrancy was reacted to in England during earlier centuries. Wallace comments:

> In passing it might also be noted that the focus upon skid row as a way of life links today's skid rower with his ancestors and thus

bridges a common hiatus. Before there was a skid row – a distinct
ecological area for homeless men in the city – there were hoboes,
vagrants, paupers and vagabonds. While there have been differences between the various historical populations of homeless
persons, basic features common to a way of life have remained.
Vagabonds, rogues and sturdy beggars of Sixteenth Century
England included women, children, entertainers, and university
students – persons not usually found among today's skid rowers.
Yet the institutional complex – the 'low' lodging houses, the
itinerant labourers, the relief and welfare systems, and the law –
existed then as now.[8]

Alcoholism on skid row

A popular image held of skid row is that it is exclusively populated by
down-and-out alcoholics. Furthermore it is sometimes asserted that
alcoholism as it manifests itself on skid row represents the total
alcoholism problem in the community.[9] However, surveys of skid
row and its institutions, both in the United States and in Britain, have
consistently revealed that the composition of the skid row population
includes teetotallers, moderate and heavy drinkers and chronic
alcoholics. Depending on the institutions sampled and the definitions
of alcoholism used by investigators, the proportion of alcoholics to
the total skid row population varies between 25 per cent and 45 per
cent. Moreover it is estimated that only a very small proportion –
somewhere in the region of 5 per cent – of our total alcoholic
population live on skid row.[10]

Alcoholics on skid row are part of a wider single homeless
population, which includes the vagrant, the casual labourer and the
itinerant navvy, the mentally ill, the physically disabled and the old-
age pensioner with no family ties. Typically the individual with a
drink problem is middle-aged, has never married or his marriage
broke down, has lost contact with all relatives, is occupationally
unskilled, and has spent some time in the merchant navy, armed
forces, or in heavy labouring and construction.[11] Britain's skid row
alcoholics are predominantly Scots or Irish. The public labels them
meths drinkers, law-enforcement officials view them as offenders, the
medical profession defines them as suffering from a disease, mission
personnel understand them as being spiritually and morally weak,

and social workers speak of them as social inadequates. When skid row alcoholics are not in one of the institutions that aim to control or change their behaviour, they are to be found in parks and open spaces, sharing a bottle of cider, cheap wine or crude spirits.

As with conceptions of disreputable poverty, terms such as alcoholic and drunkard carry with them social and moral imputations, which have consequences for the way problem drinking is controlled. Among sections of the disreputable poor repeated alcohol intoxication has been identified by shifting conceptions: during the latter part of the Victorian era problems of drinking and drunkenness among the undeserving poor were referred to as the Drink Question and habitual public drunkards became the target of moral and legislative control; today 'habitual drunken offender' and 'homeless' or 'skid row alcoholic'[12] function as tags by which professionals working with men who are repeatedly drunk in public are able to identify them. Often these terms are used interchangeably, although each is grounded in the ideological and professional predilections of specific agencies that come into regular contact with heavy drinkers on the row. The emergence of different terms by which problems of drunkenness and alcoholism are conceptualised would require a careful analysis of historical and cultural forces. As one social historian explained:

The Victorians often failed to distinguish between alcoholism, drinking and drunkenness. Temperance reformers argued that drinking inevitably led to drunkenness, and society at large failed to distinguish between drunkenness and alcoholism. The word drunkenness – 'the state of being drunk' – has been regularly used by Englishmen at least since A.D. 893, whereas the word alcoholism – 'the diseased condition produced by alcohol' – appeared only about 1860. Thomas Trotter in his *Essay on Drunkenness*, published in 1894, was amongst the earliest to describe habitual drunkenness as a disease: but he was unable to describe the condition in terms which were free from moral overtones.[13]

As the ensuing analysis will demonstrate, definitions of alcohol dependence tend to be dominated by the disease conception of alcoholism and are the product of medical theory and practical work with alcohol abusers. On the other hand, the label 'habitual drunken offenders' not only reflects the legal dimension of the problem but also underscores a Victorian concern with the control of widespread working-class drunkenness.

Ideologies and institutions of control on skid row

The labelling of certain forms of behaviour as deviant – and the consequent organisation of control by which society attempts to bring deviants 'into line' – has led to a bias in what we focus our attention on when we attempt to comprehend the nature of social problems. In particular the development of most criminology reflects an overriding concern with the individual deviant rather than the nature of deviancy. The institutions that both control and perpetuate social problems rarely come under the criminologist's spy-glass.

The study of skid row has been no exception to this general trend. It has been the single homeless man who has been the object of surveys, questionnaires and psychological tests. Little, if any, attention has been paid to the relationship and structure of the formal control institutions that make up skid row. The formal institutions of control on skid row are made up of any organisation or agency which, in some way or other, is directly committed to intervening in the life of individuals officially designated as criminal or deviant. In analysing those social control agencies which direct their energies at skid row men it is important to understand their ideological foundations, that is, the manner in which they conceptualise and act toward the problem. Once this analysis is achieved, the nature of the relationship between different control ideologies, and between control agents and deviants, may be explored. The importance of stressing this dimension – the relationship between skid row alcoholics and their guardians – will become apparent throughout this report. My claim is that no proper sociological understanding of skid row is possible without redressing the bias alluded to above by providing the scope and balance inherent in a simultaneous analysis of both deviants and control agents.

The contempory structure of skid row in Britain consists of an amalgamation of traditional and modern institutions underpinned by different sets of ideas and practices as to how best habitual public drunkards may be reformed, punished, cured or treated. At present the matrix of social control on skid row is composed, on the one hand, of institutions whose foundations are anchored in Victorian legislation and moral reform movements and, on the other, of agencies that lay emphasis on contemporary medical and social, rather than legal and moral, dimensions of habitual public drunkenness. Thus salvation, punishment, treatment and rehabilitation are the four strategies by which professionals attempt to bring about the alcoholic's re-entry into the community.

The argument presented in the ensuing analysis not only serves to define the complex response to derelict inebriates at an institutional level but also identifies which aspects of the skid row man are selected for consideration and modification when professionals attempt to achieve personal change in him. Furthermore an analysis of changes in strategies of control demonstrates how the emergence of a socio-medical approach to the problem is tending to replace concepts of moral reform and legal control. But, as will become apparent, the fact that social work and medical strategies are advocated as *replacing* moral and legal control methods remains an academic issue. This means that at present the institutional structure on skid row offers *simultaneously* moral, legal, medical and social approaches to pulling men out of the skid row treadmill. The theme of this chapter, then, is concerned with shifts in the conceptual frameworks by which skid row drinking is comprehended by personnel manning the institutions servicing single homeless men. In stressing changes in social control methods the outlines of skid row as a complex of institutions is made apparent. Against this background a closer look at how alcoholics survive on skid row and how professionals and alcoholics carve out lines of action in the light of each other's attitudes and values will be spelled out.

Spiritual rejuvenation and the skid row inebriate

Victorian philanthropy and moral reform, particularly during the latter half of the nineteenth century, linked problems of poverty with those of moral character much more closely than do most contemporary theorists and practitioners. Habitual drunkards, as one concrete expression of poverty, became a major target for reform among temperance groups and charitable institutions, particularly the Salvation Army. The emergence of the 'dangerous classes' in Victorian Britain elicited a reaction, whose impact is still reflected in some approaches to skid row today. Currently, as in the past, the existence of the common-lodging-house poor is understood and explained by the Salvation Army by invoking a philosophy of reform that focuses attention on the individual's moral and spiritual weakness.

Historically the Salvation Army viewed the casual poor through notions of pauperism and demoralisation. The public inebriate, insofar as he constantly engaged in excessive drinking, was seen to do so because he was essentially 'demoralised'. That he was unemployed could only be because work held no interest for him. He concentrated in the most squalid parts of urban centres because he was attracted by the prospect of hand-outs. The central thread in the argument of the Salvation Army was that pauperism and its accompanying vices were the product of character rather than economic forces. Notions of spiritual weakness prevailed to explain the existence of habitual drunks. As Stedman Jones pointed out in his extensive study of London's late-Victorian casual poor, the general view of the problem stemmed from a moral perspective:

Pitted against the dominant climate of moral and material improvement . . . was a minority of the still unregenerate poor . . . variously referred to as 'the dangerous class', the casual poor or most characteristically, as 'the residuum' . . . In the explanation of the existence of the residuum the subjective psychological defects of individuals bulked even larger than before . . . The problem was not structural but moral. The evil to be combated was not poverty but pauperism: pauperism with its attendant vices, drunkenness, improvidence, mendicancy, bad language, filthy habits, gambling, low amusements, and ignorance.[14]

General Booth, founder of the Salvation Army, viewed the consumption of excessive alcohol as the fundamental issue affecting the moral weakness permeating major sections of the British working class. He stated:

Darkest England may be described as consisting of three circles, one within the other. The outer and widest circle is inhabited by the starving and homeless, but honest poor. The second by those who live by vice; and the third and innermost region at the centre is peopled by those who exist by crime. The whole of these three circles is sodden by drink.[15]

In its plan to rescue individuals from the squalor of disreputable poverty the Army established a network of common lodging houses designed to offer 'the homeless poor, destitute wayfarers and incorrigible rogues' a roof to sleep under, basic material sustenance and, above all, an opportunity to renounce intemperance and replace it with a commitment to moral and spiritual rejuvenation. In its origins, then, the Salvation Army was founded as a means of spiritual salvation for the 'dangerous classes', and was based on the premise that problems of poverty are created by men ignoring the Word of God and His Son Jesus Christ. Booth, in his master plan, proposed that 'the submerged tenth' be rescued by being received into city colonies where the 'ship-wrecked' would be inspired 'with hope for the future, and commence at once a course of regeneration by moral and religious influences',[16] eventually moving to farm colonies where, in addition to moral teaching, they would receive instruction in agriculture.

Today Salvation Army men's social service centres, housing several hundred men, remain as a symbol of Booth's city colonies. As an example of one among a variety of different types of common lodging houses, Salvation Army centres are now viewed as an integral part of skid row, and not as a solution to the problem. Their physical size is held to be unsuitable for the application of contemporary approaches to skid row alcoholism as defined by socio-medical practitioners; the physical and social conditions prevailing in the centres, it is claimed, are antithetical to modern recovery techniques for handicapped (alcoholic) men. But the common lodging house as an institution, whether established as a solution to moral weakness or to pressures of Victorian housing and the casual-labour problem, remains an important and central feature of today's skid row. Its impact is such that its continued existence forces medicine and social work to include the Salvation Army within its own framework (see pp. 15–16).

Penal correction and the habitual drunken offender

For alcoholics on skid row, law-enforcement agencies have a particular character and significance by virtue of the central role they play in the men's lives. The sequence of repeated arrest, trial and imprisonment has been aptly labelled 'the revolving door'; and the metaphor is appropriate, since it pinpoints one crucial institutional circuit by which skid row alcoholics may be controlled. The police cell, magistrate's court, and local prison make up the judicial response to habitual public drunkenness. Punishment and deterrence are the official assumptions which underscore the penal model of social control but, as I demonstrate in Chapter 5, quite different rationalisations are currently articulated to justify the legal processing of public drunkards.

It should be stressed that the current legal basis for punishing the chronic drunken offender was also established during the latter half of the last century, at the same time as the Salvation Army was propagating its programme of reform. This is not to imply that the Army was influential in supporting a legal programme of control; as indicated above the essential thrust of Booth and his followers lay in their ability to develop strategies of moral suasion. But both legislation, whether penal or social, and moral reformism were a simultaneous response to the same prevailing conditions affecting the casual and disreputable poor. Moreover the relationship between licencing laws and the control of public drunkenness was much closer then than now, probably because of the dramatic reduction in public drunkenness since the time when the Drink Question held a central place in philanthropic and legislative control.

Public drunkenness first became a criminal offence under an Act of 1606 when the penalty was a fine of five shillings or six hours in the stocks. However, the first time the concept of habitual public drunkenness became incorporated in a legal statute was in the Habitual Drunkards Act, 1879. This Act followed a number of reports, commissions and official enactments in response to the temperance movement generally failing to achieve its aims through education and moral suasion and thus turning to statutory channels in order to resolve the problem of drunkenness. It is the Licencing Act, 1872, which marks the turning point in Victorian society's concern with the drink question insofar as it transferred responsibility for the problem from the moral and educational influence of temperance societies to the legal influence of the State. In fact the 1872 Act is currently invoked to regulate public drunkenness; the Act allows for the fining of the offender or, in the absence of means by which to pay the fine, a term of imprisonment not exceeding

30 days. But, as Harrison points out in his *Drink and the Victorians*: 'Punishment for drunkenness probably did little to reduce drunkenness: the police at this time aimed at rather preventing the drunkard from harming himself or the public – not at reforming him.'[17]

That Harrison is correct in pointing to the failure of the law as a deterrent is made evident by the introduction, only seven years later, of the Habitual Drunkards Act. The basis of this Act, and of subsequent legislation in 1898, was to offer treatment rather than punishment to habitual drunkards. The first Act made provision for the establishment of retreats at which the offender could attend voluntarily, but in 1898 compulsory detention in reformatories was introduced. Two types of inebriate reformatories were authorised: firstly, state institutions provided by central government and, secondly, those provided either by local authorities or in co-operation with philanthropic societies.[18]

The impact made by the establishment of special homes and reformatories for inebriates was minimal. The ethos permeating the reformatories consisted of moral persuasion, firstly under voluntary and eventually under compulsory detention. They were mostly organised and run by religious and quasi-religious charities, but by 1921 the authorities were forced to the conclusion that treatment was proving ineffective under compulsion.[19] In addition the reformatories were generally under-used, the courts had little faith in them, and the sheer number of offenders far exceeded their capacity. The reformatories were therefore closed and the provisions of the Acts were allowed to continue in disuse. In the absence of alternatives fines and imprisonment, once again, assumed the dominant strategy of control. The relevant sections of the 1872 Licencing Act continue to function today as a basis for repeatedly processing habitual drunken offenders through the revolving door consisting of street drinking, police cell, magistrate's court, prison, and back to street drinking.

Treatment and rehabilitation: the socio-medical model

When agents of social control speak of the skid row man in terms of the concept of alcoholism, they refer to relatively new developments in their social control. The concept enables them to comprehend the problem in the light of the medically and socially identifiable consequences of excessive alcohol consumption. Both moral and legal models, it was noted, do not distinguish between drunkenness and alcoholism. Instead they take the act of public drunkenness, whether it be a single or repeated experience, as the basis for judging the moral worth or the legal rights of the individual, and intervening in his behaviour. Insofar as there is an ideological shift demarcating moral and legal from social and medical judgements, the proponents of the alcoholism conception concentrate at one end of the spectrum, namely the state of addiction[20], and do not so much pass judgement on the consumption of drink or on drunkenness *per se*.

The emergence of a view that skid row is a place containing alcoholics who ought to be the target of medical and social-work expertise is reflected in the belief that therapy and rehabilitation are relevant and integrated strategies by which individuals may be rescued from there. These strategies are premised on two notions: that alcoholism, as opposed to occasional or even persistent drunkenness, is a disease, and that skid row alcoholism is a particular variant of the disease, compounded by social disaffiliation from the normal institutions of urban societies. Thus two interlocked problem areas present themselves for consideration by psychiatrists and social-work agents when working with skid row alcoholics: physical and psychological recuperation on the one hand and attainment of social stability on the other.

The contemporary collaboration of medicine (psychiatry) and social work, in which professionals from both disciplines co-operate to achieve the recuperation of skid row alcoholics, has its genesis in separate historical traditions. Firstly, the concept of alcoholism as a disease was formulated by the medical profession. The intellectual origins of the concept are exclusively grounded in notions of biochemical and psychological dependence on a psychotropic drug, and are explained in terms that refer primarily to imbalances in the personality structure of the individual. Secondly, the concept of alcoholism as social inadequacy is propounded by social workers, and can be traced back to philanthropists working with the poor through programmes of charity, poor relief and housing. But, whereas Victorian philanthropy was to a degree concerned with both the reform of society and the rescue of afflicted individuals, the contemporary social worker is singularly taken up with the task of caseworking the client while relegating to a peripheral sphere of interest the abolition of skid row as a whole. Both medicine and social work take as their focus the reform of afflicted individuals.

Where psychiatry and social casework intersect is in their common interest in, and application of, counselling techniques based on the secular assumptions and values of what Halmos termed 'the new philanthropic expertise of helping through-caring-listening-prompting'.[21] The element distinguishing psychiatry from social work, where homeless alcoholics are concerned, is more a matter of emphasis than of principle. Whereas psychiatry views the skid row alcoholic as primarily psychologically and physically addicted and therefore in need of treatment, the caseworker regards him as undersocialised and therefore in need of resocialisation.

The co-ordination of these two professional approaches in the field of alcoholism and homelessness is promoted in the policy recommendations of a recent Home Office Working Party[22] report, where a comprehensive socio-medical model is proposed as an alternative to the current penal model. In the new model medical detoxification and social rehabilitation are institutionalised in a treatment system, which includes (i) contact with the alcoholic at street level, for example through shop-fronts, crypts, shelters, and hand-out centres, (ii) detoxification centres and alcoholism units where individuals would be 'dried-out' and offered therapy and (iii) community-based hostels or half-way houses where social rehabilitation and re-socialisation would be achieved before the final 're-entry into the community'.[23]

The proposed structure of this comprehensive treatment system is cemented by an interlocking of medical and social-work conceptions, since the alcoholic on the row is simultaneously diseased and socially disaffiliated. The advocates of treatment suggest that it is fundamentally necessary for psychiatry and social work not to operate in isolation from each other if they are to fulfil their aims. Thus, in practice, while detoxification is viewed as requiring medical expertise, detoxification centres are also advocated as places where psychiatric and community-based social workers begin to work with the patient-client. Successful referral to community-based hostels is grounded in the assumption that psychiatric and social-work counsellors will make adequate assessment reports. Furthermore half-way houses, insofar as they engage in group therapy, encourage the professional collaboration of psychiatric and medical personnel.

Implementing the socio-medical model: the revolving door extended

Thus far the analysis has focused on skid row as a set of unconnected conceptual and institutional responses to habitual public drunkenness. Moral, penal and socio-medical concepts have been sketched out and the institutions representing each of the models have been specified. Figure 1 represents graphically the control matrix currently operating in response to problems of alcoholism on skid row.

Dominant ideological base	Dominant view of skid row alcoholic	Main strategy of recovery	Institutional base
Moral	Spiritually weak	Salvation	Missions
Penal	An offender	Correction	Police cells, courts, prisons
Medical	Diseased	Treatment	Alcoholism units (detoxification centres)
Social	Socially inadequate	Rehabilitation	Shop-fronts, crypts, half-way houses

Note The dotted line separating the medical and social conceptions of skid row alcoholism signifies the interdependence of these two approaches to the problem

FIGURE 1   *Skid row social control matrix*

But what is the relation between these different responses to skid row alcoholism? Inasmuch as there is a tendency for one strategy to replace another, I have hinted that socio-medical treatment is regarded by its proponents as an alternative to the processing of public drunks by law-enforcement agencies. However, the police, courts and prison, together with the common lodging house and mission, continue to perpetuate a response in which the criminal and moral character of the deviant are the focus of interest. These institutions are being supplemented by medically supervised alcoholism units and detoxification centres, and social work based street level services and rehabilitation hostels. In essence, then, the complexity of this punishment and treatment matrix is the product of conceptual and practical confusion about whether the habitual public drunk should be defined as spiritually weak, criminally deviant, mentally sick or socially inadequate. The emergence of a more complex and extensive social-control matrix – and the confusion inherent in it – is succinctly summarised in the Home Office Report: 'Whether one takes the view that habitual drunken offenders represent a penal, social, or medical problem or, as we believe, a combination of all these, the fact that the problem exists as an overt one requires some response from the community.'[24]

In spite of this complexity, it is the emergent conceptions of therapy and social rehabilitation, advanced by advocates of the socio-medical model of control, which seem to be taking over as the dominant ideological and practical response to the problem. The concern expressed by the Home Office Report underpins a set of policy recommendations that defuse the moral and penal character of the traditional responses to the homeless alcoholic. The onus of responsibility for containing the problem is seen to fall on agencies representing the socio-medical approach. In practical terms the strategy is to replace or modify those institutions associated with a penal or moral response to habitual drunkenness in such a way that the police, courts, prisons and common lodging houses are redefined in terms of a treatment and rehabilitation model.

Firstly, there is an attempt to modify institutions anchored in a moral view of the habitual drunk, that is, those agencies whose fundamental *raison d'être* is based on principles of Christian charity and quasi-religious reform. Since the vestiges of a Victorian attitude to the drink question remain as part of the common response to skid row, the work done with single homeless persons by the Salvation Army, the Church Army, missions and Christian Charitable organisations is included within the framework of a socio-medical model by redefining their function. This is done by propelling the emergent strategies of treatment and rehabilitation to their logical limits, encompassing the traditional institutions of skid row within the scope of a socio-medical strategy. 'Hand-out' agencies, and facilities such as crypts, shelters and lodging-houses are redefined as 'a very necessary element in the overall treatment system, primarily as milieux in which the potential client can be reached and an attempt to motivate him to receive treatment in more therapeutically-orientated facilities'.[25]

Both the emergence of modern social-work methods to tackle problems previously dealt with by traditional philanthropy and the introduction of medicine as a solution to problems of alcohol abuse have served to influence the current *modus operandi* of organisations based on a moral view of drunkenness. Increasingly missions and Christian charities combine their missionary work with definitions of habitual drunkenness that seek answers in professional social work and psychiatry. The human 'sciences' are invoked to fortify their moral standpoint and Christian-based skid row projects employ social workers, doctors and psychiatrists.

Secondly, the movement to redefine the skid row alcoholic as a socio-medical case attempts, in addition to modifying the moral concept, to decriminalise his status. The criminal identity assigned to habitual drunken offenders on skid row by virtue of their perennial visits to penal establishments is held to be incompatible with a socio-medical status. With the tentative acceptance of alcoholism as a disease grew an awareness of the fundamental logical weakness of processing skid-row alcoholics through police cells, courts and prisons. The contradiction inherent in controlling habitual public drunkenness through law-enforcement procedures for what came to be defined as an illness compounded by social disaffiliation has led to redefining the status of the public drunk in the eyes of the criminal law. For instance, in 1967 the Criminal Justices Act legislated in favour of the lower courts referring alcoholics to community-based hostels rather than having them punished for public drunkenness. Five years later the Criminal Justices Act, 1972, made provision for the police to take public drunks to detoxification centres.

However, the impetus to decriminalise the alcoholic on skid row has not, in practice, succeeded in removing him from the institutional reality of police cells, courts and prison. Legislation has changed the status of the public intoxicant in theory only, since detoxification facilities have not yet been implemented and the courts make little use of the limited number of rehabilitation hostels. The attempt to shift responsibility for the skid row alcoholic from an overtly punitive to an overtly therapeutic response remains therefore an ideological, as opposed to a practical, issue. Consequently penal institutions are also redefined by the Home Office Report in the function they play; their traditional concern with punishment has had grafted on to it the ideas of medicine and social work. For example, when detoxification centres are eventually established, the police will retain a vital role in ensuring that the intoxicant enters the initial stage of drying out by taking him or her to the centre. The police are invoked to think of their role in the treatment process as positive and constructive. If drying-out centres are not available and penal establishments continue to process habitual drunks, then courts are urged to make greater use of their powers to remand individuals for social and medical investigation, and prisons are recommended to increase their awareness of the problems of alcoholism through medical and welfare services.[26]

In his essay Matza implied that new conceptions of disreputable poverty tend to arise when there is a perceived failure to eradicate the problem with methods deemed as ineffective. In addition he indicated that the major purpose of word-substitution in identifying a problem is to reduce and remove the stigma, but since stigma inheres mostly in the referent and not the concept, the effort is fruitless.[27]

Conceptions of drunkenness among skid row men are currently identified by four distinct models of control: moral, penal, medical, and social. Medicine and social work, in combination, are tending to assume dominance, theoretically and in the formulation of policy, over moral and penal approaches. The original legitimacy of those institutions representing the moral and legal control of habitual drunks is being questioned. But, in reality, due to administrative and political reasons (see Chapter 7, p. 151), strategic innovations in the control of skid row alcoholism are currently being added to enduring historical control methods in the shape of those institutions whose strategies are rooted in Victorian philosophies of quasi-religious reform or punishment.

Medicine and social work, then, are expanding and reshaping the world of skid row. Novel strategies of control have been added to those historically associated with problems of drunkenness and destitution. The missions and penal establishments are being supplemented by mental hospitals, detoxification centres and community-based rehabilitation hostels. In essence the rhetoric of modern psychiatry and professional social work assumes the dominant rationale by which society attempts to control both the institutions of skid row and skid row alcoholism. This means that the institutional revolving door for the alcoholic is widening insofar as it permits the individual to be at different times a prison inmate, hospital patient, social-work client, and potential convert to a virtuous Christian life. But at all times he remains a skid row person, since the one irrefutable fact about the homeless alcoholic in relation to all forms of social control is the apparent inability of himself and his guardians to achieve the ultimate goal – 'getting him back into respectable society'.

2
Perspectives on Skid Row

Researchers and participants define the alcoholic and his situation

Sociological accounts of habitual public drunkenness among single homeless men are virtually unknown in Britain, in spite of the persistence of the problem since at least the beginning of the eighteenth century.[1] The proliferation of recent criminological and deviancy research has for the most part by-passed issues surrounding vagrancy and homeless single persons; in particular the combined problem of alcoholism and homelessness has not been the target of sociological enquiry. This absence of research stands in sharp contrast to the extensive sociological and socio-psychological literature on skid row and skid row alcoholism emanating from the United States. We know little about similar problems in this country, particularly in terms of a perspective that focuses on the relationship between the down-and-out alcoholic and those institutions – and their representatives – which in one way or another seek to control the problem.

The limited information that does exist consists almost exclusively of survey material – surveys focusing on the social, medical and psychiatric characteristics of individuals who inhabited specific skid row institutions at the time the surveys were made. We have no description and understanding of the phenomenon as defined by homeless alcoholics themselves; neither have we a sociological analysis of the matrix of social control agencies that in one way or another seek to reform, punish, treat or rehabilitate skid row alcoholics.[2] The phenomenon of skid row alcoholism is, in fact, made up of more than just those men who perennially move through the institutions of the row. We need to understand the character of those institutions, the framework within which they operate, and the reaction of skid row alcoholics to them.

This study, then, is about the relation that exists between skid row alcoholic men and agents of social control, in particular the meanings each attribute to the other and the strategies by which alcoholics and professionals organise their activities. Insofar as the study examines both the deviants' attitudes and behaviour, and society's reaction to them, it adds balance and scope to a subject of enquiry that has been marred by a bias that all too often regards the deviant as the sole object of study. Society's reaction to habitual public drunkenness needs to be examined if the social reality of the penal revolving door and treatment circuit is to be grasped. Juxtaposing within a single framework accounts of social reality as experienced by alcoholics and those professionally concerned with the problem not only provides us with an insight into the quality of their relationships, but illustrates how alcoholic and professionals define, sometimes in opposition to each other, the common ground within which they both operate.

Some skid row literature reviewed

Why alcoholics use skid row

Explanations as to why skid row exists and why men make use of the institutions of the row are prolific, and depend to a great extent on the professional framework with which pundits and experts conceptualise the problem. Numerous enquiries into the aetiology of homelessness and alcohol addiction among skid row habituees seek clues to the question of why men gravitate to and take up permanent residence on skid row in their personal characteristics and histories. The dominant assumption of much research is that problems of individual and social pathology need investigating, since it is in this area that solutions to personal rehabilitation may be located.

Thus, for example, the National Assistance Board report on homeless single persons focused exclusively on the individual and social characteristics of men living in common lodging houses or government reception centres, or living rough. Although the report was not officially concerned with providing answers to the problems of homelessness and vagrancy, it nevertheless concluded as follows:

> . . . homelessness or social instability appear to be frequently a manifestation of a deep-rooted and long-standing [personal]

situation or difficulty . . . many of the residents [of common lodging houses and hostels] appeared to need individual help . . . [and] have problems which ordinarily are recognised as requiring help and support from community services.[3]

A similar theme underpins the policy-directed government report on habitual drunken offenders. Recommendations to develop socio-medical treatment and rehabilitation facilities as alternatives to arrest and imprisonment were made against a background in which the medical and socio-pathological dimensions of alcoholism and homelessness were stressed. In particular, medical terminology is continuously invoked to explain why men become habitual drunken offenders: pathology, symptoms, diagnosis, and disease are key concepts by which the phenomenon is explained. The report states:

. . . of the various diagnostic elements which may be observed in the habitual drunken offender it seems that the basic medical exposition of the causes of alcoholism is very appropriate to an understanding of how the drinking problems of this group of men originate.[4]

In fact the stress on aspects of individual causation is held as central in suggesting policies by which the problem may be contained. There is little evidence, at least as far as Britain is concerned, for any change being advocated other than that which lays emphasis on rescuing or rehabilitating individuals from the revolving door of penal and treatment institutions. In the United States the solution to the chronic poverty, disease and deprivation inherent in skid row areas is sometimes sought through the implementation of urban renewal programmes.[5] The absence of any major identifiable skid row area in Great Britain precludes any necessity to tackle the problem at this level, although the redevelopment of inner city zones and the upgrading of large working men's hostels is held by professionals to be one of the reasons for the subsequent shortage of cheap lodging-house accommodation and the increase in the numbers of persons sleeping rough. Nobody is born into skid row, but once there homeless men construct a life style that agencies find difficult, if not impossible, to remove them from. Consequently two main questions inform most research into skid row men. Firstly, what adverse social and psychological forces did individuals experience before their arrival on skid row? Secondly, what social and psychological pressures do they experience after their arrival – pressures which appear to contribute to a total commitment to a skid row life style?

From a review of the literature it is quite evident that social workers, medical personnel, psychologists and sociologists regard the problem as a prime manifestation of individual and social pathology. Bogue, for example, aptly represents this dominant view. He advances two levels of explanation – the socio-psychological in which 'it is important to underscore the concept of abnormality [which] . . . apparently results from mistakes in childrearing or, from contact with models of deviant behaviour';[6] and the sociological in which skid row is defined as an area that 'provides continued survival for familyless victims of society's unsolved social problems while these persons are in the terminal phase of their affliction and after society at large has abandoned all hope for them and has ceased to rehabilitate them'.[7]

One of the most widely propounded sociological theories to explain the arrival of problem drinkers on skid row is the 'undersocialisation' hypothesis, as spelled out in one of the earliest American studies of the chronic police inebriate.[8] Pittman and Gordon argue that police case inebriates are inadequately socialised during early life and are therefore unprepared to meet the demands of adult life. In particular the authors stress unstable family and home backgrounds coupled with the development of emotional handicaps as preconditions to alcohol dependency. In short, unstable family situations encountered in early life cause excessive drinking, which, in turn, leads to chronic alcoholism and eventually homelessness. Variants of the undersocialisation theory are to be found in the work of Straus, in the work of Bahr (who explains the skid row man in terms of disaffiliation) and in Merton's theory of anomie and retreatism.[9] What essentially links these theories is their common view that personal and social inadequacies in the individual hold the answer to why men fail to conform with the broad expectations of society, and therefore turn to drink and fall back on the institutions of skid row for survival.

An alternative approach to the sociological understanding of skid row, used not so much to explain why men in the first place gravitate to homelessness but to understand how they survive once there, and why attempts to return them to the community so often fail, has been developed in the tradition of subcultural theory and research.[10] It is the socialisation of men into a permanent state of homelessness rather than any evidence of undersocialisation before arrival on skid row that becomes the primary object of study. Crucial to this approach is an attempt to analyse attitudes and behaviour, and the meaning of life on skid row, *as defined by skid row residents themselves*. What especially distinguishes such studies from surveys of carefully selected samples is the emphasis attached to appreciating the social organisation of life on skid row as told by the men who experience it. The distinction is an important one, because in subcultural studies the anlysis is not cast in terms of concepts such as undersocialisation, anomie and disaffiliation, but, on the contrary, the inhabitants on the row are perceived as purposeful creative men engaged in adapting to problems of chronic poverty, deprivation, social control and, in the case of alcoholics, problems of addiction.

Subcultural studies of skid row do not totally ignore explanations of the socio-psychological forces which, in the first place, cause disaffiliation and homelessness. But by paying more attention to how men 'make out' and confront daily the myriad of agencies that in one way or another seek to intervene in their lives, they make the 'here-and-now' of the skid row life style the central point of enquiry. Indeed, the complexities of becoming a skid row habituee are often taken as a basis for offering a critique of theories of anomie, disaffiliation and undersocialisation. For instance, American studies of the social organisation of drinking among derelict alcoholics have served to undermine the dominant image of problem drinkers as being inadequate isolates.[11]

Handling the skid row alcoholic – two accounts of institutional control

Two recent accounts that pay special attention to skid row alcoholism and direct critical attention to the institutions of control are Nimmer's *Two Million Unnecessary Arrests* and Wiseman's *Stations of the Lost*.[12] Nimmer, interested in problems of policy implementation, is concerned with an analysis of the administration required in removing a social service problem from the criminal justice system. He explores 'the question of how policy, practice, and facilities might best be altered to reduce the criminal law role while not impairing, but perhaps improving, the quality of the handling of the men.[13]

In posing this question he is driven to examine the policies of the traditional system by which skid row men become the target of law-enforcement practices as background to the difficulties and problems of providing and implementing an alternative socio-medical treatment system. Replacing punishment by treatment is identified by Nimmer as the main thrust by which the structure of control is being reformed. The author argues, however, that the two major assumptions underlying such reform – that the basic issue of socio-medical treatment is an appropriate response to public intoxication and that arrests cannot be terminated unless new treatment alternatives can be provided – cannot be viewed as absolute guides to policy. The reasons advanced for this position are as follows: 'The needs of skid row men are substantial and diverse, and it is this very diversity that makes it undesirable to predispose the service issues by defining the problem a priori as one dealing (simply) with public intoxication.'[14] Chronic poverty, long-term unemployment, stigmatisation and exploitation are all issues interrelated with problems of public intoxication. The skid row drunk is continuously harassed and arrested by the police, made the object of moral reform at the hands of institutions with a paternalistic bias, or treated and rehabilitated on the basis of a poorly understood medical conception of alcoholism.

Some of these issues receive attention in Wiseman's book. In her account the juxtaposition of deviancy and social control is achieved by describing and analysing law-enforcement and rehabilitation strategies, simultaneously including the viewpoints of alcoholics and agents of social control. Of special interest is the author's insight into the different frameworks within which law-enforcement and rehabilitation personnel organise their policies and practical activities, since it is the contradictions that emerge between how alcoholics and professionals define what are objectively the same situations and institutions which, it is claimed, lie at the root of the failure to 'return these men to society'. Wiseman's perspective is a major advance in our sociological understanding of the total skid row scene, if only because for once there has been a sustained attempt at focusing on the relationship that develops between deviancy and social control as opposed to the traditional and exclusive concern with the deviant.

Given that skid row alcoholics move through a closed orbit consisting of drinking on skid row and being dried out in one institution or another, Wisemen sets out to test the assumption that this cyclical phenomenon profoundly affects the lives of both alcoholics and the professionals who man the agencies 'on the rehab loop'. She discovered that both parties hold somewhat polarised views about the world they interact within. As the relationships between alcoholic and professional personnel are at present constituted, the divergent frames of references held by both sides stand as an obstacle to the efforts of agencies to re-establish alcoholics within the community. This difficulty is compounded by what Wiseman terms the lack of social margin[15] skid row alcoholics possess. Implicitly re-entry into the mainstream of 'normal' social relationships, i.e. full employment, family membership, sobriety and a fixed address, requires the re-accumulation of social margin by acquiring those social attributes by which personal, social and economic stability may be identified. Wiseman refers to this process as replacing an old by a new biography:

> The plan to re-enter society, then, must of necessity be a plan to recreate a new biography for a marginless person who has fallen drastically behind in his personal timetable. The agent of social control, while acknowledging the many difficulties, and stressing the time and patience it takes, believes new margin can be created.[16]

But this can only be done by changing the existing relationships between alcoholics and professionals, and between the different institutions operating on skid row. For Wiseman, the nature of those relationships is the obstacle to change – not the imputed inadequacy and recidivism of the inebriate.

Dual views on skid row and its men

So far my analysis has consisted of an outline of the structure of skid row and a review of some of the literature on skid row, its men and institutions. Three distinct approaches by experts to the skid row phenomenon have been touched upon. Broadly speaking, each of these approaches addresses itself to different problems. Firstly, surveys ask the question: who are skid row men and why do they gravitate to skid row? Secondly, studies with a subcultural emphasis focus on the problem of how men manage to survive once they become permanent residents on the row? Finally, shifting the focus to include the viewpoint of the agencies and the role they play *vis-à-vis* homeless alcoholics, the main question becomes: what problems of definitions and action are agencies confronted with in order successfully to interrupt the cycle of drunkenness and treatment and how can more effective services to skid row men be provided? In the introduction to this chapter I argue that any explanation of the skid row scene gains in scope and balance, and therefore in adequacy, if the account views the phenomenon as one in which alcoholics and professionals present two distinct sets of reality. This claim was made as a prelude to reviewing some of the approaches used by research experts to understand skid row. In the remainder of this chapter some of the preoccupations held by professionals and skid row men, as opposed to research experts, are examined. I ask: what views of skid row and skid row men do professionals hold? And how do skid row alcoholics view themselves?

Agents of social control view skid row and its men

Generally speaking, professionals in their face-to-face work with homeless alcoholics come to grips with the problem of bringing about personal change in their clients by operating within fairly well demarcated frameworks of theory and practice. Whatever the assumptions held by different professionals and no matter how ideologically distinct are their rationales for acting towards the homeless alcoholic, all the institutions on skid row are essentially concerned with 'putting the skid row alcoholic back in the community'. This is not to say that there are no marked disagreements about what professionals believe to be the most effective means by which to attain their ultimate objective. Further on I will interpret the disagreements that exist among different control strategies; suffice it to say at this stage that representatives of treatment and rehabilitation agencies are not only in conflict with one another, but are in fundamental disagreement with the judiciary system, which seeks to bring skid row men into line by repeatedly processing them through police cells, courts and prison.

To begin with, then, how do professionals view the twin problems of homelessness and alcoholism (as opposed to how they typify or characterise homeless alcoholics)? Reviewing definitions of the problem as a whole serves to outline some of the broader issues that arise – issues that go beyond personal encounters between professionals and deviants.[17]

Firstly, the extent of the problem, its public visibility and the inadequacy of cheap accommodation and treatment facilities are linked into a single argument and held as a valid platform from which to demand an extension and improvement in resources. In particular the numbers of single homeless persons 'sleeping rough', and the closure of large common lodging houses, are linked to the pressure for rehabilitation agencies to offer accommodation and treatment. Pressure on skid row facilities is annually viewed as 'a crisis situation', especially during the winter months.[18] The following statements[19] reflect this concern. A vicar, addressing a meeting about the imminent closure of a common lodging house argued:

> There is a crisis in accommodation for the homeless single person in London at present. A Salvation Army captain informs me that on one Saturday night he turned away 30 people requesting a bed. It is difficult to estimate the total number of homeless single persons but it is clear that all the hostels are filled to capacity.

A government reception centre manager explained:

> We can try to contain the problem and give the men some hope. But I cannot see how this can be done properly when the numbers being referred to hostels and the reception centre are so numerous that it is evident all of us are working under a great strain.

The crisis, in the eyes of one social-work organisation, could be met by expanding facilities.

> In a survey we carried out we found 1600 dossers sleeping rough in London. We think these figures do not represent the real number . . . we need a general expansion of facilities . . . more cheap hostels for itinerant workers, more soup runs, more rehabilitation hostels and more shelters.

Secondly, in the context of the modern Welfare State professionals working with homeless men are conscious of the fact that problems of single homelessness, vagrancy and alcoholism are very low in the hierarchy of priorities that determine the allocation of central and local government resources to agencies in the field. A social worker illustrated this ranking of social problems by stating that if a pop-chart of society's concern for social problems existed, then vagrant alcoholics would probably always remain at the bottom. This ranking is not unconnected with popular images of skid row alcoholics, of which more further on. The peripheral nature of the problem was reflected in the uneven public response to problems of homelessness as a result of Sandford's television dramatisation of two types of homelessness in his plays *Cathy Come Home* and *Edna, the Inebriate Woman*. A social worker captured the differential reaction to family homelessness and that of the single inebriate in the following manner:

> Our society fails to identify with this type of person [the homeless alcoholic]. Furthermore, the difference between Cathy and Edna is that Cathy constitutes an example of a political issue, namely housing. On the other hand alcoholism is in no sense a political issue in our society.

Discrimination by the Welfare State against single homeless persons is one reason often advanced as to why voluntary and charitable organisations dominate the field. It further compounds the often expressed view that these organisations are the only ones interested in what, through charity and philanthropy, the Victorians referred to as 'the undeserving and disreputable poor'. Vestiges of this attitude are in fact still offered as further evidence for working with the homeless and rootless. The social worker explained:

> Our project operates on the principle of the open door. We felt we had an obligation towards those individuals who had been turned away by other [statutory] services. Hospitals and some social service departments are the worst offenders – we have had men literally dumped on our doorstep – in one case a man was brought 200 miles and left with us.

However, in spite of the Welfare State's peripheral interest in the vagrant alcoholic, a third major issue raised by voluntary agencies revolves around the demand for action from and the co-operation of both central and local government to achieve a successful shift in responsibility for homeless alcoholics from the penal to the medico-social sphere. In spite of general agreement on all sides that habitual public drunks are best dealt with in detoxification centres and rehabilitation hostels rather than in courts and prison, agencies at the forefront of the reform campaign are consistent critics of the disparity between government intention and practice in achieving this shift in responsibility. Detoxification centres where men will be dried out and sufficient rehabilitation hostels to cope with patients being discharged from the centres are promoted as alternatives to arrest and imprisonment. But delay in implementing such reform is held as a further obstacle to coping with derelict alcoholics adequately. A campaign letter to achieve major reforms stated:

> It was agreed that . . . a working group . . . be elected whose task would be to seek implementation of the major recommendations in the Habitual Drunken Offenders Report 1971 by organising and maintaining pressure through CHAR on relevant Government Departments . . . We are sure you appreciate . . . the gravity of the present situation; individual representations to the Government . . . have been unproductive and we now believe that concerted effort is necessary to prompt the Government into action.[20]

Thus far the emphasis has been on outlining some of the main social policy issues preoccupying agents of social control. But how do the personnel manning skid row agencies define the homeless single man? Obviously definitions will vary according to the institutions professionals align themselves with, the ideological framework within which they operate and the manner in which they organise their daily activities. In official terms the police, magistrates and prison officers define the alcoholic dosser as an offender, psychiatrists as someone suffering from a disease, the mission staff as a person morally and spiritually weak, and social workers as someone socially inadequate. What binds all these professionals is their common concern to exert some kind of control over the skid row drunk. The alcoholic's commitment to a life of heavy drinking and drunkenness, and his inability to extricate himself from the revolving door of institutional and public life, clearly place him beyond the boundaries of an acceptable moral order. Repeated relapse gives rise to a generally pessimistic outlook among professionals for the future recovery of the alcoholic dosser. Numerous comments by agents of social control reflect the vagrant alcoholic's status as being that of the complete outsider. As one writer put it:

> It is not so much that he is a deviant as that he is outside the usual system of sanctions, and hence his behaviour cannot be predicted with any certainty.[21]

The following themes are consistently articulated by professionals. For example, the alcoholic on the row is perceived as rootless:

> These men have no social supports whatsoever, like a family or relatives – *psychiatrist*.

A major obstacle to the alcoholic's recovery is that he is often regarded as unco-operative and beyond redemption:

> The difficulty is that some of these men keep appearing in court on drunkenness charges but don't accept they have a drinking problem or are alcoholic – *social worker*.

> . . . they are not rewarding patients – *general practitioner*.

> I interviewed a man who'd been in prison 150 times for drunkenness – what are you going to do with a man like that? – *prison probation officer*.

Furthermore, skid row alcoholics are said to be morally and spiritually weak:

> The homeless alcoholic is really being controlled by Satan – unless he changes he will go to hell – his life is not complete without Jesus Christ – *mission director*.

Finally, apart from overcoming all these problems, alcoholics are also perceived as dishonest and work-shy:

> A significant number of these men are committing fraud, especially the meths boys . . . they sometimes claim they haven't drunk for ages and that they don't want to stay in a common lodging house because it is lousing them up. But they are mostly conning us . . . they want the money to go on a binge – *social security officer*.

At one time we were recipients of the loafer whom we could make to work. Now they become mere guests of the State. They just live on social security – *Salvation Army officer.*

Other defining phrases used to characterise the alcoholic dosser include such terms as 'inadequate', 'lacking in motivation', 'unemployable', 'wretched and filthy', 'psychotic', 'incoherent in thought and word'. The images conjured up by these terms are not unlike those used by local citizens complaining about public amenities and open spaces being 'taken over' by vagrants and drunks.

The London Bridge station area has become a social cesspit of human decay. There has, over recent months, been a massive increase in alcoholic tramps using the vicinity as an open air dosshouse. Visitors to Southwark Cathedral and City workers like to sit in the sun and eat their sandwiches in the cathedral gardens, in peace and quiet, but this tranquillity has been shattered of late, by foul-mouthed, drink-sodden tramps accosting the public for money and behaving in the most offensive way imaginable. No doubt 'Christian Charity' could be advanced as a reason for not driving these derelicts away from the cathedral but I for one cannot see how they are being helped by being able to loll around in alcoholic stupefaction, littering the gardens with refuse and empty bottles. Similarly, these alcoholic tramps may be seen on the station approach staggering about, shouting incoherent abuse at all and sundry . . .[22]

Commuters and shoppers generally have little direct contact with homeless men. Mostly an indignant silence is maintained in the face of public drinking. But, unlike most deviancy, drinking among skid row men is done publicly and collectively. As a result the alcoholics' demeanour, appearance and inebriety in the midst of normality occasionally elicit open moral indignation from members of the public. Complaints to the police, holding local meetings 'to do something about this problem', and letters to the local press are methods by which expressions of abhorrence, disgust, indignation and retribution are expressed.[23]

Now, if these stereotypical images of alcoholic derelicts are widespread even among professionals who come into daily contact with them, how is it that attempts at control and treatment, attempts that repeatedly fail to bring these men 'into line', are not entirely discredited in the eyes of their advocates? Further on I explore this question in greater detail. Suffice it to say that whereas most methods of control and treatment continue to be upheld in spite of little evidence of success, many professionals and voluntary workers, as individuals, opt out after relatively short-lived workspans with homeless alcoholics. On the other hand, quite clearly committed agents of social control interested in the welfare of their clients do not view them as hopeless. The chronic relapse rate of the skid row alcoholic, his apparent commitment to a deviant life style, his entrapment in the revolving door of institutional control, are all hallmarks by which skid row drunks may be labelled with negative traits. Yet, against this pessimistic portrayal, the efforts of society to cope with the intractability of the homeless alcoholic are a testimony to what Wiseman perceived as 'the magnificent indomitability of the human spirit, for men who fail rise to try again and again'.[24] This faith was articulated by a number of professionals:

> The people who come to the reception centre are not to be written off as commonly supposed . . . our visiting medical officers can sometimes be overwhelmed by what would appear to be the intractable character of the problem. (In spite of) this repetitive cycle the men keep going through . . . it is still worthwhile helping them – *reception centre manager.*

> We must not write off these damaged men. They have got potential. New and better ways of treating homeless alcoholics will arise out of the battle between the optimists and the pessimists . . . I too can be overwhelmed . . . but one has to start somewhere, do it intelligently, exploring new ways of treatment and care – *social worker.*

> Ninety-nine per cent of the men fail on the first day they're out of prison. However, we must continue to give them an opportunity (at rehabilitation) every time they're in here – *prison welfare officer.*

Skid row alcoholics define themselves

In the course of participating in the life of down-and-out alcoholics the absence of any open discussion as to one's personal condition and status soon became apparent. Other observers of the skid row scene have remarked that its inhabitants rarely, if ever, exchange views about their reasons for being on skid row. To talk about past troubles is taboo. This absence stands in sharp contrast to the professionals' and researchers' concern to tease out elements in the alcoholics' personality and life experience that led to heavy drinking and alcoholism. In addition little is said about the impact that alcohol is making on individuals in terms of the likelihood that it is impossible for men to pull out of the skid row life-way. Conversations among homeless men are more likely to focus on whether the company they drank with was good or not, the amount and type of drink consumed, and their dealings with agencies of social control, in particular the police. Other topics raised include the whereabouts of other skid row men, the availability of casual work, and information about horse racing and betting.

An important dimension of contrast with the world of rehabilitation is the relative lack of awareness among skid row alcoholics as to the competing theories and definitions of alcoholism prevailing among professionals interested in the problem. In particular the disease conception of alcoholism holds little, if any, meaning for the homeless man. The internal debates as to whether the problem is best tackled through moral reform, medical treatment or social rehabilitation are not part of the alcoholic's perspective. The forces operating in favour of changing the social control structure from punishment to treatment do not influence the derelict alcoholic's view of the world. Of much more crucial importance to men on the row is an awareness of how best his immediate surroundings and the social relationships he maintains with his peers and guardians may be turned to advantage. Problems of survival override all other considerations.

This is not to minimise any awareness of the role that alcohol plays in the life of homeless men. Quite evidently the relationship between the structure and process of an alcoholic's life on skid row and the excessive consumption of alcohol is a very close one. But the meaning that is ascribed to alcohol, as a consciousness-altering drug, does not reach the level of articulation as is found, say, among certain groups using marijuana or LSD. Observers of drug-using youth cultures have noted that the meanings attached to drugs by hippies and others emphasise their symbolic quality in 'allowing the passage through a barrier separating the "straight" from the "hip".'[25] To smoke marijuana or 'drop acid' is to achieve a level of consciousness in which 'the search for a distinctive spirituality and awareness' becomes paramount.[26]

Skid row men, on the other hand, do not articulate a conscious philosophy around the use of alcohol. Alcohol is not a means by which homeless men in any way attempt to reach a state of existential awareness. Quite the contrary. On the few occasions that alcoholics exchange views about the impact of alcohol it is in terms of its potential quality to distort or blot out reality. To those who remain sober, the heavily intoxicated alcoholic is someone who engages in 'drink-talk' (i.e. incomprehensible conversation), is likely to be uncooperative or even aggressive and, most significantly, attracts the attention of the police. To those who get drunk, alcohol relieves physical and psychological symptoms of withdrawal and lubricates social relationships among those drinking together (men slightly intoxicated often refer to 'having a good crack amongst the boys'). Much of the monotony of living on skid row is blotted out and any recollection of events experienced when heavily intoxicated is erased.

Occasionally homeless men will discuss their low social status in terms of its negative consequences for their identities as persons considered somewhat less than human by the conventional world. The alcoholics' relationship to agents of social control and the public in general (skid row men are highly visible deviants, even when sober, by virtue of their appearance and demeanour) is obviously not expressed by them in the abstract language of sociological analysis. However, alcoholics do sense, and sometimes articulate, the fact that their position at the very bottom of the social hierarchy is responsible for the way the world at large views them. Homeless men are unwashed, sometimes scarred or physically disabled, wear ill-fitting clothes, constantly pass the day on the street and in public places, beg, drink, get drunk, live rough or in institutions, and are repeatedly moved on or arrested by the police. All these factors act in concert to remind the alcoholic constantly of his low status. The essence of his condition is crystallised by the fact that all homeless men know that the police, magistrates, prison staff and personnel manning the treatment and rehabilitation agencies do not judge him so much by what he does, as by what he is.

The alcoholic's self-conscious awareness of his situation *vis-à-vis* the conventional world is a reflection of that world's definition of vagrants and homeless men as standing on the very lowest rung of the status ladder. But, within the social boundaries of skid row, alcoholics construct their own terms of reference by which they can measure their personal condition and behaviour against that of other alcoholics and inhabitants of skid row institutions. There is a continual struggle for status among homeless men.[27] Skid row pub drinkers hold street drinkers in low esteem, while among the latter the cider and wine drinkers consider themselves superior to habitual methylated and surgical spirit drinkers. Alcoholics rate each other according to the main strategies they develop to survive on skid row. Developing a particular skill in order 'to make out', such as begging, thieving or conning the social security system, confers status on, or is used as a basis for discrediting, other alcoholics. The skilful beggar looks down on men who depend on state aid for money. Others view begging as below their dignity and pride. Men who depend on Salvation Army centres for shelter are criticised by those who sleep rough. Finally, all long-term alcoholics on the row consider themselves far more respectable than the mentally ill who rely on hospitals, common lodging houses and reception centres; the young heroin addict, whom they see using a syringe in parks and public toilets; the sexual offender, whom they read about in newspapers or come across in prison; and homeless women who drink in public.[28]

To an outsider the physical conditions and social relationships that prevail on skid row appear to be objectively the same for all its residents. Men who are homeless, drink in public, and are arrested for drunkenness, are referred to in blanket terms: they are all homeless alcoholics. However, from the perspective of the inhabitants of skid row the objective fact of being a resident there is interpreted along a variety of dimensions. A finely spun web of informal status categorisations is formulated and exchanged among drinking group members and institution inmates. Exclusion from the mainstream of conventional society would appear to narrow the lives of homeless men radically. Although this is undoubtedly the case, a countervailing force comes into operation as individuals become increasingly immersed in the subculture; alcoholics learn to construct a status system which, psychologically, permits them a degree of self-esteem not accorded to them by inhabitants of the conventional world.

3
Strategies of Survival

The alcoholic makes out on skid row

Most conventional portrayals of deviant behaviour are made from the standpoint of experts and professionals who have a vested interest in eradicating problems of crime, poverty and deviancy. Consequently emphasis is laid on those attitudes and behaviour of the deviant that serve to highlight his difference from members of the conventional community. In particular the causes that led individuals into deviant behaviour are regarded as fundamental knowledge and as a prerequisite to any recommendations appropriate to correctional or treatment programmes. Problems of aetiology are resolved within an analytical framework dominated by concepts of individual and social pathology. Deviants, by definition, are said to be leading pathological, irrational and meaningless lives.

Now, whether the typifications used to identify skid row alcoholics emanate from experts or laymen, their view of the phenomenon is constricted and partial – inevitably so – as a result of the social distance separating the world of the deviant from that of the social control agent. Not only are the definitions applied to the deviant grounded in concepts that reflect the particular professional frameworks of individuals making statements about skid row men, but these statements often contain messages of moral indignation, reproval and condemnation, prejudice, cynicism and hopelessness. This is not entirely unexpected from agencies concerned with correcting or treating individuals who not only appear to be totally 'outside society' but seem to be committed to remaining there in spite of numerous entries into both correctional and rehabilitation systems. On the other hand, there are important consequences for our understanding of skid row alcoholics when the definitions of the phenomenon are offered by the men themselves. The basic question that then needs asking is the following: what meanings does skid row have for the alcoholic? In greater detail this basic question allows the investigator to discover how derelict inebriates view themselves and others on skid row, by what means they overcome problems of homelessness, poverty and addiction and, finally, how they define the world of punishment and treatment they so often find themselves in.[1]

The advantage of adopting a perspective in which deviants are allowed to speak for themselves is that social reality takes on a dimension which counterbalances the dominant views held by rule-enforcers. When the investigator approaches his subjects from this perspective, he does so by applying a methodological principle that is summed up in the axiom 'let the deviant tell it as it is'. By taking this approach the world of skid row, as will be demonstrated in both this and the following three chapters, takes on a complexity and sophistication transcending the usual description of derelict alcholics as isolated and inadequate individuals. But how do those differences in our conception of skid row alcoholics arise in the first place? Wallace, in his *Skid Row as a Way of Life*, answers this question. He points out that when investigators arrive on skid row with pre-coded, pre-tested, survey questionnaires, they do so with the implicit assumption that the person is a failure and ask why. Consequently the picture they construct is of an individual who is isolated and inadequate, engaged in meaningless behaviour. On the other hand, sociologists who attempt to elicit the native point of view by listening to men and observing their experiences *in situ* are able to go beyond superficial appearances and discover a complex set of values by which derelict alcoholics give meaning to and organise their activities and relationships on the row.[2]

Two fundamental and interrelated problems face skid row drunks: their chronic poverty and their dependence on alcohol. In both this and the following chapter the analysis is concerned with what may broadly be termed the alcoholics' strategies of survival. Given that down-and-out alcoholics are homeless, property-less, without the support of family and regular work, a question often asked of them is how they manage to make out in overcoming the problems they encounter. The ensuing analysis reveals the means by which problems of poverty and addiction are met, interpreted and adapted to. New recruits to skid row, through a process of gradual acculturation into the skid row life-way, perpetuate these strategies of survival beyond the life span of any single individual or generation of men on the row.

Furthermore, as individuals become increasingly immersed in the skid row life-way, their identities as stable working men are eventually replaced by identities that reflect their overriding concern with drink and the problems of overcoming the deprivations inherent in poverty and homelessness.

In this chapter the research material on strategies of survival is organised around two main themes: shelter and money. The selection of these two needs is not entirely arbitrary; rather, they represent two areas of concern that not only preoccupy the majority of adults in western societies but also those individuals who, by definition, are urban outcasts.[3]

Money

All skid row men suffer from chronic poverty. Long-term unemployment and a meagre, irregular income are two dimensions by which down-and-out alcoholics may be defined. Almost all adults in advanced industrialised societies require money with which to purchase the basic needs of survival. The skid row man is no exception; but his low status places him outside the usual formal and structured opportunities by which most of us obtain wages and salaries. Wiseman writes:

> When the skid row man thinks of getting money he . . . must show ingenuity in creating something out of nothing. Thus, he thinks in terms of objects, relationships, or short-term tasks that can be converted into enough cash to take care of current needs – liquor, food, shelter, incidentals.[4]

A recovered skid row alcoholic stated:

> An experienced dosser knows there is always something to be had if he looks around hard enough. Magazines, books and food can be sold to a Sally Ann dosser; lead can be stripped from a new derry; someone he knows as a soft-touch can be begged. He's always on the look-out for something that can be turned into money.

In obtaining money there are a number of channels – some of them illegal – which the homeless inebriate exploits. Begging, petty thieving, claiming welfare payments from the state, taking on unskilled short-term casual work, and picking the pockets of other derelicts or relatively wealthy middle-class drunks were all either observed or reported during fieldwork. Of course, how particular skid row alcoholics make a livelihood is dependent on which specific skills they develop and their ability to manipulate the urban environment.[5] The same survival skills and modes of adaptation are not found in all down-and-out inebriates. Thus, for example, whereas some men employ a number of sophisticated begging techniques, others are unable to beg at all. 'Working the charities' or even making legitimate claims on the state social security system, although engaged in by some men, is often regarded by others as demanding too much effort.[6] An account of different ways of making money follows.

Begging

Begging is one of the most common and sophisticated strategies by which homeless men earn their livelihood. Wiseman asserts that the different begging techniques 'reveal their users to be shrewd students of commonsense psychology'.[7] However, begging is by no means a universal skill at the hands of every alcoholic, though probably all men on the row have at some time engaged in begging. By definition begging means a relationship with another person, no matter how brief and transient that relationship is, in which the victim is persuaded to part with a (usually) small amount of money with no expectation of any goods or services being given in return.[8]

A useful way of looking at begging is in terms of such a relationship. In his study of blood donors and recipients, Richard Titmuss drew attention to a number of propositions characterising relationships centred on the giving and receiving of blood. An adaption of most of Titmuss' propositions to the begging situation will illustrate their relevance:

1. The gift of alms often takes place in impersonal situations.
2. The recipient is not personally known to the donor. (But, unlike in the blood donor – receiver relationship, personal expressions of gratitude are offered because of the essentially face-to-face nature of begging.)
3. There are no personal, predictable penalties for not giving; no

socially enforced sanctions of remorse, shame or guilt. (But there are, of course, penalties for the receiver, since begging alms is a statutory offence.)

4. For the giver there is no certainty of a corresponding gift in return, present or future.
5. No givers require or wish for corresponding gifts in return. They do not expect and would not wish to be the recipient of alms.
6. There is no obligation on the recipient himself to make a corresponding gift in return.
7. To the giver his gift does not lead to economically harmful consequences. To the receiver, the gift may be everything.[9]

The relevance of the above propositions to begging is that they focus on a relationship in which the two participants are essentially strangers and in which communication is short-lived. When the participants are known to each other, as in cases where skid row alcoholics beg from social workers and others with whom they are personally acquainted, the nature of the relationship is somewhat altered.

Within the framework of the above propositions the alcoholic applies specific rules and techniques of begging by approaching carefully selected victims in appropriate surroundings:

When you've been drinking for years around the East End you get to know by sight who the local people are. So you don't beg from them, only from strangers, people who you haven't seen around in the area before.

A place like Waterloo Station is a good place to beg because it's really no-mans land – it's only used by commuters.

If you haven't been up the West End begging then you'd better start now. Around here [a commuter railway station] it's no good – there's too many men already doing it.

Asking for the price of a sandwich or cup of tea ('I'm hungry')[10] explaining that one needs help with a fare home or to one's ship ('I'm stranded'), or, if one's appearance is particularly destitute, passively begging alms with an outstretched hand ('I'm down-and-out'), are all gambits by which men obtain the price of a bottle. Moreover the entire process is carried out as unobtrusively as possible; the victim must not be openly upset or made indignant at the request, he must be persuaded to part with his donation within the shortest possible time, and the alcoholic must escape the attention of police patrolmen. Most alcoholics who specialise in begging claim that the entire process is faciliated when they 'have a bit of heat on' but are not drunk enough for the victim to be put off. Tourists, commuters and pedestrians are all favourite targets for the skilful beggar; and railway and tube stations, entertainment areas, parks and busy shopping thoroughfares provide the appropriate anonymity for begging to be done unobtrusively. Although begging skill is learned through participation in the collective life of the skid row culture, it is a skill invariably practised on its own. The art of persuasion and diplomacy inherent in begging can only be successfully applied if the alcoholic, making the initial contact and request on his own, is able to hold the victim's attention and interest. 'Two-handed begging' would only unbalance a tenuous relationship, in which the alcoholic is placed in an inferior status, both as a result of his request and because of his general appearance and demeanour.[11]

The police sometimes use begging statutes as devices by which to control persons and situations defined as undesirable rather than as means by which the overt act of begging is proscribed.[12] In other words, the authority of the law is directed at derelict alcoholics and vagrants for what they *are* rather than what they *do*. Their condition or status constitutes sufficient criteria for police intervention. This means that a criminal category is invoked against persons who appear idle, have no visible means of support and are suffering from chronic poverty and destitution. Skid row alcoholics are aware of the arbitary power the police hold over them. One man explained: 'It's too difficult to do any panhandling on this station – the last time I got stopped for it the coppers told me that if they saw me doing it again they'd have me put away.' Another homeless man, in court on a charge of begging alms, explained to the magistrates: 'The police are picking on me – I'd only just come out of the off-licence with a bottle of wine when they picked me up.' During fieldwork one homeless man was observed to inadvertently beg from two plain-clothes policemen. The following day the man appeared before a magistrate's court on the more serious charge of suspicion. Several alcoholics reported that 'being done for sus' is one strategy by which the police conveniently ensure their removal from the scene for periods longer than prison sentences arising out of begging and drunk-related charges.

In addition to commuters and pedestrains, agencies that in one way or another offer help and treatment are also used by homeless men in their efforts to obtain money. Hospital and hostel personnel, social workers, probation officers and missionaries are all at some time requested for financial assistance. Begging from professionals who are in the business of treatment and rehabilitation very often changes the nature of the begging relationship that exists between the total stranger and the alcoholic, because the participants are personally known to each other or they are at least aware of the 'official' expectations that bring them into contact with each other. In these cases the following proposition may be added to the seven outlined above:

8. When donor and recipient are known to each other, then morally enforced sanctions characterised by a variety of subtle expectations and sentiments come into prominent play.

In particular, professionals working at the rehabilitation of skid row alcoholics find it sometimes difficult to resolve the dilemma between giving money they suspect or know is to be used for drink and refusing the request at the expense of adversely affecting a casework relationship. This last proposition is applicable because the continuation of a professional relationship between alcoholic and expert is always premised, for the professional, on the hope that the client will at some time in the future make a genuine request for treatment. As Titmuss points out:

> . . . the personal gift and counter-gift, in which givers and receivers are known to each other, and personally communicate with each other, is characterised by a great variety of sentiments and purposes . . . Within all such gift transactions of a personal face-to- face nature lie embedded some elements of moral enforcement or bond. To give is to receive – to compel some return or create some obligation.[13]

In the final analysis social workers, mission personnel, psychiatrists and others hope that their patience and perseverance will be rewarded; in the meantime experts accept that they, and the agencies they work for, are frequently redefined by derelict alcoholics as potential sources of money and other hand-outs.

Just as with begging from strangers, the skid row drunk prefaces his request for financial aid from professional workers with a hard luck story:

> I told them [the staff at the hospital emergency clinic] that I'd been staying at the Blackfriars Sally Ann but that I'd damped down my bed and they wouldn't let me back in unless I paid the ten bob fine. I told them straight why I needed the money but it didn't work. But the next day I got the money off a social worker.

From the alcoholic's point of view, though, begging from experts also carries with it a number of hazards. Aware of the beneficiaries' status, experts are likely to subject the alcoholic to lectures about his condition, his past and the need for help and rehabilitation. In the process the derelict man is obliged to play along with the picture offered by the professional if he is to achieve his object. In particular inexperienced social workers newly recruited to the rehabilitation scene are considered a relatively 'easy beg'; but even then this begging technique does not always work. Professionals experienced in working with homeless men are apt to refuse requests for money:

> Nine out of ten times some smug cunt who's all dressed up ends up telling you what you've done wrong, how you got on the wrong foot, and instead of getting help you get all confused. So you begin rearing up inside yourself because of what he's saying and because of his fancy office and job. Eventually he might offer you five shillings but you tell him to stuff it.

> I expected I'd get ten bob off the probation officer but I only got two. You know, she made me sign for the money. Not only that, she asked me if I did any drinking and when I said 'no' she tried to smell my breath.

A third source of begging consists of other alcoholics and heavy drinkers, especially from men who are sober, living in a rehabilitation hostel, and probably earning a working wage. If skid row drunks manage to retain any contacts with men who confine their drinking to pubs, particularly former working and pub-drinking companions, then the latter will also be approached for the price of a bottle. Occasionally skid row men are joined by alcoholics whose visits to skid row are either temporary or intermittent. These men often hold regular jobs and live with their families, but heavy drinking sprees force them to suspend their family and work responsibilities. Such cases are viewed as a source of relative wealth by the skid row habituee and are worked on as 'an easy touch'. For the price of joining in group drinking the visitor to skid row finds that wage packets are rapidly translated into bottles of cheap wine and cider. The 'live wire', then, means the real possibility of comparatively large returns of money or alcohol in return for minimum begging effort. The 'live wire' is the drinking groups' benefactor *par excellence*. Lastly, men who are sober, living in a rehabilitation hostel and earning a working wage are also used as a begging source. Recovering alcoholics find it difficult to refuse their companions who are still drinking, since the rules of mutual aid that govern collective drinking on skid row are carried into the rehabilitation environment. The sober alcoholic knows that to turn down a request for money is to run the risk of being heavily criticised should he break out and return to his drinking school (see Chapter 4, pp. 66–74).

State welfare money

Claiming social security benefits from the state is a further source of money for the single homeless man. In London the Department of Health and Social security has created two offices that cater exclusively for men who are officially labelled as having no fixed abode. The special function and clientele of these offices mark them off from similar offices servicing the local, estabilished community. The following material taken from my field notes, describes one of the offices:

> The clients using this office are characteristic of the typical skid row population . . . the homeless alcoholic, the vagrant, the old age pensioner living in common lodging houses, men from the government reception centre . . . the first thing that struck me was the overall mood of despondency, dereliction, destitution. It is as if skid row . . . had artificially been brought together by virtue of the function of this office. There must have been close on 200 men

occupying long benches facing the interview booths. The office, although clean, was bare and functional. There was an air of 'suspended time' as men waited to be called for interview, sometimes for as long as one or two hours. The impersonality and neutrality of the surroundings contributed to the institutional character of the place . . .

The counter clerks interviewing applicants sit behind a wire grille, which extends up to the ceiling. Some men read newspapers, some merely wait, others talk to their neighbours, while still others may drink from a concealed bottle. The atmosphere is occasionally punctuated by arguments between counter clerks and applicants sitting in the interview booths.

The effort required to obtain money from a social security office is often regarded with ambivalence by derelict alcoholics; men legally entitled to assistance know that to obtain a cash grant is like taking an obstacle course, of which the major hurdle is being interviewed by the counter clerk. In addition, for those men who are sleeping rough, their right to state welfare benefits is only guaranteed following a request that the applicant first take up residence in a government reception centre or common lodging house. In a discussion with a group of alcoholics the participants agreed with the comments of one man that booking in at these institutions is not worth the money: I don't bother going to Scarborough Street or Marshalsea Road [social security offices] because they would only send me to the Salvation Army hostel, and I wouldn't go there if you paid me.' Of course, derelict alcoholics do from time to time work the system of booking into reception centres and lodging houses as a means by which they can apply for welfare benefits. This is one of three tactics which virtually guarantees the beneficiary a cash grant. Two informants explained:

You sign on the dole on a Monday, get a 'casual' on the Tuesday and with the money from that book in at the Sally for a couple of nights. On the Wednesday you tell the Labour Exchange you weren't able to get a job. You work another 'Casual' on Thursday, stop the night in the kip house, and on the Friday you're down to Marshalsea Road to draw benefit. Men who go through this procedure have a cast-iron alibi – they can't get a knockback. Mind you, that makes it a busy week for the dosser. A Jack-drinker *might* get round to doing this, but it's difficult. It's the cider and wine drinkers that are more likely to have a go.

Sometimes two men would book in on one ticket in a kip house – that would cost six bob. But then both men using that ticket might pull £16 at the NAB.

A second tactic is for the alcholic to obtain a doctor's sick note. Many skid row men are not registered with a general practitioner; those that are rarely make their way to general practices because of their habitual drinking, appearance and demeanour, or because they do not find themselves in the area were they are registered. However,

Getting money from the NAB is worthwhile when you give them a sick line because they can't give you a knockback – they can't even ask you to book in at the Sally Ann. You see, you can sometimes work a doctor – I did – he'd write out anything I'd say on the certificate.

I've been getting a certificate for my bronchitis from my doctor for the past two months. With that I can get a few quid each week from the NAB.

Finally, every homeless man is entitled to benefit on release from prison. Since habitual drunken offenders are imprisoned for their inability to pay the fines imposed on them – not for drunkenness – payment of the fine by someone outside the prison secures the early release of the prisoner. Occasionally alcoholics turn this arrangement into a financial advantage. A prison officer explained how shortening a man's sentence as a result of a fellow alcoholic paying off the outstanding balance of his fine could benefit both alcoholics financially.

A man discharged from prison is entitled to £2.50 from social security. He'll hold back £1 of that to obtain the early release of a friend whom he left back in here the morning he got out. All he does is come up to the prison gate and pay the pound. Not only does his friend get out early but he's entitled to *his* £2.50. If he's released on a Saturday, we have to give him the money in cash because the social security office is closed. Sometimes the men outside know how much is outstanding on the fine of someone they know who's inside – then they'll put their money together and get him out that way.[14]

From the homeless man's point of view probably the most intolerable aspect of obtaining welfare benefits at the specially set up state welfare offices is the interview procedure at which the claimant's entitlement to benefit is established. Alcoholics know that their spoiled identity opens them to morally loaded allegations from counter clerks, such as they will spend all the money on drink. The applicant is confronted by a battery of questions about when he last worked, what his wages were, whether he has attempted to obtain work, where he last resided, what benefits he has been receiving and whether application for benefits have been made at other offices. The relationship between counter clerk and claimant is marked by underlying hostility and suspicion.[15] The manager of one office put it this way:

> The better the tale this type of bloke can tell the more money he's going to get. Their stories are embellished . . . we've got to try to sort this kind of thing out when interviewing the claimant.
>
> There are a significant number of men who come to our office who are committing fraud, especially the isolated and hardish bodies, the meths boys.

On the other hand, an alcoholic viewed the interview as follows:

> The interview is nothing but a battle of wits. The man behind the counter will try to catch you out but you've always got to have a ready answer for anything he asks you about – they'll ask two or three times the dates you've entered in your sickness certificate. It's no good rearing up on the man, but you can't help it sometimes. This place is enough to drive you crackers.

Another alcoholic had this to say:

> Every time there's a drunk in the NAB, fuck me, out of every twenty dossers in there, he'll break the harmony and rear up. I've seen many tramps – those men that are just tramps – get a knockback and the man just accepts it. Well, you won't get this from a drunkard, dry or sober . . . especially when he's sober. Your

man cannot stand it – his nerves won't take it – he'll rear up on the man from the NAB and finish getting fucked out of Marshalsea Road – sometimes by the police.

In the context of such feelings of mutual distrust and antipathy between claimant and benefactor it is not surprising that alcoholics, even when legally entitled to claim, prefer to take up begging, casual work and petty thieving as means by which to survive on skid row.

Casual work

Historically the structure of the casual labour market and the availability of casual jobs for the chronically poor has radically altered since the turn of the century. London, in particular, was traditionally defined as possessing the largest casual labour market in Britain owing to its concentration of small non-factory work situations. As opposed to capital-intensive manufacturing centres, such as in the Midlands and the North, which require a consistent disciplined labour force, London's economy was based to a large extent on commerce, trade, and a production system that was broadly based on the 'sweating' method of employment[16] During the first half of the twentieth century the Victorian casual labour market was gradually replaced by three interrelated major developments: the enormous expansion of the consumer market forced the 'sweating' trades into factory-type production; secondly, the shift to factory-centred production opened the way for the unionisation of labour; and finally, this second development signified the decasualisation of traditionally casual occupations. However, the availability of casual labour in London has not entirely disappeared. Although dock work, and occupations associated with transport, factory work and some miscellaneous trades and jobs are now closed to any form of casualisation, the building and construction industry, for instance, still retains a proportion of casual labour. The development of tourism and the related expansion of hotel and restaurants in London has probably increased the opportunity for casual work in terms of kitchen portering. London's central wholesale markets also remain a source of casual work. Finally, residual and miscellaneous occupations such as sandwichmen, touters and newspaper vendors are occasionally filled by homeless single men.

The fundamental difference between the Victorian casual labour market in London and its contemporary counterpart, apart from the dramatic shrinkage in the size of the market, is the social composition of its work force. Evidently a sizeable proportion of London's permanent casual labour force were family members whereas now casual work is taken up by single homeless men.[17] Stedman Jones, in his study of the late Victorian casual labour market, draws a distinction between ordinary casual labourers and vagrants who temporarily filled certain casualised occupations. Although he found it difficult to draw a precise line of demarcation between the two groups, the distinction was warranted on the basis of the geographic immobility of the permanent casual labour force and the mobility of the vagrant.[18]

In spite of the dramatic shrinkage, casual work remains an important source of money for the skid row alcoholic. There are a variety of criteria by which casual employment may be defined[19] but, from the homeless alcoholic's point of view, 'a casual' means immediate cash for short-term tasks. It consists of unskilled work paid on a daily basis, in which no formal contract of employment is drawn up, and does not call for either the employer or worker to pay taxes and national insurance contributions.

A range of casual work is available to the skid row population, of which labouring on construction and demolition sites, kitchen portering in hotels and restaurants and holiday camps, unloading lorries and portering in wholesale markets, are some of the most common. Among other tasks homeless men occasionally reported taking on were newspaper vending, sandwich-board advertising, and general labouring work in East End 'sweat' shops and scrap metal yards. Sometimes the down-and-out alcoholic does 'casual work' in which he is essentially self-employed, such as gardening, offering to wash parked cars, tool sharpening, peddling boxes of matches or carrying and looking after travellers' suitcases. Somewhat rarely, co-operation with newsmen, interviewers and film-crews making documentaries for the media on 'the down-and-out problem' is granted in return for cash payment. In general the skid row alcoholic learns to develop an awareness of his immediate environment in terms of the possibilities it offers in making sufficient cash to buy alcohol.

Each of these jobs are assessed along a number of dimensions. They are evaluated by homeless alcoholics according to their financial rewards, the amount of time required to complete the job, the physical strength and stamina demanded and the flexibility and freedom it offers to take up and drop work when required. Thus:

> Demolition work is a good casual in terms of pay – a man may get six pounds a day for this type of work. At the other end of the scale you get £1.50 to £2.50 at best for several hours kitchen portering in an hotel.

> Micky and I got ourselves a good labouring job this week. We start work on Monday. It's a good casual because they're paying our fares to the job and back and we're getting a £3 'sub' to start off with.

But with increasing age and as alcohol addiction tightens its grip the homeless derelict is forced to take up less demanding, short-term low-paid work or learn how to earn a livelihood through other techniques of survival:

> A lot of dossers who stop in a kip house hold onto a regular casual, like kitchen work. These men are very steady in their own way, they might lose some of their money gambling, but they book in regularly at the Sally and they can drink three pints in a pub and walk out. A real alcoholic can't do this – if he's booked in for a kip he soon gets barred because he's drunk or damped down his bed. Maybe an alcoholic will do some kitchen portering just to get off the road for a while but it doesn't last long.

> Once you're skippering and drinking heavy you give up any idea of a regular casual.

> At Billingsgate fish market I used to get sixpence for a push of the barrow up the hill. But if the market men know you they might give you a shilling, or one-and-six, or even two bob for a heavy load. A man might be able to make ten bob in two hours – sometimes I could make a quid in a morning . . . A lot of the casual workers there were jack drinkers.

Eventually, physical debility brought on by alcohol dependence forces the alcoholic to abandon work almost completely, occasionally turning his hand to one-off improvised tasks – for example, peddling match boxes. Instead new strategies, such as begging and 'working' the agencies, are adopted as means of cushioning the deprivations of poverty and addiction.

Thieving

Stealing and selling small and easily disposed of items is probably a less frequently used strategy by which the habitual drunk is able to survive. The derelict inebriate has a very restricted clientele when it comes to disposing of shop-lifted goods and other items, since the people he most frequently meets are fellow alcoholics and other poverty-stricken skid row men. Only younger men, whose heavy drinking is balanced by periods of sobriety and who are not fully assimilated into the skid row culture, may occasionally engage in organised small-scale thieving. Once men find that drink plays an increasingly important role in their lives and they take on the identity of derelict alcoholics, their new status has the effect of severing any real connection they may have had with the social organisation of 'cons', thieves and 'fences'. In any case, the number of men who have taken part in organised thieving before becoming homeless alcoholics is probably very small.

However, petty thieving and shop-lifting are occassionally used as means by which money can be obtained. Clothing, food, ball-point pens, magazines, paperbacks and other small items are peddled to the marginally better-off regular common lodging house residents. Portable radios, lighters and watches are either sold in pubs or pawned. But one common and relatively lucrative source of cash is stripping lead and copper from newly vacated and derelict buildings. Those men who regularly sleep rough not only assess derelict buildings as potential shelters but also as a source of ready-to-hand materials that may be sold to scrap dealers. A homeless man, on being informed by a friend that he had recently located a newly vacated house to sleep in, enquired whether the house contained any lead or the gas and electricity meters had been emptied. He was answered: 'You don't think I'd look over a skipper without findings out these things. There was fuck all in the meters but we might be able to screw a little lead.'

Finally, taking money (and drink) from other alcoholics when they are heavily intoxicated is one method which, from those skid row men who do not engage in it, elicits strong condemnation. Rolling or 'bugging' other drunks is, however, practised by some men. The victim becomes particularly attractive when he is suspected of carrying relatively large sums of money – for example, middle-class drunks and skid row men who earn money from regular casuals or who have 'broken out' after a period of sobriety in a rehabilitation facility and carry with them their savings.

Shelter

Modern approaches to the treatment of derelict and homeless inebriates stress that it is the individuals' problem drinking that primarily requires attention. Until the alcoholic admits that the excessive use of alcohol is damaging his physical and psychological make-up, professionals argue that there is little point in attempting to resolve what are viewed as the secondary problems of housing and unemployment. The attainment of personal sobriety can only be acquired through the transformation of the 'inner' man, either through group psychotherapy, spiritual regeneration, or social rehabilitation, depending on the theoretical premises the treatment programme is based on. Fundamental readjustments in the personality and outlook of persons undergoing treatment are viewed as necessary prerequisites to acquiring a steady job and permanent home in the community.[20]

However, to the down-and-out alcoholic drinking heavily on the row, his homelessness is a major preoccupation, not in terms of acquiring a permanent and fixed abode (habitual drunkenness, poverty, and repeated institutionalisation prevent this) but rather as a means of adapting the urban environment to his immediate needs for shelter, warmth, sleep and privacy. How, then, does the vagrant alcoholic meet these basic human needs in a essentially hostile world? The following material focuses on two basic methods by which alcoholics resolve this problem: their adaption of what homeless men refer to as 'skippers', that is the public facilities, derelict buildings and open spaces informally transformed into places for sleeping rough; and their use of the formal institutions of skid row, in particular common lodging houses and reception centres.

Skippers and skippering

Of the total population living permanently on skid row the importance of resolving the problem of shelter is probably most acute for
the alcoholic, since habitual drunkenness (especially if compounded
by bed-wetting) is the primary justification advanced by agency
personnel for banishing homeless men from lodging houses, shelters
and rehabilitation hostels. In these circumstances the inebriate is
forced to adapt the surrounding physical environment to meet the
needs of shelter, sleep and privacy.

For the most part, when not incarcerated, hospitalised or resident
in charitable institutions, skid row men resolve these needs by 'doing
a skipper'. Broadly speaking, skippers are any facilities which the
homeless men use for sleeping in and which do not require any
monetary resources. Since skid row pockets are usually found in
older commercial and working-class districts, homeless men are able
primarily to sleep in derelict houses, empty offices and warehouses
scheduled for redevelopment. However, although these buildings are
the most frequently used type of skipper, an almost interminable
range of places and situations may be adapted for the purposes of
shelter and sleep. The following facilities, organised under five main
headings, were either observed or reported as places used for shelter
and accommodation:

1. *Transport facilities*: railway and underground stations; underground trains; railway carriages (in stations and sidings); buses in
   bus depots.
2. *Public facilities*: parks and open spaces (benches, park shelters,
   under bushes, on grass); car parks (underground); hospitals (in
   emergency clinic, under hot-water ducts); cemeteries (in disused
   chapel); all-night laundrettes; public lavatories; telephone kiosks;
   all-night cafés.
3. *Redevelopment sites*: abandoned and derelict houses, shops, fac-
   tories, cinemas, blocks of flats, warehouses and churches; bombed
   sites and demolished buildings (in cellars and basements).
4. *Miscellaneous*: abandoned motor cars; under railway arches; on
   pavements (next to warm-air grilles, under bridges, next to
   bonfire); in roadside sand box; in an oil drum; in cupboards turned
   on their backs with the door acting as a lid.
5. *Skid row facilities*: common lodging houses (under an occupied

bed in a booked cubicle); government reception centre (in an out-of-door shelter); in an 'off-the-street' night shelter.

This list probably does not exhaust all the situations or facilities men adapt as alternatives to more conventional sleeping places. Moreover they only reflect how the *urban* environment is manipulated to meet the need for shelter; homeless men also use a variety of places in the country when moving from one town to another. As Spradley points out in his analysis of the different kinds of 'flops' used by American skid row men, objects in the physical environment may conventionally be defined by their form, but their meaning also arises from their function.[21]

It has been claimed that single homeless men sleep rough by choice rather than conform to the standards and expectations of the wider community. If beds remain empty, then, the argument goes, homeless men must be freely choosing not to make use of them. However, the opinion of seasoned alcoholics suggests that discrimination against them by hostel and lodging house personnel renders such choice a purely academic issue. Furthermore, awareness of the physical and institutional conditions prevailing in large common lodging houses is regarded as sufficient reason to avoid them. Men often state that 'it is better to do a skipper than stop in a doss house'. Thus, although habitually sleeping rough is viewed by outsiders as the final stage in a downward process of human dereliction, many skid row alcoholics regard the use of mission shelters, hostels and common lodging houses, particularly if drunk, as opening them to the risk of harassment by both officials and other inmates. Sleeping rough is not only perceived as a possible, but also preferable, alternative:

> I would never go back to the spike [government reception centre] again because it's full of mental cases . . . nutters. Then there's the heavy gang [the porters] – they're always fucking you about, telling you what to do. I like my freedom . . . to do a skipper gives me freedom.

> I'd sooner sleep rough than in the Sally, because you get loused up in those places. Another thing – you know you can't get a job. Employers don't want to know if you give the Salvation Army hostel as an address.

> The Sally Ann is only in this business for financial gain . . . we're being exploited.

In addition, not using skid row facilities as somewhere to reside enables the alcoholic to avoid being subjected to religious sermons, invitations to be reformed, and requests to perform menial tasks and chores, or comply with institution rules and regulations.

However, although sleeping rough frees the dosser from the constraints imposed on him by living in large common lodging houses and reception centres, to the uninitiated skippering can be an added hardship, especially during the winter months. One man said of a drinking companion who managed to retain a fixed private address:

> Bob is in danger of losing his steady job because of his drinking. If that happens he'll go back to drinking meths and skippering. He's only done that once before back in the winter of '68. It nearly killed him.

Another alcoholic, for the first time experiencing the hardships of sleeping in derelict houses, put it this way:

> I haven't got as low as these boys yet but I've just started skippering. Mind you, I'm feeling it more than them. I'll tell you what I'd like most at this moment – a hot bath. These boys are used to skippering – they do not miss the comforts of life . . .

A few weeks later the same alcoholic reported that he had booked in at a Salvation Army lodging house because he was unable to tolerate sleeping out during the cold winter months. But within time, forced by heavier drinking, banishment from skid row institutions and lack of funds to book a bed elsewhere, the alcoholic is forced to adapt to the hardships of living rough. Asked if the cold winter nights were a deterrent to sleeping in derelict buildings,[22] an alcoholic replied:

> If you're living in a skipper day after day you get used to it. When you're steamed up you don't even feel the cold nights. But it's difficult for the man who starts skippering in the winter – he soon gets browned off.

Skippers, apart from their obvious function as a source of free shelter, offer the homeless alcoholic some security and privacy from the vicissitudes of a continuous public life. Consequently skippers are judged along two criteria: their comparative degree of comfort and the protection they offer from police intervention. It is in this context that newly abandoned buildings, structurally intact, with easy access, unlikely to be under police surveillance, and still containing useful items such as a bed or mattress, are highly prized: 'I'm skippering in a garage down Fleet Street. It's a good skipper, even got some heat in it. The coppers don't bother me there – so long as you don't get up to any mischief, they leave you alone.'

The derelict alcoholic often keeps the location of a skipper secret, only sharing the knowledge of its comforts and whereabouts with trusted drinking companions:

> It's one of the best skippers I've ever had. We light a fire, even fry up some potatoes in the morning. But I'm not telling no-one where it is. You know what it's like if the word gets around – you're fucked – every dosser in London will be there.

But sometimes it is not long before a new location has to be discovered, either because buildings are demolished or for the kind of reasons given by the following alcoholic:

> When you've got a good skipper you pick men of your own choice – the men you like. You want to have men who respect the place, who do not shite and piss in the same room you're kipping in. But then all that can be cut short if you break the rules yourself when you're drunk, by asking a stranger along to the skipper. You regret it next morning – it's either you or him that moves.

The relative security and privacy that skippers offer reduce the opportunity for the police to maintain surveillance over derelict alcoholics. The likelihood of harassment and arrest is minimised if men skipper in derelict buildings as opposed to those places, such as railway stations, archways and parks, which are open to regular police patrols. Adapting these types of readily accessible situations for the purpose of shelter and sleep increases the possibility of being arrested for trespassing, hosed down by street-cleansing authorities, or merely asked to 'move on'. However, the use of secluded shelters and derelict buildings does not mean that homeless men totally escape the hazards of using such places at night. For, when living in derelict houses, the right to privacy normally accorded to citizens possessing a home is suspended. The police and other intruders are liable to enter derelict houses unannounced. Several alcoholics mentioned that, particularly when drunk, they were at the mercy of young vandals and the harassment of the police. Measures to prevent detection or the invasion of their privacy, therefore, need to be taken:

> When we get into the skipper we barricade the door from inside – that way we can stop anyone trying to get in from outside.

> If the police see you going into a derry they'll come in and chase you. You've got to slip in quick.

> The other day some kids set fire to an old derry two doors away and that brought the fire brigade and the police round. Well, Alec, who was steamed up, began rearing up that he was going to get those kids for creating all the trouble. I had to keep him quiet, if not the law would have come in.

In spite of these intrusions and dangers, regular users of derelict buildings regard them as the only source of privacy in an otherwise totally public and institutionalised world.

Shelter in formal skid row facilities

Fundamentally four types of formal institutions are used by homeless men for the purposes of shelter: common lodging houses, cheap commercial hotels, government reception centres and night shelters run by voluntary agencies. Other facilities, such as small private lodging houses, are sometimes used but the price usually places them outside the range of the alcoholic's pocket. In any case seasoned alcoholics, faced with spending what little money they have on either booking a bed or on drink, will more often than not favour the latter choice. To be booked in on a regular basis at a commercial hotel or lodging house requires a relatively steady income through casual or permanent work, and means that either one is not a heavy drinker or is undergoing a period of self-imposed sobriety. As pointed out in the previous section, for the heavily intoxicated man, harassment and banishment from shelter and rehabilitation facilities are all too common; as a result, sleeping rough is often regarded as preferable.

The common lodging house is probably the most frequently used skid row shelter facility.[23] Sleeping quarters in them consist either of partitioned cubicles or communal dormitories. At any one time several hundred men may be sheltered in any one lodging house. The 1965 National Assistance Board survey, for example, reported that the majority of men were in establishments catering for 100 persons or more, and about 37 per cent (10,095 men) of the surveyed homeless single population were in establishments with 300 beds or more.[24] Bahr's description of an American skid row hotel cubicle could be accurately applied to the British scene:

> The cubicles in skid row hotels are very small, perhaps five by seven feet. The partitions between them reach only part way to the ceiling. The tops are covered with wire netting to discourage thieves from crawling over. The cubicles are open at the top, and sounds from other men on the floor are clearly audible. Inside the cubicle there is a stand of some kind – sometimes merely an apple box – and a cabinet attached to the wall. The other furnishings are a metal cot, a chair, and some hooks or nails in the wall.[25]

If cubicles are not available, then the next best thing is to book in at a lodging house with dormitories. The dormitories are usually large, with long rows of beds tightly packed together, separated by a chair used for hanging clothes on. By normal standards the physical and social conditions prevailing in the dormitories are inadequate. Once again Bahr sums up the conditions:

> Even in the best lodging houses a man is cramped for space, and in the worst he is assaulted by noise and foul smells, attacked by vermin, and constantly exposed to filth, disease, and the depredations of other men.[26]

In general alcoholics will rate common lodging houses according to the amenities available and the regime imposed on them. Establishments with cubicles and run by commercial organisations are preferred insofar as they offer relatively greater privacy and allow men more freedom to come and go as they please. But facilities with a philanthropic or religious orientation are viewed with hostility.

Inmates are requested to vacate the premises if they choose not to attend religious services; during the day men are forced on to the streets, since many Salvation Army centres close their doors; the quality of the food and the beds, and the behaviour of other inmates, are criticised. Personnel manning the booking hall, lounges and canteens are viewed with mistrust, especially if they are known to be recruited from the ranks of skid row men. Above all, alcoholics experience a sense of exploitation when booked in at Salvation Army lodging houses. The following comments by alcoholics sum up a prevalent view of shelters with a predominantly religious outlook on the problem:

I keep well away from the kip houses. You see, when you're in one of the Sallies [Salvation Army centres] your time is not your own. You're better off skippering, what with the nut cases and other men rearing up on you. There are too many rules in those places.

Some of these kip houses are just like the nick – the people that run them are no different from screws.

If I'm given a voucher for the Salvation Army I just tear it up – it's no good to anyone, not even for flogging because who would go to the Salvation Army, their beds are dirty and loused up.

The government-run reception centre is viewed in an equally critical light. A number of men commented in the following vein:

Once I tried to stop in the spike [government reception centre] when I was drunk but they made me stay outside in the shelter till I sobered up. The heavy gang [the porters] are always on to you there. But I can come in here [a commercial common lodging house] steamed up and no one will bother me.

The advantage of the reception centre over other large residential institutions on the row is that homeless men are permitted to stay there without having to pay.[27] The physical conditions are acknowledged by residents as having improved over recent years and are generally accepted as being better than in common lodging houses. But its disadvantages, from the men's point of view, often outweigh these factors. The regime, strictly enforced by porters and welfare officers, is the most common target for criticism. Since on average 500 men are handled in the centre each day by no more than 15 officers and assistants, and the centre is officially attempting to resettle men passing through the centre, a strict programme of control, super-vision, interviewing and referral is adhered to. The control system necessitates moving large batches of men through the waiting shelter, booking-in lobby, bath-house (where inmates must undergo in-spection, have their clothes fumigated, be deloused and bathed), dining hall, dormitories, welfare interview offices and workshops. At many points inmates are forced to wait in queues. Alcoholics frequently complain about the way they are handled through each of these staging posts within 'the spike'. A distinct animosity exists between the assistants and the men. Although fights and scuffles occasionally occur between assistants and inmates, homeless men take isolated assaults as evidence for roundly condemning the entire institution and its staff.

The attitudes many homeless alcoholics hold about sheltering in common lodging houses and reception centres are quite clearly based on feelings of animosity toward the personnel in authority. Yet it is quite evident that many alcoholics do occasionally seek shelter in these facilities. Among reasons given for booking in at the Salvation Army centre, commercial hotel or reception centre were the follow-ing: to avoid living rough during the winter months, take a rest from drinking and build oneself up physically, escape harassment by the police or, for those seeking treatment, take advantage of the chance to be referred to a more comfortable, small rehabilitation hostel. The more regular patrons of these establishments either learn to adjust to the institutional atmosphere or find themselves in the earlier stages of alcohol addiction, in which case, intermittent drinking may be tolerated by the management. Veteran skid row alcoholics know, however, that their residence in formal skid row facilities is inevitably a short-term expedient strategy. Sooner or later they will either be banned from the premises for transgressing house rules, sent to jail by the courts, move to another district or town, or decide that the money in their pockets is best spent on a bottle of cheap wine rather than on a bed ticket. In any case to settle down in one lodging house, pay a regular rent, tolerate the regime and a company of several hundred other men is to be labelled as not being 'a real alcoholic'. One veteran explained: 'Regular doss house users may have a bit of a drink problem but they are far from alcoholics. Some of them work a regular casual, book in at the Sally every week, and spend the rest of their money in the pub and on the horses. They are very steady men in their own way.' And another man pointed out: 'I know I am an alcoholic because I am always making sure that I have got some beer in the locker [some alcohol in me]. If I haven't I'm not happy. A real alcoholic is always on the move for a drink – that is, when he hasn't already got one. You'll never find an alcoholic just sitting around.'

4
Drinking Schools

The social organisation of drinking on skid row

Alcohol is one of the most easily acquired and widely used drugs in our society: its availability and consumption are not generally proscribed by law, except on licenced premises for persons under age. In fact, social drinking is actively encouraged at all levels of the social system, and even drunkenness, as long as it occurs within specific culturally defined times and locales, is often tolerated. Kessel and Walton, in their book *Alcoholism*, introduce the subject in the context of society's view of alcohol as a drug widely accepted as a social lubricant:

> We live in a society where it is customary to drink. It is the abstainer who strikes us as the more abnormal. With alcohol we offer hospitality and display our sociability. Though we frown on drunkards we are suspicious of teetotallers. Over a glass we enjoy old friends and make new ones, proclaim our loyalties, discuss affairs, negotiate and seal bargains. Repeated minimal intoxication is expected of our leading figures, soldiers, statesmen, businessmen, dons. We know that this sort of drinking, open and well moderated, is, for the most part, harmless and seems to conduce to good relationships.[1]

In Britain, pubs and off-licences are the most common outlets for the sale of alcohol; in addition drinking, as a normal social activity, takes place in restaurants, hotels, bars and in our homes.

But once excessive drinking and repeated drunkenness begin to impair individuals' social and economic functioning, a range of sanctions imposed by different social groups comes into force.[2] When individuals repeatedly transgress conventional rules as a result of drinking excessive quantities of alcohol, they take on a new identity. Habitual drunks, in contemporary terminology, become known as alcoholics. For alcoholics the consumption of alcohol and its social consequences take on a significance that markedly separates them from the rest of the community. The attitudes and behaviour of alcoholics, in concert with reactions to them, result in a realignment of their moral status. In short, confronted by a variety of problems arising out of excessive drinking, alcoholics need to make personal and social adjustments both to their own condition and that of society's reactions to them.

Viewed from the perspective of groups whose interests are related to handling alcoholics, alcohol addiction is often couched in terms that describe habitual drunkenness as an asocial act consisting of uncontrolled and often bizarre and aggressive behaviour. A common view of alcoholics is that they are out of control when 'under the influence'. The following quotation, although alluding to crude spirit drinking, illustrates a commonly held stereotype of vagrant alcoholics in general:

> Unwashed, evil smelling, incapable of work, occasionally emerging from his psychotic drunken state . . . his condition gives rise to contempt . . . Such persons tend to cause offence or annoyance to members of the public, if only by reason of their unkempt appearance and slovenly behaviour, and in the small open spaces where they are most often found it is difficult to avoid coming into contact with them. In addition, their uncontrolled urination gives rise to offence, whilst in the toilets an objectionable smell remains which is almost impossible to get rid of. [Crude] spirit drinkers are moved on by the staff . . . but they are often aggressive and the police are frequently called on for assistance in removing them. The position is aggravated by the fact that the drinkers usually congregate in groups.[3]

This quotation not only reflects the social distance between deviant and moral entrepreneur but, in the language of the layman, also helps convey an image perpetrated by many social theorists interested in the skid row phenomenon, namely, that men on skid row are disorganised and undersocialised (see pp. 20–3). In spite of these widely accepted attributes an examination of the social organisation of drinking on skid row reveals that drinking and drunkenness are not the apogee of an asocial world but are governed by norms, attitudes and sanctions appropriate to the alcoholic's survival on the row. In the final analysis, in spite of the illicit nature of methylated and surgical spirit drinking or the excessive use of socially approved alcoholic beverages such as cheap wine and cider, it is not drinking and drunkenness *per se* that determine the shape of social control but rather the general life style and status of the homeless alcoholic.

In keeping with the general argument of this report the analysis of the social organisation of drinking among homeless men is designed to counter the commonly held view that the abuse of alcohol on skid row is nothing but a reflection of irrational and pathological personalities who are merely to be understood as physically and psychologically addicted to a legalised drug. To be sure, sustained alcohol abuse does have marked deleterious effects on the physiological and psychological make-up of individuals. For example, skid row alcoholics suffer from malnutrition and vitamin deficiency. The proper functioning of the stomach and liver may be affected. The nervous system is adversely affected, and prolonged and excessive intake of alcohol induces abnormal mental states, especially in the form of withdrawal symptoms. When alcoholism is compounded with homelessness and chronic poverty, other ailments and diseases are likely to arise. Skin infections, pulmonary diseases and tuberculosis are prevalent. Among regular crude spirit drinkers premature blindness is likely to occur. Finally, mortality rates amongst homeless men are high in comparison with the population at large. In his study of skid row in American cities, Bogue concluded that 'Skid Row appears to be one of the last domains of avoidable and unnecessary death'.[4]

Yet, despite the adversity of physical and psychological illness, the deprivations inherent in alcohol addiction, homelessness and chronic poverty are countered, and given meaning, by a network of social relationships structured around the alcoholic's central activity – drinking. From the vantage point of the skid row alcoholic, drinking takes on a meaning that is directly related to his status as a skid row man. Derelict alcoholics organise their drinking around a finely spun web of norms and sanctions, which they have created as a workable answer to their problems of addiction, homelessness and poverty, but which also take into account their vulnerability to external controls by police and other persons in authority.

This does not mean that there is a uniform response in the drinking patterns of homeless men. Not all men who drink heavily and live in skid row institutions organise their drinking activities around street drinking, and neither, as is commonly believed, are all homeless alcoholics inveterate (or even occasional) crude spirit drinkers. Rooney, referring to American skid rows, distinguished between 'tavern' and 'street' drinkers, claiming that the former tend to be labelled 'drunks' and the latter 'winos'. Other writers have distinguished between two types of street drinkers – 'lushes' and 'winos' – while Jackson and Connor have referred to a third type of drinkers known as 'dehorns' or 'rubby-duds'.[5] Lushes and winos may be grouped together, since they concentrate on legitimate alcoholic beverages (fortified wine), whereas dehorns and rubby-duds are a quite separate group. The authors defined them as follows: 'Dehorns or rubby-duds are habitual drinkers of non-beverage alcohol, chiefly bay rum and canned heat . . . these men may also resort to shaving lotion, paint thinner mixed with water, and rubbing alcohol.'[6]

The significance of these distinctions as they apply to the American scene is the remarkable parallels they have to drinking patterns among homeless men in Britain. Fieldwork has revealed two broad patterns of skid row alcoholics. Firstly, there are men who are able to frequent pubs located in areas that are serviced by other skid row institutions, especially common lodging houses, and are run by managements tolerant of their clientele. Cider and beer are the most common beverages consumed in this setting, although cheap wine is also occasionally drunk. Secondly, there are men who almost exclusively confine their drinking to public locales, such as streets and parks. In this case the majority of alcoholics organise their drinking around small groups known as drinking schools, although some men are known to drink on their own. Street drinkers may be sub-divided into two categories: cider and cheap wine drinkers and, making up a small minority of homeless alcoholics, crude spirit drinkers.

Now these divisions are not watertight, but should be regarded as ideal types. The pub drinker may occasionally drink cider and wine on the street when his funds are low, when he finds that he is unable to confine his abuse of alcohol to pub licencing hours, or when he is, for a number of reasons, banned from pub drinking by the management. Conversely, cider and wine street drinkers occasionally drink in pubs. Habitual crude spirit drinkers, however, very infrequently make their way into pubs but sometimes will join cider and wine drinkers at street level. Moreover the progression from one type of addictive drinking to another, no matter how long men remain on skid row, is not inevitable. Some long-term residents on skid row remain exclusively heavy cider drinkers throughout their skid row lives; others only drink crude spirits very occasionally; still others become habitual consumers of 'jake'.[7] Each type of alcoholic on skid row, according to the type of drinking situation he frequents and the kind of alcohol consumed, confers different meanings on his drinking status and that of others. A complex hierarchy is constructed in which regular skid row pub-drinkers regard street drinkers as having a lower status, while cider and wine drinkers who confine their activities to the street view the habitual crude spirit drinker with disdain and antagonism. Finally, members of the latter group not infrequently justify their drinking and personal situation in relation to other skid row alcoholics by claiming that meths drinkers are the only '*real* alcoholics' and that cider and wine drinkers are merely ordinary drunks who do not qualify for full membership of the 'jake' drinking fraternity.[8]

The skid row drinking school

The most visible form of deviant drinking on skid row is the 'bottle gang' or 'drinking school'. Although the social organisation of bottle gangs has been studied in the United States, no comparable reports focus on the drinking school phenomenon in this country. This is not surprising, since it is often the more unorthodox elements of any deviant phenomenon that remain unexplored.

One major preoccupation of those researchers interested in the internal structure of American bottle gangs has been to test the thesis that alcoholics on skid row are not necessarily undersocialised isolates. A reading of the limited literature focusing on bottle gang structure and behaviour serves to undermine the view that derelict inebriates can only be understood as individuals engaged in meaningless activities. Both Jackson and Connor, despite their professional psychiatric interests, and Peterson and Maxwell arrived at similar conclusions about different types of alcoholics on the row. Both 'lushes' (a prestige group of alcoholics who take up temporary residence on skid row) and 'winos' (permanent residents) are not social isolates. Both sets of authors instead concluded with the opposite view, summed up as follows:

[Skid row alcoholics] are found to live as social beings in a society of their fellows. It is a society which prescribes and provides mutual aid in meeting the problems of survival: food, drink, shelter, illness and protection. But more than that, it is a society which also provides the emotional support found in the acceptance by, and the companionship of, fellow human beings.[9]

Similarly Rooney perceived bottle gangs as fulfilling both the social and psychological needs of their members, and thereby partially undermined the prevalent view that alcoholics are under-socialised, inadequate and isolated.[10] However, Rooney qualifies his conclusions by pointing out that the collective search and consumption of alcohol is mainly an instrumental activity and does not reflect any permanance of personal relationships among bottle gang participants. Once the need for alcohol is satisfied, he found that relationships are dissolved, and therefore concluded that bottle gangs, as groups, are 'not characterised by intimacy or mutual trust and identification'.[11] Finally, Rubington offers a detailed description of the ritualised dynamics of bottle gang members in terms of the stages the gang goes through from the moment it comes together to its dispersal. He divides the process into six specific stages: salutation, negotiation, procurement, consumption, affirmation, and dispersal.[12] Each of these stages reinforces the members' sense of participation in the collective life of skid row and provide a basis by which group drinking may be meaningfully structured.

'Bottle gang' and 'drinking school' are synonymous terms, respectively applied by American and British skid row inhabitants to group drinking. Rubington's definition of a bottle gang is, for the most part, applicable to a drinking school:

> . . . [the term] 'bottle gang' refers to the typical form of street drinking in which indigent unattached men engage. The men appear to be heavy drinkers by conventional standards and are usually referred to as alcoholics, or in slang terms as 'bums' 'drunks', or 'winos'. Generally they meet on the street, pool meagre funds, send a member to a package store to buy an inexpensive bottle of fortified wine, share the bottle in some public place (e.g. alley, doorstep, park or street corner in rooming-house areas, urban slums, or Skid Row quarter) and separate once the bottle is emptied.[13]

To the outsider drinking schools appear to consist of small groups of drunks – between two and six men – who congregate in railway stations, parks and other open spaces with the sole purpose of drinking and getting drunk. Very often they are taken to represent the 'down-and-out problem', although all systematic surveys of skid row populations show that the majority of men who inhabit lodging houses and reception centres are either abstainers or light drinkers as defined by the standards of the wider community. Although drinking schools nearly always congregate in a public place, since they are denied access to legitimate drinking locales, such as pubs, its members nevertheless often manage to conceal their presence from police and public by drinking in common lodging houses, derelict buildings and other secluded places.[14]

For derelict alcoholics, drinking schools act as a convenient vehicle through which they are able to minimise the impact of addiction, poverty and police control. Drinking schools become a substitute primary group, since they act as a familiar homing device by which men are able to participate meaningfully in their culture. One informant explained:

It's more habit where you frequent. You do so for your own security and safety, and because you know what the score is, who your mates are, and how they will react. When you pick a new drinking scene you feel everyone is watching you, you feel all out of place. Till you get drunk, that is, then you don't give a fuck.

But it is as a regular source of alcohol that drinking schools fulfil their most important function. Members of drinking schools know where they can obtain a drink even if they are penniless:

When I wake up in the morning I've often got the sickness and the first thing I want is a drink. Sometimes I've got some cider left over from the previous night or four bob with which to buy a bottle. If not the first place I go to is Camberwell Green – I know I can get a drink there.

A good man, even when he's broke, will get a drink from his pals. He'll go to where the school meets but he doesn't join them – he'll sit to one side and wait for his pals to call him over. To be invited into a school is better than making your own way in, you get more drink in the end.

Two crucial dimensions, which determine the structure and functioning of drinking schools, are explored here. They are, firstly, the internal economic and social relationships governing the behaviour of drinking school members, and, secondly, their relationship with external forces of social control, in particular the police.

Drinking schools: their social and economic function

The membership of drinking schools varies in size, and is usually made up of two to six men. Such a membership reflects the optimum size by which alcoholics collectively pool their limited economic resources. Frequenting the same drinking locale, a regular core of alcoholics will drink and maybe beg together, and will sometimes live in the same common lodging houses .or derelict buildings. The economic function of group drinking is crucial to the schools' adequate performance. Usually an individual's access to a drinking school is guaranteed on the strength of being able to make a contribution towards the next bottle. However, absence of any monetary resources does not exclude homeless men from sharing in drinking; for, as observers of group drinking processes on skid row have noted, alcoholics not only contribute financially in return for the immediate consumption of alcohol but do so in the knowledge that on future occasions they will be able to participate in drinking on the basis of past donations. Moreover unequal contributions to the funds of a school are made in return for equal consumption of alcohol. Thus a fine balance is created, on the one hand, between one's performance and reputation as a drinking school member and, on the other, one's right to participate in the sharing of a bottle without making a financial contribution to it. On countless occasions derelict alcoholics were heard to judge others for their willingness to contribute to a school's economic strength. To give money when others are unable to do so is to reinforce the sense of reciprocity and mutual aid that cements the drinking school members together. Thus:

> When I've got money I put it towards a bottle. You only get a regular drink if you give your share. That's the way it is.

> When you're new to a school you've got to put something into it. The regulars may give you a drink from the bottle when you first arrive but if it looks like you're not going to give them anything

then they'll fuck you out of the company . . . you've got to put your piece in.

If you're on the toby and you're thinking of moving on you leave a drink with the school. I would do a wee fiddling job or get some money off the N.A.B., and give the lads a pound. Then if I come back in a year I'd know where to find the same men. They'd welcome me back.

The importance attached to sharing money and drink is highlighted by the consequences for those individuals who fail to comply with the ethic of sharing. Men who fail to share their money acquire reputations for meanness, are forced into solitary drinking and become labelled as loners. Some of the men commented on the rules:

A drinking school can always tell a mean man.

Andy 'the Pole' gets a pension every Monday. He tried to keep it secret but the dossers got to know about it. You'll never see him buy a bottle – I could never do that, go around with money and not spend it with the lads. He's not a man, is he?

Furthermore, alcoholics who are allowed to join in the group drinking activities of a school they do not frequent but who hold on to the bottle too long, attempt to drink more than their share, or depart without making a contribution after a bottle is consumed, are heavily criticised.

However, there is one rule which, if broken, opens the alcoholic to heavy sanctions. When a school has pooled its economic resources, one member acts as 'runner' to the off-licence or liquor store. Usually this person will be the least drunk, most respectable looking and best trusted member of the school. Those remaining behind will wait patiently for the return of the 'runner'. However, to 'pull a stroke' on the school, that is, to fail to return with the bottles, is to break one of the most strongly adhered to rules of skid row. The uncompromising denunciation of anyone who 'pulls a stroke' illustrates the significance attached to the norm of mutual trust and reciprocity. Only one valid excuse exempts individuals from the inevitable criticism and rejection that surrounds the act of making off with the pooled funds of a bottle gang, and that is to be arrested while carrying out the mission. In conversation among drinking school members the principle of trust in connection with making 'a run' to the off-licence was articulated on a number of occasions:[15]

> If I were given ten bob by someone for a bottle of wine I would never fuck off with it because I'd never be able to show my face again. You're not a man if you pull a stroke on the school.

> It's almost professional ethics to return with a bottle once you've been given money by the company.

> Mary is not to be trusted – she'll make off with the money if we're not careful. I'm going to make sure we're going to get a bottle of wine out of that money by going with her to the off-licence.

Alcoholics who attempt to make their way into group drinking without contributing to its resources, who choose to drink on their own when in a relatively strong financial position, or who 'pull a stroke', gain reputations for meanness and unreliability, reputations which are spread through the skid row grapevine. Mutual obligation and trust, then, serve to bind drinking schools together and allow them to function adequately. But, as Rubington correctly pointed out, the infraction of bottle gang norms are frequent, and although sanctions are imposed on those who contravene drinking rules, they are not imposed uniformly and consistently. The criticism and rejection directed at those who break the rules, although not necessarily forgotten, are often suspended when the infractor at some later date offers 'the price of a bottle as an entrance fee to the school'.

If the application of norms and sanctions is sufficiently inconsistent as to deny their ultimate validity, what impact do they have, if any, on the quality of social relationships among street and park drinkers on skid row? American observers of the skid row scene have debated whether the social relationships thrown up by the structure of group drinking are essentially based on notions of mutual friendship or whether they reflect somewhat fragile and instrumental relationships based merely on economic expediency. In a useful review of the bottle gang literature Bahr claims that on balance American authors have concluded that the members of bottle gangs are interchangeable and that 'the most important thing about a member of a bottle gang is that he "belongs" because he has bought his way in'.[16] There would appear little to bind members together except the function of drinking and getting drunk. In essence Bahr asserts that skid row alcoholics are friendless and isolated, and that informal relationships among them are impermanent and weak. The derelict alcoholic is basically untrustworthy. It is not surprising, therefore, that Bahr's evaluation of bottle gangs is made within the following framework:

> Since social control derives from the ability to exercise sanctions, and sanctions stem from organisations, the more impermanent a group, the less it is able to level sanctions effectively . . . The greatest sanction the men in a bottle gang can muster – exclusion – is quickly neutralised by the proceeds from a few minutes' panhandling.[17]

However, the conclusions arrived at by Bahr and others cannot be uniformly applied to the structure and quality of social relationships among skid row alcoholics in Britain. For certain, a common identity amongst homeless alcoholics as 'park drinkers' or 'jake-drinkers' does not preclude personal relationships developing on the basis of genuine mistrust and antipathy, on the one hand, or on solid friendship, on the other. Observations and accounts of social relationships among drinking schools showed that skid row men do make marked distinctions between a 'good man' and a 'blaggard', between a 'regular' and a 'stranger', that the personalities involved in drinking schools do matter, and that friendships and antipathies are based on factors beyond the ability, or lack of it, to provide the funds for the next bottle. Generally speaking, friendship and personal antagonism are expressed within drinking schools, and these attitudes are determined by the 'mix' of permanent and temporary members. A regular core of four to six members does not congregate merely 'to pull liquor' and drink; rather the members' affinity with each other is often based on friendships struck up before their full-time residence on skid row, while working as seamen or labourers and confining their drinking to pubs, or occasionally even earlier, as in the case of men who were brought up together in the same village or town.[18]

It is those alcoholics who join drinking schools temporarily and who make their membership short-lived that are regarded with antagonism and distrust. Comments made by regular members of a drinking school on the relationship between themselves and temporary members illustrate the divisions that may arise:

Some of these strangers come up to us asking where the off-licence or the 'Spike' is. But they do so because they're trying to get in with us regulars.

You get strangers who join the school but don't know what the score is. This man was holding onto the bottle too long so I asked him 'Are you trying to marry that bottle that you're holding onto it? In this gang we pass the bottle round quick.'

Keep an eye on that stranger.

A stranger knows that he's only a temporary member of a school and that he's open to being excluded at any time. When he's drinking with the lads he knows that, without saying it, the regulars are telling him 'don't be coming the dog'.

Since they opened the new court next to this park we can't drink in peace here no more. Men we've never seen before come out of court and make straight for the park. They're nothing but trouble-makers, fighting and rearing up. In the old days the real regulars could drink all day on the Green and not be bothered by anyone. This park is fucked now.

New arrivals to the scene are unaware of the particular nuances that bind regular drinking companions together. Neither have they any sense of the subtleties and norms that operate in particular public locales so as to minimise the school's visibility and possibility of external sanctions being imposed on it by the public, park keepers and, in particular, the police. Yet, occasionally, a stranger will be welcomed into the regular company of a school, as the following field notes revealed:

Jock was a new man to all the members of the school. But he was allowed to join us on the basis of a generous contribution towards five bottles of cider. Moreover, Jock was sober. He entertained the school with accounts of past experiences on skid row. Stories were exchanged about begging exploits, 'beating the law', and 'conning the agencies'.

Once the school had pooled their money Eddy asked one of the regulars if anyone was familiar with the new face amongst them, a younger man sitting a little aside to the gang. A short discussion followed as to whether he should be allowed to join the school. The alcoholic holding the funds settled the argument by saying 'The man has made a contribution, so he should be allowed to join us and drink his share of wine.'

Patterns of friendship, therefore, have to be understood not only in the context of the deprivations inherent in chronic poverty and alcohol addiction but in relation to how strongly personal allegiances are developed and sustained over time, and how these affiliations contrast with those temporary relationships based on the expedient need for a drink. It is not sufficient to infer from the impermanence of drinking schools' membership that alcoholics on skid row are invariably isolated and friendless. After all, any permanence in drinking school relationships, even among its core members, is made impossible as a result of the frequent institutionalisation of derelict alcoholics by social control agencies. Skid row habituees are able to structure their relationships around such interruptions to the extent that even relatively long absent members, on returning to skid row drinking, reforge links with their previous drinking companions.

Crude spirit drinking[19]

Is the social organisation of crude spirit drinking in any way radically different from that practised by cider and cheap wine drinkers? The number of men who exclusively drink methylated or surgical spirits is comparatively small, although most homeless alcoholics report consuming crude spirits intermittently. Certainly men addicted to non-beverage alcohols are aware of the redefinitions imposed upon them. The illicit nature of this type of alcohol consumption markedly separates 'meths drinkers' from other alcoholics on the row. In their chemical composition alone crude spirits are radically different from socially acceptable beverage alcohols. Consequently, among skid row men and social control agents, crude spirit drinking takes on a special meaning. In turn, meths drinkers, as one small section of the skid row population, acquire an identity that reflects the special problems associated with the habitual consumption of 'jake'.[20]

In the first place, cider and wine alcoholics view crude spirit drinking with a marked sense of caution and apprehension. Aware of its immediate and long-term toxic effects, they frequently turn down the offer of a drink from men who regularly consume 'the queer stuff'. However, the most common justification advanced by wine and cider drinkers for the initial drinking of crude spirit is economic destitution coupled with a desperate need for a drink. Most alcoholics learn to appreciate from acquaintance with veteran crude spirit drinkers the physical, psychological and social consequences inherent in its regular consumption. Here are some comments made by cider and wine drinkers:

It's is a big step down when you begin drinking the jack. You feel that you're degrading yourself since when you're a cider or wine drinker and you see the rough boys then you know you haven't got to the bottom yet.

Once you drink the jack you've had it.

Tracey is a regular jack drinker – his mind has gone. You can tell that, he doesn't give a fuck for anyone except himself.

I tried to beg someone I know in a pub last night but when he smelt the jack on me he gave me a bollocking and I didn't get anything.

I've always been afraid of meths drinking. Then there's another thing about meths drinking schools – I didn't like the scene – the smell of meths drinkers' piss put me off.

Dependence on non-beverage alcohols is a secondary form of addiction, that is, it is an addiction found in individuals who already, in the first place, are addicted to legitimate alcoholic drinks. Of course, the progression from socially acceptable beverages to crude spirits is not inevitable, as is clear even with those individuals who may drink it only itermittently. But for those alcoholics who do make the transition, the process of adaptation to crude spirit drinking on a regular basis necessitates a careful appraisal of its acute toxic effects. This appraisal includes learning how to become a jack drinker. A number of informants explained:

When it comes round to drinking the jack for the first time an alcoholic might be told to drink it carefully. I was with a couple of friends who were experienced meths drinkers. They bought a couple of block busters [large bottles of methylated spirits] and Danny showed me how much meths to mix with cider and V.P. wine . . . I was told to sip it . . . I took to the heavy stuff like fish to water.

> A friend of mine told me how to drink the jack . . . you've got to sip it . . . if you drink it too fast it goes to your head too quickly and you're likely to be knocked out.

> I found that it took a lot of cider to get drunk so I mixed it with the jack to make it stronger.

Both methylated and surgical spirits are almost invariably diluted with water or mixed with cider, wine and other beverages. Since seasoned jake drinkers are able to tolerate higher concentrations of non-ethyl alcohols in the mixture they make up, novices are often sick on their first attempt to share a bottle with the veterans.[21]

> A jack-drinking gang knows that a wine drinker who makes an approach to them is doing so because he is desperate and not out of love for the drink. They'll offer him the bottle and might tell him that 'if you can keep it down you're with us'. But if it's the first time he's tried it he'll be sick. The gang might then make up a lighter mixture which the man will be able to take. He thus begins to acquire a taste for the hard stuff.

Habitual crude spirit drinking also produces a number of readjustments in the social organisation of drinking schools. Generally speaking, the rules and norms around which members of cider and wine drinking schools structure their activities are also evident among methylated and surgical spirit addicts. However, a number of factors bring about crucial realignments in the social relationships among jake drinkers.

Firstly, the jake drinking school is a much more closed group. A school will rarely consist of more than three or four members, who consistently drink together.[22] As opposed to cider and wine drinking schools, the jake gang is unlikely to have temporary and peripheral members join its activities. This is probably due partly to the relatively small number of seasoned meths and surge alcoholics. But, more important, the school does not augment the quantity it drinks on the basis of occasional outsiders buying their way into the school; rather they will confine their drinking only to permanent members who are prepared to work for their share of the bottle.

> Meths drinking schools can't afford to carry a non-producer. If a man can't beg or do a bit of thieving then he won't be tolerated. Put

it this way: if you don't come up with the pay-off, then eventually you'll get run out of the school. The men in a meths gang stick together more, beg together, and pool their money. Only if one of the regulars is very ill or going to snuff it [die] will he not be expected to work. The others will carry him.

I'd get up to the fish market early in the morning and do a wee casual. I'd make enough money to buy two blockbusters before ten o'clock . . . if the lads knew I was bringing the message I would be alright for the rest of the day . . . I didn't have to buy another drink.

Secondly, men who are often dishevelled and unkempt, and who gain reputations for crude spirit drinking, find that chemist and hardware shops which are prepared to sell them crude spirits are limited. To overcome this difficulty drinking schools are anchored in locales where their presence passes relatively unnoticed and they have access to a ready source of supply. Alternatively, members are forced to travel some distance within large urban centres to acquire crude spirits from unsuspecting or permissive shop attendants. Consequently habitual crude spirit drinkers need to establish a tighter and more stable internal structure to their drinkting school. Becoming a known meths drinker is to consolidate one's identity as a total outsider. Both social control agents and other alcoholics on the row frequently help in consolidating this new identity by consistently portraying meths drinking as the last step in alcoholic oblivion, directly responsible for mental atrophy, creeping blindness and eventual death.[23]

Drinking schools and the police

The analysis so far has focused on the internal dynamics and norms governing drinking school behaviour. In Chapter 5 I concentrate in some detail on the interaction between homeless alcoholics and law-enforcement agencies – organising the material in relation to the traditional framework by which skid row drunks are controlled. Police control and arrest, trial, and imprisonment are viewed simultaneously from the standpoint of deviants, on the one hand, and police, magistrates and prison personnel, on the other. But it would be useful at this stage to extend the analysis to include the meaning skid row alcoholics attach to police intervention in drinking school behaviour.

Alcoholics on skid row perfectly well understand the significance of drinking and drunkenness in relation to police practices toward them. The high visibility of drinking schools opens them to police surveillance and intervention. Chronic intoxication often leads to the rules and norms binding drinking groups together being openly broken. In particular the rules of admissible personal conduct are transgressed. Men break bottles, urinate in public and sometimes fight. To the outsider, and in particular to the police, all the attributes by which skid row drunks become labelled and stereotyped then come to the fore. Alcoholics are aware that in situations of this kind the police shift their control tactics from peace-keeping – the regular surveillance and occasional breaking up of drinking schools – to law enforcement – the arrest and prosecution of habitual drunks. Thus those men who remain comparatively sober attempt to control, warn, or cajole those who are inebriated into maintaining, as far as possible, acceptable standards of public behaviour. To draw attention to the school is to place those men who are not technically infringing the law in a position where they are as likely to be arrested as those who are. A dosser explains:

> There's no point in rearing up on anyone in this park – you just get knocked off. When you're drinking in a school the first thing to do is to remain completely cool: keep your eye on the bottle, on the other dossers, and on the police. When I'm drinking and the men begin rearing up I always keep a lookout to see if the park keeper is watching us. As soon as he makes a move to his hut I know he's going to 'phone for the law.

The high visibility of drinking schools using public spaces quite clearly opens alcoholics to police harassment and sanctions.[24] It is important, therefore, to examine the optimum size and visibility of drinking schools in relation to the likelihood of police intervention.

The possibility of external controls being imposed on drinking schools arises especially when three factors, often interrelated, come into play. Firstly, the optimum size of drinking school membership is exceeded. Secondly, members who are chronically intoxicated lose control over personal behaviour and that of others. Finally, individuals whose membership is incidental transgress the established nuances of personal conduct within the drinking school. These factors in combination are often invoked as explanations for the interference of the police in the activities of the school, especially when individuals are arrested or, on occasions, when police conduct mass clean-ups of parks and open spaces. On such occasions drinking schools over six or seven in size are defined as 'heavy gangs', relatively unknown men or strangers are labelled 'troublemakers', and individuals engaging in drunken behaviour are accused by those who remain 'in control' as being unable to hold their drink. Chronic drunkenness, a 'heavy gang' and the possibility or actual display of violence, are all taken as appropriate cues by which to condemn others for attracting the attention of the police or public.

The nature of public drunkenness and its control by the police needs to be understood in the context of the fact that skid row men do not have any substantial claim to the institutions of privacy: their day-to-day lives are conducted exclusively in public or within formal skid row institutions, which, by their very function, lack the privacy the majority of us take for granted. When persons do not have access to the institutions of privacy, the likelihood of being investigated, arrested and prosecuted is increased. Stinchcombe sums up this problem:

A man entirely without access to private places is legally unfree . . . if a man is not a member of some organisation or family or other group that have control over a 'private place . . . then he has to satisfy a policeman that his occupation in the area is lawful and has to make visible his means of support . . . Few of us ever see a policeman in those places we spend most of our time; a 'tramp' sees one wherever he goes, and the policeman has the discretionary power to 'run him in.'[25]

Drinking schools, therefore, seek to minimise their public visibility. Bottles are secreted on the person when not doing the rounds, empties are discarded in litter baskets, contact with the public (except when begging) is kept to a minimum, bizarre behaviour and horse-play are controlled. Moreover drinking schools use territorial areas in urban centres that both alcoholics and police regard as 'netural' zones of public conduct, that is, areas where public drinking by homeless men is to a degree tolerated by police and public, and therefore partly legitimised. An alcoholic recounted:

We used to drink in an abandoned cemetery because the place was all overgrown and the grass was long. You could drink and get steamed up, and lie in the grass and no one would know about it. That place is not so good now because the council cleaned the place up and removed the gravestones – you're made more visible if you drink there now . . .

When we drinked at 'The Ramp' we did whatever we liked because the public did not use it as a thoroughfare. From time to time the police would come to see that everything was in order . . . but on the whole they didn't bother us regulars. If they found a younger man there – someone new – they'd chase him.

There are a number of reasons why the police view skid row drunks within a wide range of discretionary power (see Chapter 5, p. 93). Nevertheless, since homeless alcoholics are *repeatedly* at odds with the police, all skid row habituees are able to recount situations where at one time or another patrolmen employed techniques of control that included threats, harassment, unwarranted arrest and, occasionally, brutality.[26] How do derelict alcoholics, drinking in gangs, react to police interference? The powerless position of homeless men generally results in them developing strategies of avoidance. Members of drinking schools keep a lookout and warn others of the approach of patrolmen; move away voluntarily if arrests are imminent; attempt to persuade the police that nothing untoward has happened and that everything is 'normal'; or accede readily to requests to 'move on', sometimes helping to remove those companions who are too incapacitated to remove themselves. Reacting to police harassment has little to commend it:

You've got to keep cool when it comes to the police. I myself get mad with them but I know I cannot beat them. You've got to remain cool and think. It's no good losing your mind – you only end getting knocked off by the law.

We used to drink by Bloomsbury Square but the coppers around there were pure bastards, so we eventually decided to move to Red Lion Square.

In other words, although interaction between police and homeless alcoholics is perceived by the latter as one in which police discretion as to how they handle the men is very wide, they are aware that not only their behaviour but their status is sufficient cause for arrest and prosecution. In this context derelict alcoholics invoke a multitude of social skills by which they attempt to conceal their deviant behaviour and status in situations of maximum public visibility.

Skid row alcoholics who learn to participate in the collective activities of drinking schools are able simultaneously to transcend problems of addiction and chronic poverty, on the one hand, and society's attempt to control them, on the other; for, as Rubington has indicated:

> Finally, as [they] become more deeply involved in a drinking-centred existence, statuses and roles, beliefs and norms all revolve around this axis. In the process, the usual urban complexities change in meaning and shrink in scope. Now obvious social failures can sustain a life which is to be understood in terms of the metaphors of deviant social drinking, with all its rewards and punishments. Obtaining and maintaining a supply of drink in accordance with a set of rules provides a schedule, a calendar, a routine and a morality all its own. The net effect of this life-style is to deny failure in the pursuit of drink in company.[27]

The aim in this and the last chapter has been to demonstrate that for men habitually engaged in public drinking, who are homeless and chronically poor, their world becomes defined primarily in terms of the construction of appropriate survival strategies. Drinking schools not only function as an informal institution through which collective drinking takes place, but as a means by which its participants learn to attach specific meanings to their social situation and society's attempt to control or modify it. Individuals take on identities that fit in with those they most frequently live with and direct their activities in relation to the problems encountered on skid row. Insofar as the analysis has stressed the essentially social nature of skid row drinking, the account offered is at variance with the dominant view held by most outsiders that skid row 'is composed largely of discontented and semi-isolated individuals, who have few if any close friends, and who survive by being suspicious of everybody.'[28]

5
The Penal Revolving Door

Interaction in the world of law enforcement

In the previous two chapters the analysis focused on how homeless alcoholics define and overcome problems of survival and drinking on skid row. Money, shelter and alcohol were taken as the three central needs of the derelict inebriate; how these needs are resolved reflects a particular meaning and complexity when viewed from the alcoholic's standpoint. Merely describing the down-and-out drunk as poverty-stricken, homeless and addicted conceals or denies the finely spun web of attitudes and values the alcoholic himself attaches to these problems.

So far, however, the alcoholic's view of his world and the activities he engages in have been spelled out in isolation from attempts by society to intervene in the skid row life style. Only limited reference has been made to police intervention in the attempt by homeless men to 'make out' on skid row. In both this and the following chapter an understanding of how homeless inebriates and agents of social control define each other is offered. Their respective views are located in the context of the penal and rehabilitation institutions within which interaction unfolds between the alcoholic and his guardians.

The impact that law-enforcement agencies make on the life of skid row drunks extends beyond face-to-face encounters with police patrolmen. Sooner or later the entire apparatus of law enforcement – the police, the court, and the local prison – take on immediate relevance for vagrant alcoholics. Each of these institutions plays a part in moulding the deviant identity of men on skid row,[1] since a crucial factor about them is their frequent intervention in the drinking careers of street alcoholics.

On the other hand, the personnel manning the institutions of law enforcement – policemen, magistrates, and prison officers – view the handling of habitual drunken offenders along lines which reflect a widely held opinion that these men are beyond redemption, take up inordinate resources in relation to the nature of their offence, and are only peripheral to the overriding concern of the criminal justice system's endeavour to control *serious* crime. Above all, the recidivism of the drunken offender, coupled with his low social status, confirms the cynicism and contempt with which law-enforcement officers often regard drunkenness offenders.

It is the repeated processing of skid row alcoholics through police stations, courts, and occasionally prison, that has given rise to the term 'revolving door' as an appropriate metaphor to identify the closed cycle in which many men are trapped.[2] Hollister comments on the American skid row revolving door as follows:

> The 'revolving door' cycle, one extremely unfortunate sociological outgrowth of alcoholism, affects the homeless man in particular. Such a person is inextricably caught up in the cycle of intoxication, arrest for being publicly in that condition, conviction, confinement, release, and return to the street where, because of his complete lack of control over his drinking, the cycle begins again.[3]

Hollister's description is appropriate to the British scene. How alcoholics and agents of the law define each other, and how each party carves out lines of action in the context of the revolving door process, is taken up in greater detail in the remainder of this chapter.

The objectives and structure of the penal revolving door

Drunkenness only becomes an offence in English law when it is committed on a 'highway or other public place, whether a building or not, or on licenced premises' (Licencing Act, 1872, section 12). The same Act also provides powers for the police to arrest persons considered as being guilty, while drunk, of riotous or disorderly behaviour or, to use the more common term, 'drunk and disorderly'.

There is no scope in this book to explore in depth the social and political climate in which current laws affecting public drunkenness emerged during the latter half of the nineteenth century. However, it is evident that Victorian legislation on drunkenness was implemented against a background quite distinct from the social and political conditions prevailing today in relation to the problem. The 1872 Licencing Act – under which public drunks are presently arrested – arose out of an intense temperance and licencing reform movement, a lengthy moral and political debate about the dangers of the 'drink problem' among the working classes, and a belief that the control of public drunkenness could be achieved through punitive measures.[4]

Since the control and reform of habitual public drunkards in institutions traditionally based on a philosophy of deterrence and punishment is not achieved, any justification for invoking existing drunkenness laws is open to question. Thus, as already noted, penal institutions are being redefined in their task of handling homeless alcoholics. The Home Office Report on *Habitual Drunken Offenders* concludes unequivocally that the traditional objectives of the penal system are ineffective:

> Certain principles concerned with the law and its administration were . . . very much our concern. They are indeed principles on which much of our thinking . . . is founded. The first is that *punishing* the habitual drunken offender is seldom an effective method of dealing with his drinking problem. Arresting and prosecuting him therefore is not likely to be useful for that purpose except insofar as it ensures that he receives treatment of which he might not otherwise have taken advantage. The second is that as long as the courts have to continue to deal with habitual drunken offenders, they will need a wider range of measures from which to choose. For practical purposes this means an adequate spectrum of treatment facilities in the community. Third and last is the . . . concept behind section 91 [of the Criminal Justice Act 1967]: while prison is clearly not the most appropriate place in which to treat the habitual drunken offender it is important that changes in the law that would have the effect of curtailing the power of the courts to sentence such offenders to imprisonment should not be introduced until suitable [treatment] alternatives are available.[5]

In short, punishment and deterrence as means of achieving the reform of skid row alcoholics are declared obsolete, and are to be replaced by treatment and rehabilitation. However, in the absence of extensive treatment services, the penal circuit remains as the central and most significant institutional complex seeking to control skid row men. At best, a treatment rationale has only been theoretically introduced into the penal system as justification for the continuing legal processing of alcoholics.[6]

The skid row penal revolving door consists of four basic parts: skid row itself, the police station, courts, and prison. These stages in the processing of derelict inebriates are closely interrelated in that they make up a closed circuit on which alcoholics and agents of social control continuously come into contact with one another. Each stage in the revolving door brings the alcoholic into direct contact with agents of the law, thus reinforcing his deviant identity. With each arrest, conviction and prison sentence his powerlessness and low social status are confirmed.

A diagrammatic representation of the penal revolving door is shown in Figure 2. It is important to note that although arrest by the police is essential to entering the revolving door, it does not mean that the alcoholic is inevitably processed through each of the main stages of the circuit. Statistically the number of homeless men passing through each of the main stages of the revolving door (the police station, court, and prison) progressively diminishes, since at each station on the circuit there are exits that allow for the release of the drunken offender. In fact, the most frequent contact homeless alcoholics have with law-enforcement officers takes place on skid row itself, but without a formal arrest taking place. Once in the police station the alcoholic is sometimes granted bail to appear in court the next morning, but often fails to do so. At the court stage a fine is imposed in the vast majority of cases and the defendant is once again released. Of the minority who are imprisoned, a few pay outstanding fines before completing their sentence. The factor that links the release of homeless men from each of these stages on the penal circuit is their return to drinking on skid row, where the process is more than likely to begin again.

Recent legislation does provide powers for the lower courts to deal with drunkenness offenders other than by fines or imprisonment. The Home Office Report, in a brief examination of the law relating to drunkenness, touches upon alternatives to fines and imprisonment and outlines the statutory abolition of imprisonment for 'drunk and disorderly' under section 91 of the Criminal Justice Act, 1967.[7] However, magistrates avail themselves of forms of treatment in only a very small number of drunkenness cases owing to the lack of community-based socio-medical facilities. Consequently, although

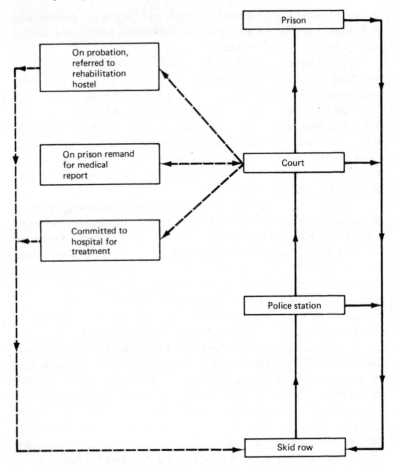

FIGURE 2   *The structure of the penal revolving door*

the structure of the penal revolving door does formally include treatment-oriented provision (see Figure 2), the vast majority of homeless alcoholics are managed by the law in terms of either moving men on, arresting and holding them till sober in a police cell, processing them through a lower court, or confining them to prison.

Each of the main stages in the revolving door will now be described from the point of view of the alcoholic and of the personnel administering his passage through the penal system. Interaction in the world of punishment reveals a set of relationships in which both sides hold both complementary and divergent views of each other's roles.

Police control and the public inebriate

Homeless men can be distinguished from other citizens in the community, and even from other deviant subcultures, by virtue of their total commitment to skid row as a way of life. Rarely are derelict alcoholics able to forge solid connections with the world of steady work and family relationships. At every point in their career as skid row men they are open to some form of intervention designed to change their life pattern. But such intervention rarely makes a lasting impression.

The police represent the most concrete example of society's attempt to 'do something about the problem'. Of all the different types of social control agents operating on skid row, it is the police that hold most relevance in the skid row man's life style. This is reflected in the fact that not only do specific illegal acts (being drunk in public, begging, thieving) open him to legal sanctions, but his very social status and demeanour are taken by the police as sufficient grounds for interference.

The police view of the down-and-out drunk

There are two basic situations where the police come into contact with skid row men: in public places (usually streets, parks and public buildings) and in the police station. Each of these situations is looked at in turn.

Bittner,[8] in an incisive study of police practices on an American skid row, highlighted the two main stances the police adopt towards the control of vagrant alcoholics: keeping the peace and enforcing the law. Each of these approaches plays an important part in determining the outcome of face-to-face encounters between police and alcoholics.

Peace-keeping is by far the most frequently employed method of control. It occurs whenever the police, by their very presence or by directly intervening in the activities of skid row men, ensure that bottle gang members suspend their activities, temporarily break up and disperse, or voluntarily remove themselves from the scene where they are begging, sleeping rough, or merely hanging around. Clearly, in such cases where the police are exercising social control but do not arrest homeless men, they are seeking to resolve the problem in the field; they regard enforcing the law as unnecessary and thereby avoid the need to dispose of the case in the courts.

The decision by police patrolmen to exercise a peace-keeping function is not arbitrary: a number of specific circumstances determine their actions. For example, in some cases directives are issued by officers in charge of police stations to limit the number of arrests of down-and-out drunks:

> When I came to this police station I told my men to cut down on arresting the drunks. You see, its a waste of police time and money. These men are a nuisance.

> I know that with some stations run by the City [City of London] police they are reluctant to get involved with drunks because it's so easy to move them out of their patrol areas into districts run by the Metropolitan Police.

> If we kept to the letter of the law and arrested every drunk we came across, then in some areas we'd have the police cells full up in no time. On top of that the courts wouldn't cope.

In addition police on foot patrol are guided in their approach to skid row men by the exigencies of particular situations and with little regard for any long-range effects on individual persons. Patrolmen employ an approach viewed as appropriate to the *ad hoc* nature of skid row life. For instance, officers gave the following reasons for not arresting men on sight: some drunks show evidence of being booked in at a common lodging house in the vicinity and are likely to arrive there unharmed; particular individuals are either too well known at the police station, are troublesome when arrested, or have a reputation for being too dirty or lousy; the police cells already contain their quota of homeless drunks or are occupied by persons facing more serious charges; and handling drunks of the skid row type is administratively inconvenient, time-consuming, distasteful and, above all, ineffective. Faced with the dilemma of having to be seen administering the law while at the same time having to avoid arresting every skid row inebriate they come across, patrolmen achieve a working balance, sometimes by simultaneously maintaining the peace and enforcing the law. Bittner's description of police-alcoholic interaction reveals a not infrequently observed ploy of police behaviour, which manages to achieve a compromise:

> . . . even where there is no apparent risk of proliferation of trouble, the tactic of removing one or two persons is used to control an undesirable situation. Thus, when a patrolman ran into a group of men sharing a bottle of wine in an alley he . . . arrested one man – who was no more or no less drunk than the others – and let the others disperse in various directions.[9]

Of course, when arrests do take place, the enforcement of the law becomes the official justification for intervening in the habits of street and park drinkers. The homeless alcoholic is then legally defined as either drunk and incapable or, less often, drunk and disorderly or drunk and indecent. But every policeman with experience of arresting habitual drunken offenders knows of potentially critical situations that justify the arrest of homeless men, although such justifications have no basis in law. Here are some informal reasons advanced for arresting derelict inebriates:

> Sometimes we'll arrest men when drunk if there's a chance that they might get into a back street where they'll get robbed.

> By arresting the drunk itinerant we recharge their batteries – this way we keep a percentage of these men alive.

> Some of these men get knocked over by cars. If one of the men does get knocked over it involves us in even more work and report writing. So we get him off the street by arresting him.

> Handling the habitual drunk is nothing but a waste of time – they're not even criminals. The only real advantage of bringing these men into the station is that they act as a basis for training police recruits; all this business about charging men, filling in forms and property books has to be done for everyone that is arrested. Arresting men and charging them with drunkenness gives young police trainees a bit of confidence in their new jobs.

Complaints from local merchants and residents that open spaces are being 'taken over' by vagrants and alcoholics is one of the more usual reasons for seeing that homeless men are temporarily removed from the scene. On such occasions the police sometimes organise 'mass clean-ups', occasionally arresting men who are sober and charging them with offences such as begging or being a suspected person.

The other crucial situation where the police come into contact with the alcoholic is in the police station. Holding alcoholics overnight or over the weekend presents the police with a number of practical problems. Complaints about the men's physical condition override other considerations, as on arrival the police are obliged to search and remove the arrestee's property. Some men may conceal physical injuries (such as broken bones), which do not become immediately apparent. A major preoccupation is the possibility of alcoholics dying in the cells. Although deaths are infrequent relative to the number of men processed through police stations, nevertheless they bring the police into coroner's enquiries and cause detailed paperwork. One major theme expressed in the police station *vis-à-vis* holding the homeless alcoholic centred around the officers' resentment at having to put up with men regarded as being primarily a social nuisance.[10] This theme was expressed in a number of different ways but was best summed up as follows:

> The trouble with these drunks is that they take too many of our men off the streets. We're under-staffed as it is. Now, one of our main jobs is crime prevention. The point is that while police officers are dealing with drunks, taking them to hospital or bringing them back to the police station, a crime can be taking place in the community. While we're involved with the drunk we are not preventing crime.

Alcoholic's view of the police assignment

In the previous chapter the role the police play in controlling public drinking and drunkenness was touched upon in relation to its effect on the organisation and structure of drinking schools. Drinking school members were shown to develop specific responses to police surveillance (see p. 77). In this section a broader question is posed about the alcoholic's perception of the police: what attitudes do homeless men hold of the police's assignment in maintaining the peace and enforcing the law?

Repeated encounters with the police, sometimes over a period of years with the same patrolmen and station officers, enables alcoholics to gain considerable insight into the way police regard the problem. Homeless alcoholics know, for example, the dilemma they present to the police:

> We know that the law is fed up nicking us. On the one hand the police see it as their duty to do something about the complaints they receive from the public. But at the same time taking a dosser in might mean the station sergeant saying 'Is that the best you can do? Bringing in a loused-up drunk!'

Skid row men are aware that police operate on the basis of a wide range of discretion as to how in practice they dispose of situations they encounter on their patrols. Of peace-keeping, skid row residents had the following to say:

> They regard us as more of a nuisance than anything else . . . they'd rather not have the job to do. I've seen the police give a drunk three or four chances to get away before he's arrested.

> Part of the job of the police is to keep a constant check on us. They know that when new faces appear on the scene there's bound to be trouble. It's the coppers' job to learn who these men are.[11]

> Sometimes it only takes a copper to make an appearance [on a railway station concourse] and we'll hide the bottle or move off. But once he's gone we come back again.

Although the police are generally held in low esteem by the homeless alcoholics, there are occasions when the former show a degree of tolerance towards drunks:

> There was a time in this park when we could drink in peace. One or two of the policemen would come over to us and have a chat, and then continue on their beat.

> The police were called by the hospital staff because we were drunk in the emergency clinic . . . we were escorted out but not arrested.

But it is harassment and repeated arrests that men on the row most frequently comment on. The enforcement of the law and the police behaviour that accompanies it are often the subject of conversation among skid row residents. Informants gave a number of reasons why they felt the police had carried out arrests rather than giving them a warning or merely asking them to move on: men were either seen fighting, breaking bottles, urinating in public, or failed to leave a public building or open space when requested to. Such occasions almost inevitably lead to arrest when individual patrolmen come across homeless alcoholics in the normal course of their beat. In addition park and street drinkers know that a number of arrests are inevitable when the police are engaged in a 'mopping-up campaign of vagrants and other undesirables'. The simultaneous arrival of a police van and several officers warns alcoholics that they are open to arrest whether they be technically infringing the law or not.[12]

For a skid row alcoholic an arrest needs to be understood in the context of numerous previous encounters with the police, an awareness that his 'crime' is not regarded as at all serious, and that any official punishment meted out to him will probably consist of at most a day held in a police cell and a nominal fine for being publicly drunk. Homeless men thus become resigned to frequent arrest and prosecution. Instead it is a feeling that they are the targets of unwarranted harassment and brutality that elicits the strongest comments about police behaviour:

I was on Waterloo Station once and I wasn't even drunk when three policemen in plain clothes came up to me and said 'What do you want to be done for: drunk, begging or sus?' Naturally, I picked the easiest – being drunk.

The other day we were sat at the roundabout when a copper came up to the school, took a full bottle of cider from us and poured it all over the ground. He then asked us to move . . . he had no right to do that . . . the police are just a bunch of bastards.

I saw Paddy down on the ground with a couple of policemen standing on his hands . . . when you get the law onto you like that you come round to thinking they have it in for you. There's nothing much you can do about it.

The coppers stopped me coming out of the skipper and belted me all over for about 20 minutes.

In addition it is *in* the police station that the alcoholic is likely to be subjected to taunts about his condition and his low status; sometimes he is harassed or even occasionally physically assaulted, especially when drunk.[13]

From the alcoholic's point of view one central feature that marks police–alcoholic encounters is their unpredictability. The criteria by which the police shift their stance from peace-keeping to law enforcement is not always readily apparent to men on the row. Alcoholics are perfectly aware that the police operate on the basis of a wide range of discretion when it comes to handling homeless men. But it is precisely this range of discretion that places low-status alcoholics in a position of not always knowing how the police will act toward them.[14]

The apparent powerlessness of the vagrant alcoholic in the face of police authority does not necessarily render him entirely helpless. The analysis of drinking schools demonstrated how skid row men do inject a measure of control into their situation, thus minimising the risk of police intervention. Which areas are relatively safe to drink in and which police stations operate policies of toleration or repression are crucial knowledge to street drinkers. But in the end every alcoholic on the row learns that the police assignment as it affects him is one in which both parties are caught up in a process where neither side wins. A police inspector summed up this view as follows: 'The problem is one that no one has done anything about it . . . we keep seeing the same faces again and again.' And an alcoholic commented on witnessing a police swoop on a park: 'They'll never solve this problem on Camberwell Green.'

With every intervention by the police the alcoholic is reminded of his lack of connections with the ordinary world. Continuously under surveillance, repeatedly asked to remove himself from the scene, often harassed, arrested, and held in a local police cell, the skid row man takes on an identity that confirms his status as that of the complete outsider. Being released on bail to appear in court the following morning may be one way whereby the homeless man temporarily avoids the remainder of the penal revolving door; but sooner or later the magistrate's court takes on as much relevance for the alcoholic as does the police patrol and the police station.

The judicial system and the habitual drunken offender

Public drunkenness is a non-indicatable offence dealt with by the lower courts in our judicial system. Magistrates are empowered to impose a maximum penalty of £5 for 'simple drunkenness', that is, for being drunk and incapable. Imprisonment cannot be imposed in such cases. However, when it comes to offences referred to as 'drunkenness with aggravations', i.e. 'drunk and disorderly' or 'drunk and indecent', the court has the power to impose a maximum fine of £10 or up to one month's imprisonment. The yearly total number of convictions for all types of drunkenness offences in England and Wales (excluding drunken driving) has currently reached a figure of approximately 100,000.[15]

It is difficult to estimate accurately what proportion of the total offences are committed by habitual[16] drunken offenders. The Home Office report arrives at a figure of approximately 5,000.[17] Habitual public drunkenness is largely confined to inner city areas and only then to commercial and working-class districts. Consequently certain magistrate's courts handle a disproportionate number of such offenders. The way in which these courts and recidivist drunks interact is the subject of the following two sections.

Magistrates' view of the habitual drunken offender

In *Stations of the Lost* Wiseman uses the term 'assembly line justice' as an appropriate metaphor to describe the American process by which large numbers of homeless men are sentenced in court for being publicly drunk.[18] The judicial system in England and Wales in its approach to drunkenness offenders closely resembles Wiseman's analysis of the process, as the ensuing account reveals.

For example, in a talk delivered by a magistrate on the work of the lower courts, judging drunks was described as follows:

> The court proceedings usually begins its day's business with what we might broadly term 'the hopeless cases' – the rapid-fire types which can be dealt with in a very short time. There is very little we concern ourselves with except the actual sentencing of the offender. The clerk will read out the charge, the defendant nine times out of ten pleads guilty, and the court policeman inform us whether the

man has any previous convictions for drunkenness at the court in question. Usually, all that remains to be done is set the offender a token fine.

Other magistrates expressed a similar viewpoint:

> Behind the thinking of every magistrate when he deals with the homeless destitute is the thought: 'How can we get these chaps off-stage as quickly as possible without losing the decency ascribed to British justice?'

> . . . we must remember that it is a question of proportion. We have to deal with all the cases before us in a day and our time is limited. That is why we deal with drunks so quickly.

Only one important feature would appear to distinguish the American from our approach: American lower courts often sentence 50 to 100 men within an hour, in batches of 10 to 25 men at a time.

Three main factors determine how magistrates dispose of the homeless and habitual drunkard. Firstly, public drunkenness is regarded as a relatively minor misdemeanour. It is handled with less formality than probably any other type of lower-court case. Thus, in contrast to other, more serious, offences, the court does not require the arresting officer to be present to give evidence about the circumstances surrounding the arrest; neither is the defendant expected to request legal representation. In answer to the usual plea of guilty the magistrate will ask the defendant if he has anything to say, but this is more by way of formality rather than a genuine request for information, which might help the magistrate to arrive at a decision about particular cases. In passing sentence there is no official consideration taken of the defendant's social and economic circumstances. Neither probation officers, social workers, friends nor relatives speak for the homeless man. Consequently the administration of justice in relation to drunken offenders consists of a rapid turnover of defendants; individual cases often take less than a minute to dispose of, and any effort to establish the facts of the case and the circumstances surrounding it are almost non-existent.

Secondly, the repeated appearance of homeless alcoholics before the same court, sometimes over a period of several years, produces in court officials a feeling of inevitability and familiarity about the 'stage army of drunks' standing trial. This is what one magistrate had to say: 'I know some of these men so well by sight that on each occasion the offender appears before me I meet him with a smile and almost regard him as a friend.' The sense of inevitability behind the reappearance of alcoholics before a magistrate's court is confirmed by their state of dereliction, their lack of any permanent or fixed address and, above all, by a widespread feeling that these men 'are beyond redemption'. Here are some comments made by magistrates:

> The homeless alcoholics that unfortunately come before us . . . there is very little we can do for them.

> When we are confronted by habitual drunks we have a feeling of helplessness rather than thinking we have another rogue in front of us.

> . . . we see them going downhill so rapidly and getting so filthy.

> Magistrates have accepted a degree of failure in controlling the drunk who repeatedly appears in court.

Additionally court officials feel the time spent in administration unwarranted, considering the nature of the offence and the short time taken to convict the defendant. In short, just as with the police, the court personnel place the habitual drunk at the bottom of the list in any informal ranking about which groups of offenders constitute worthwhile targets of crime prevention and control.

Finally, despite the prevalent view that few, if any, habitual drunks will ever extricate themselves from the penal revolving door, magistrates feel strongly that some useful function is served by handling these men through the judicial system. Taking drunks off the street, holding them in a police cell, and having them brought before the court is justified in terms of protecting the individual from himself, even if it is for less than 24 hours. This can be the only justification offered (beyond arguing that the law must be administered by police and courts), since in the vast majority of cases habitual drunken offenders are released from the court immediately after having received a nominal fine or alternative sentence of one day.

However, a comparatively small number of habitual offenders are sent to prison.[19] in the majority of cases as a result of failing to pay fines imposed for drunkenness and for not appearing in court on previous occasions when released on bail from the police station.

Most magistrates argue that it is futile to fine or imprison the homeless alcoholic, given that neither form of punishment deters the individual from committing further breaches of the law.

Jailing the skid row alcoholic is, nevertheless, regarded positively by magistrates as an expedient answer to the deleterious effects of protracted heavy drinking and living rough. Temporarily removing the individual from alcohol and partially restoring his health make up the pragmatic objectives that lie behind sending men to prison. This is how magistrates see it:

> When a man is getting to the end of his tether I see a drying out period in prison as a positive sanction.

> Some of these men appear in a bad state of cleanliness . . . 14 days in prison has the positive effect of having them cleaned up.

> Sending these men to prison is a life-saving act. To put the man back on the street is to ensure the man's early death. Prison is really an informal drying out centre where the rule of no drinking is enforced on the men.

> A remand in custody for a medical report means that at least we are keeping the man warm, fed, and off the streets.

Recent legislation, in particular the two Criminal Justices Acts passed in 1967 and 1972, has in theory created alternative socio-medical means by which the courts and police can dispose of public drunks. Magistrates collectively have supported the formulation of policy that seeks to remove drunken offenders from the penal system and into the field of therapeutic care and treatment.[20] But, as has been made evident, the lower courts are confronted by the reality of having to handle individuals for whom socio-medical provision is not yet widespread. This section has drawn on some of the major adjustments magistrates make to handling the dilémma between what they believe ought to be happening and what is happening in the sentencing of habitual drunkards.[21] On the whole a pessimistic tone is struck by magistrates as a result of seeing homeless men come through the courts. But how does the homeless alcoholic define his relationship with the judicial system?

An alcoholic's perspective on the magistrate's court

Magistrate's courts as agencies of law enforcement are a central component in the life of chronic public inebriates. Indeed, the vast majority of homeless alcoholics become as familiar with the lower courts as they do with the police.

Being charged with contravening drunkenness laws does not signify for alcoholics that they will inevitably appear in court. Homeless men know that should they sober up sufficiently, the police might release them on bail. The likelihood of a pre-trial release is increased if offenders are not wanted for other outstanding offences, including previous drunkenness offences and breaches of bail committed in the court catchment area where they were arrested.[22] Furthermore, the police bail system has little, if any, effect in compelling homeless alcoholics to attend court. Although failing to appear in court is viewed with seriousness by the police, alcoholics are perfectly well aware that the issuing of warrants for their arrest is not actively pursued:

> Mickey got stopped in the street by the law and asked why he hadn't appeared in court to answer a drunk charge. He told the copper that he'd managed to get a job that morning. When the law heard that Mickey was stopping in Carrington House [a common lodging house] he said 'That's alright then, so long as we know where you are.' I suppose they'll wait till he's knocked off again for being drunk. Then they'll throw the book at him.

> The police won't do anything about me not appearing in court till they find me drunk again. Then they'll hold me overnight and *take* me to court. That's when I'll be faced with two drunk charges *and* not turning up in court . . . I could get sent down.

However, as both the above statements imply, in the end alcoholics with no fixed abode are compelled to appear before a magistrates' court.

By the time a derelict alcoholic stands in the court dock he has spent long hours in a police cell, probably over the weekend, been transported to the court, and held in a court cell. He may be feeling physically and psychologically weak from the symptoms of alcoholic withdrawal. His appearance and demeanour reflect his low status. In addition repeated drunkenness offences dealt with by the same court – maybe even by the same magistrate – establish his reputation as an incorrigible drunk. The alcoholic has learned that under these circumstances his processing through the judicial system is merely a formality. Both he and court officials are concerned with getting through the formalities as quickly as possible – the magistrate in order to move on to more serious cases and the alcoholic that he may effect a quick release in order to recommence drinking.

Thus with straightforward cases of simple drunkenness, once the clerk has read the charge, identified the place where the alcoholic was arrested, and asked the defendant how he pleads, cases can be concluded within a minute. The exchange below between court police, magistrate and defendant is typical of most trials; it followed the request for the alcoholic to plead guilty or not:

Defendant   Guilty.
Police   Two previous convictions for drink.
Magistrate   Have you anything to say?
Defendant   No, sir.
Magistrate   £1 or one day. And make sure you keep away from here in future.

Cases of 'drunkenness with aggravations' ('drunk and disorderly' or 'drunk and indecent') are similarly dealt with, except that the court police offer a very short report of the defendant's behaviour leading up to arrest.

Pleading guilty is by far the most common response of alcoholics to charges of drunkenness. The speedy conclusion of the case, usually by the imposition of a nominal fine, is assured by entering a plea of guilt. But, as the remarks below reveal, there are other considerations skid row men take into account:

If the magistrate already knows you, it doesn't matter what you say, he won't believe you. Sometimes you get picked up when you're not drunk, but if he's seen you many times before and each time you plead guilty, then there's no point pleading any other way. It's a waste of time pleading not guilty.

I wasn't feeling fit. I had been drinking heavily and all I wanted was for the case to be over with.

Whether you were drunk or not it doesn't matter, it's always best to plead guilty. If you plead *not* guilty the case has to be put back so that the arresting officer may appear as a witness. Well, you see, if you haven't got an address, you look rough, and you're well known then to plead not guilty might be seen by the magistrate as you're trying to challenge the court. In that case he might place you on remand for a week in Brixton Prison for a medical report. I tell you, that's worse than doing time in Pentonville.

For the derelict alcoholic the outcome of an appearance in court is much more uncertain if he is confronted by a string of outstanding drunkenness charges and breaches of police bail. The likelihood of being jailed, either as an alternative to a fine for being drunk and disorderly or drunk and indecent, for failing to pay past fines, or for not turning up in court, is increased. Habitual drunken offenders often feel that in such circumstances magistrates are unpredictable and inconsistent in how they dispose of drunkenness cases.

Three strategies in particular are open to homeless men in an attempt to reduce the uncertainty and chances of being sent to jail. Firstly, alcoholics manage to gain some knowledge about how specific magistrates generally dispose of their case-load of drunks:

Before you come up in front of the bench you know if you're going to get a good or a bad magistrate because you ask the copper on duty. Once you know something about the magistrate then you know how to approach him when you come into the dock. If he's a bad one then you know that you'll be sent down, and no amount of talking will make him change his mind.

Every time I appear before Mr. Grant I get a rough deal.

Today's magistrate was a good man. He generally lets everyone off lightly.

Mr. Grant – he takes likes and dislikes. If he dislikes you then God help you. With me, he sees me as a menace.

I overheard a policeman say in the corridor leading into the courtroom that 'the mad major' was hearing the cases. Once I heard that it was an ex-army man on the Bench I said to myself 'I'll beat the law this time.' I went into the dock, stood to attention and referred to the magistrate as 'Sir'. When he asked me if I had anything to say I told him that I'd been in the army where drinking had got the better of me and that I couldn't settle down in 'civvy street'. He didn't send me down.

In his account of the moral career of mental patients Goffman touches upon a general phenomenon bearing on the careers of different types of deviants. He indicates that having taken on a deviant identity an individual will handle his encounters with agents of social control by taking one of two lines of approach to his current situation. Either the person's line stresses that he is not responsible for what has become of him, especially if his past and present are extremely dismal, and thus engages in telling what Goffman calls 'sad tales'; or, conversely, he shows the operation of favourable personal qualities in the past and a favourable destiny in the future, in which case he puts across a 'success story'.[23]

Both the use of 'sad tales' and 'success stories' are employed by homeless alcoholics with a view to affecting the outcome of the magistrate's decisions. Their use constitute an apologia by defendants to excuse their repeated court appearances for public drunkenness and other related offences. An apologia, then, is the second strategy which skid row men bring into play before a court. Here are some typical 'sad tales' offered in reply to the magistrate's request for an explanation of defendant's behaviour:

I can't help it – I'm an alcoholic.

I apologise, sir. I'm being picked on by the police.

I only came out of prison this past Tuesday.

You see, sir, I really can't remember anything. I'm on the sick and have been taking tablets given to me by my doctor.

'Success stories', on the other hand, consist in convincing the magistrates that one has made attempts in the past or is currently endeavouring to lead a sober and regular life. For instance:

I was taken to court on my third arrest in a week. But then I told the magistrate that I'd been sober for eight months, had kept in touch with my Probation Officer, and that I would like to have another go at sobriety. My probation records were brought down to the court and read to the magistrate. That's how I come to be here [a rehabilitation hostel] and not in the nick. A Probation Officer referred me from the court.

I'd like to be given a chance. I've just started work yesterday and went to work this morning – they let me come along to court.

I told the magistrate that a place had been found for me in hospital by my social worker. The case was put back till later in the morning while he had this story checked out. When I reappeared he said 'Mr. Walsh, it's a good thing to hear the truth spoken in this place – I'm going to allow your social worker to have you taken to hospital!

But the lack of connections skid row alcoholics have with *bona fide* persons, whether welfare workers or other professionals, means that the 'sad tale' technique is by far the most frequent type of apology offered in attempts to 'beat the law'.

The final strategy employed by the skid row man is requesting from the magistrate that he be given time to pay a fine. The possibility of avoiding jail when confronted by a penalty of a fine or an alternative of imprisonment is markedly reduced for the alcoholic as a result of his chronic poverty. Unable to pay any fines on the spot, the derelict skid row person will often, as a last resort, request time to pay his fine. It is not unusual for a court to grant a period of seven or fourteen days in which to pay small fines. However, faced with the chronic public inebriate who has outstanding fines, drunk charges, and breaches of police bail, the magistrate will often refuse the request. The factors that determine this refusal and thus ensure the jailing of the skid row alcoholic have already been explored in the previous section. An account of how jail is viewed by the skid row man and his guardians concludes this chapter on the penal revolving door. But some indication of the habitual drunk's attitude to being sentenced to jail is reflected in the following comments:

Sometimes I look forward to doing 7 or 14 days because it gives me the chance to have a bit of a clean up and a rest. Mind you, it all depends. On one occasion in the middle of summer a magistrate gave me 14 days when I didn't want to go into prison at all. I had just come out after doing a 12 month sentence and I didn't think I'd had enough freedom.

The local prison and the alcoholic inmate

The local prison is one of the more important institutions that make up the matrix of social control on skid row. Most homeless alcoholics at some time in their long skid row careers are put in jail; indeed, a few men use prison as a way station on the penal revolving door with such frequency that phrases such as 'doing life on the never-never' or 'doing life on the instalment plan' typify the regularity with which they pass through the prison gates.

Sparks, in a study of a local prison, wrote about its inmates:

> In one sense . . . the men who make up the resident population of the general locals are distinguished chiefly by their inability to obtain any better conditions in which to be punished; they have been 'inside' too often, and for crimes too petty. Very few are dangerous; but they are poor candidates for 'treatment' of any kind offered by the system, and the prospects of their reform are considered bleak. They are the residue which remains when the best of the prison's input has been skimmed of its star prisoners and dangerous criminals; they are thus the lumpen proleteriat of the whole English penal system.[24]

The 'stage army' of alcoholics regularly sentenced to short terms in jail are part of the prison lumpen proleteriat; they neither respond to treatment nor is the system capable of effecting any personal change in them. Their status as drunks is defined in such a way that both prison personnel and other inmates regard them with contempt and cynicism.

For the purpose of this book Pentonville Prison was selected for study. Pentonville is a large Victorian prison catering mainly for recidivist offenders serving sentences of 12 months or under. Because of the relatively short sentences and the consequent rapid turnover of the prison population, the prison authorities have found it necessary administratively to divide the population into two groups: those men jailed for 3 months or less and those being held for periods over 3 and up to 12 months. Homeless men imprisoned for drunkenness offences are usually committed for periods ranging between 7 and 30 days. Thus crucial to an understanding of how both prison personnel and alcoholics view each other within the prison context is the short duration of the drunken offenders' sentences.

One further point should be made about the general character of Pentonville as a local prison before going on to explore in detail the officers' and men's perception of their situation in it. Although all prisons are organised around a set of formally laid down rules and procedures, often strictly adhered to, it was evident from talking to both inmates and prison staff that Pentonville has a relaxed atmosphere as far as relations between staff and alcoholics go, especially in comparison with long-term and maximum security prisons. Phrases such as 'easy going', 'not run by the rule book' and 'a holiday-camp' were used to illustrate the general atmosphere prevailing there.[25]

The prison officers' perspective on the alcoholic inmate

Two aspects are explored in this section. Firstly, comment is made on how prison personnel concerned with administering the reception and discharge of skid row alcoholics regard their charges. Secondly, the views of prison officers responsible for the welfare of the drunken offender are explored in some detail. Both these sets of views are closely determined by the short period alcoholics spend in prison and the frequency with which many of them return to serve further sentences.

The inmate as an administrative unit

An important part of the organisation of prisons is taken up by the administrative handling of inmates on arrival and discharge. Surrendering one's personal property, having biographical details entered in the prison records, bathing and changing into prison clothes, attending a medical inspection, being classified according to one's offence, length of sentence, and general state of health, and being allocated a wing, floor and cell in addition to a specific workshop or tasks, form part of the routine all inmates undergo on arrival. Because most alcoholics spend only 7 or 14 days in prison[26] Reception (the official name of the department handling both arrivals and discharges) features largely in the officers' encounters with alcoholics.

The officers manning Reception focus on three areas around which they construct their opinions of the alcoholic inmate. These are the following: the contrasting physical condition of alcoholics on arrival and discharge, the regularity with which some men return to prison, and the function the prison plays in prolonging the skid row alcoholic's life.

Above all, officers supervising the intake of new prisoners complain recurrently about the physical condition skid row alcoholics arrive in:

> The smell is something terrible.[27] Since I've been put on Reception I've been bitten by more fleas than I can remember. This is why we wear these white coats – so that we can spot the bugs easier.

> Some of these men refuse to have a bath when they come in – the 'red bands' have to force them into a bath with disinfectant – we call it a 'double-bubble'. These fellows literally have to be scrubbed. Mind you, some of them don't even feel it – they have no sensitivity.

> The trouble with the police is that they don't want to know about the dosser's injuries when he's arrested. There have been occasions when we've had to get a doctor to the man immediately he arrives in prison.

The prisoner's physical weakness and lack of cleanliness,[28] in particular with men who have been drinking methylated or surgical spirits and sleeping rough, is the subject of derisory comment and joking among officers. The prisoner is sometimes forcibly reminded of his status and condition, as the following interchange of words reveals:

Officer   Bill, you're in for drunk this time – what were you in for the last time?
Alcoholic   Drunk.
Officer   And the time before that?
Alcoholic   Drunk.
Officer   And before that?
Alcoholic   Drunk.
Officer   You're not going to fall all over me, are you now? You're in a filthy condition . . . Been living rough, have you?
Alcoholic   Yes.
Officer   I can see that – fucking condition you're in.

When alcoholics are discharged from prison, they pass once more through Reception, receiving back their personal belongings, including any items of clothing that were salvageable on arrival. However, some alcoholics are issued with a new set of civilian clothing. Their appearance stands in sharp contrast to that on their day of arrival. An officer in charge or fitting out men explained:

> When the dossers come off the van I can tell which are the alcoholics, just from their appearance. But when they leave this place they look just like ordinary people, they're dressed respectably and they're healthy. You see, they accept this place as a home for themselves, where they can be properly fed and looked after.

But handling the discharge of homeless alcoholics is conducted with a marked degree of cynicism; the prospects that the inmate will return to drinking and to prison are considered extremely high. This feeling was expressed in a variety of different ways within Reception:

> . . . some of these men do pretty well if they manage to stay out of this place for more than 3 weeks – they're totally dependent on this institution.

> I've heard men complain about being let out too early in the morning – they like to time it so that they can make it for when Tesco's opens at 8.15. They can buy a bottle of VP Wine there and start all over again.

> I won't give this man a pair of shoes because I know what he'll do – as soon as he gets out he'll flog them down the road and get an old pair out of the bins. More than likely we'll be seeing him back in here next week.

The high recidivist rate of the skid row drunk is taken as evidence that some men keep returning to prison in preference to living on the row. Regular meals, sleep, and shelter are taken as the prime reason behind their return. Consequently the cost to the taxpayer of keeping homeless men in prison was on occasions mentioned as a way of illustrating the argument that jailing alcoholics was nothing but a waste of resources.

Officers working in Reception find little justification in having men pass repeatedly through prison when their only offence is related to public drunkenness. Prison neither punishes nor offers adequate long-term treatment (in the therapeutic sense of the word) but merely interrupts heavy drinking bouts carried out in a hostile environment. At best repeated short sentences help to prolong the skid row alcoholic's life:

> We put the man in prison and let him dry out – that's all you can do for an alcoholic.

> We don't like men to die in here, you know. Mind you, one man died last Christmas but he would have died in any case . . . The treatment is second to none in here . . . If a man is sick we have to call the doctor or medical orderly, doesn't matter what the man is in for.

> Alcoholics sometimes come into prison with the shakes in which case they'll see a doctor, and get an injection, tablets and vitamins. I think we're prolonging their lives because when you see them three days later after they've come in they're jumping around like lambs.

Beyond redemption, repeatedly deprived of his liberty for a misdemeanour, dependent on prison for his survival, holding little if any esteem when out of jail, the skid row inmate is viewed with contempt. Even within prison skid row drunks are regarded by the prison staff (and other inmates) as occupying the lowest status in the inmate culture. At all times, both in and out of prison, they are regarded as the lowest of the low.

The inmate as a target for rehabilitation

In spite of the above portrayal Pentonville Prison has implemented a policy designed to provide alcoholic inmates with opportunities to tackle their drinking problem. This policy is in keeping with contemporary penal philosophy, stressing the treatment and rehabilitation of offenders.

In 1968 the Deputy Governor of Pentonville had the following to say about the role prison could play in the treatment of alcoholics:

It is often said that effective treatment of the alcoholic or the drunkenness offender cannot be achieved in prison. Several reasons are put forward, such as the element of compulsion, the resentment felt by the prisoner, and the general prison conditions. In my opinion, the reverse is true. Prison has several advantages as a place for treatment such as:

(1) The subject is sober, even if it is an enforced sobriety.
(2) Many subjects seem motivated, even if only temporarily, to gain control over their drinking.
(3) The prison has full-time medical, psychological and social welfare staff, and three full-time chaplains.
(4) There are now trained prison officers who are especially interested in the treatment of men with a drinking problem.[29]

The Deputy Governer concludes that prison can achieve more in terms of treatment than any other agency on the basis of professional assessment and classification of each inmate, group therapy, adequate medication, and co-operation with extra-mural alcoholism hostels and hospital units. Provision is made for the alcoholics to 'gain insight into their own resentment, to change their attitudes, and to recognise their opportunities'.[30] But how does this policy square with reality as experienced by prison staff attempting to put these objectives into practice?

Official responsibility for the welfare, rehabilitation and after-care of imprisoned drunks falls to uniformed officers manning the Liaison Department. This department focuses its efforts exclusively on short-sentence inmates (under 3 months).[31] Its objectives include sorting out the accommodation, employment and treatment needs of the prisoner. With those men addicted to alcohol, treatment and rehabilitation override other immediate problems, such as ensuring the inmate has a job to go to on release. Consequently Liaison officers handle skid row alcoholics with a view to (i) referring men to prison discussion groups specialising in problems of alcoholism and (ii) making arrangements with outside voluntary agencies, especially rehabilitation hostels, to accept prisoners on their discharge.

The in-prison group discussions, sometimes conducted with the outside assistance of professionals interested in alcoholism, are viewed ambivalently by officers running the Liaison department. On the one hand:

Alcoholics in for seven, fourteen or twenty-one days usually end up in the Light Textiles workshop. But we've started a day-time group where we encourage men to talk about their problems, to see if we can help them. It's better than stamping out beer mats.

If the groups don't do anything else for them at least it keeps them thinking about the problem – they keep turning it over in their minds. Take a man I know who comes in here regularly. Now that he's in prison he's thinking a lot about his problem. He's talking about it and that shows that there is some motivation for him wanting to stop drinking.

I think we can help them here by sending them to the Alcoholics Anonymous group meetings . . . the men like those classes.

However, group discussions are also viewed sceptically:

The A. A. classes seem popular but if you ask me they don't seem to do anything for the men.

. . . the men only go to the discussions because they know they can get free cigarettes from the people who visit the prison to conduct the groups.

Referring the alcoholic from compulsory detention to voluntary residence in a rehabilitation hostel is the second important goal. In theory there are close links between the prison and some community-based rehabilitation agencies. Prison officers believe it crucial that if an alcoholic is not to relapse immediately he walks out the prison gates, then he needs to be guaranteed a place in a rehabilitation hostel. But the co-operation of rehabilitation hostel staff is not always forthcoming, as the following remarks demonstrate:

A staff member from one of the rehabilitation hostels told me the success rate for men admitted straight from prison is nil – he believes they are not genuinely motivated to come off the drink.

In practice, asking a man to wait for a few days after he gets out before he's accepted into a house means that he'll go on the drink.

I know there is some substance in the principle that a man should be self-motivated to get to a hostel on his own if he really wants to have a go. But there are a lot of men who need taking by the hand . . . there should be more of actually meeting the man outside the gates, taking him to the hostel. London is a big place!

The major blame for the ineffectiveness of attempts to bring about any personal change in skid row alcoholics is attributed to the conditions prevailing inside the prison. The large numbers of drunkenness offenders present in jail at any one time coupled with the rapid turnover of the skid row population are a major hindrance to the officers' work.

Last year I saw over 1,000 men in here with an alcoholic problem.

Of the men whom I deal with the most rapid turnover is with alcoholics. Most of them we don't devote much time to. We can't deal with them adequately enough.

I've seen a fellow for the first time today [Tuesday] and he's going out on Saturday – what can you do for a man in that time.

There is widespread agreement among officers handling the welfare of homeless men that in the final analysis the prison is considered an inappropriate long-term treatment environment. As with their colleagues in Reception, Liaison officers believe that jailing men for very brief periods only fulfils a first-aid function in temporarily restoring the inmates' physical health.

However, the homeless alcoholic himself does not escape blame:

Seventy per cent of the alcoholics who come through here we already know all about them – they come in so often that we don't even look up their case-cards. I've seen some of these men coming in and out of prison for years.

I know one man who's been coming in here since I've been around and he's slipped down from Grade 1, to Grade 2, and now Grade 3 in fitness. These fellows are slowly killing themselves.

You're getting lower and lower as you get older. [Said to an inmate who admitted drinking methylated spirits.]

Both these men I'm about to interview I hold no hope for whatsoever. They prefer being in Pentonville to anywhere else judging by their short-lived excursions into the outside world.

Time, numbers, unrewarding inmates and an inappropriate treatment milieu, then, result in officers holding alcoholics in low esteem and defining the prison as an inadequate treatment milieu.

All this does not mean that the efforts of the prison personnel go totally unrewarded. Occasionally skid row alcoholics make it to a rehabilitation facility; but more often than not reality, to the rehabilitation arm of the prison service, is summed up as follows:

> As soon as the alcoholic is out of the front door he's a free agent – whatever he promised us in here he needn't do it when he gets out.
>
> I remember one man . . . for whom we had the system all tied up with a referral to a rehabilitation hostel where he could be treated for his problem. He didn't turn up!

The alcoholic inmate defines the prison and its officers

Students of prison life have tended to focus on inmates completing medium- and long-term sentences. The impetus behind this interest derives from the assumption that sudden and protracted severance from the mainstream of life outside the prison has radical consequences for the social and psychological make-up of the inmate.[32] It is argued that not only do prisoners take on a new identity in response to the material and psychological deprivation inherent in prisons; but they also give meaning to prison life against the background of their deviant enterprise and the links they maintained with their families and friends outside. But how do men who are typically homeless, unemployed, with few if any family contacts, and who are usually imprisoned for very short periods, view prison life?

The meaning that prison holds for skid row alcoholics needs to be understood in the context of their own commitment to a life style already effectively separating them from the rest of the community. Prison is an integral part of the skid row institutional treadmill; it serves to interrupt for short periods at a time the drinking career of the homeless man.

'Doing time': prison as a refuge from skid row

The criteria by which alcoholics judge 'doing time' are directly related to their status as skid row derelicts, the hardships endured when drinking on skid row, the short sentences they normally receive, and the general character of the local prison. Here are some prevalent views on how alcoholics define prison. They reflect the easy-going atmosphere of Pentonville Prison referred to earlier.

> There's no getting away from it, we all know this is a jail but it's different from most of them. In here nobody takes any notice of what you're doing except for one or two screws who go by the book. In other prisons life is all aggravation. But in here there are some officers you can talk to as if they were your own brother.

> It's a prison that suits the drunks and the dossers.

> Pentonville is the best doss-house in London.

> If the authorities were to open a wing in here for dossers to which they could come in voluntarily it would be filled up in no time.

> On the whole the screws are alright in here.

Inmates repeatedly stressed the laxity of the regime when compared with other establishments holding long-term prisoners in which they had been occasionally jailed. The men are aware that the prison authorities regard alcoholics and other derelicts as prisoners who cause little trouble.

Any impact that prison may have in severing men from their families, friends and work is minimised for the homeless alcoholic. He is more than likely to meet inside prison someone whom he drinks with or knows or who has news about drinking acquaintances and daily events on the row.

> The 'rag shop' [Light Textiles workshop] is like getting round the bonfire in a skipper – you know everything that is going on, who's been in prison, who's about to go out, and you hear about fellows who are drinking in other 'manors' [areas].

> On one occasion the doctor in Reception tried to classify me as grade 1 but I wanted to be grade 2 so that I could be placed 'on the

level' [ground floor landings] and in the 'rag shop' so that I could be with my mates. I exaggerated the shakes and got myself downgraded.

We never see ourselves as prisoners or criminals,[33] but as drunks. We bring the outside world into the nick, the *only* difference being that we haven't got a bottle in here . . .

The physical and psychological hardship inherent in continuous heavy drinking on skid row, and in living rough or in common lodging houses, means that, when jailed, alcoholics interpret their loss of liberty in terms of the short-term benefits they derive from prison life. Although not always accepting a short sentence as desirable, alcoholics are in accord with one of the main justifications advanced by the personnel manning law-enforcement agencies, namely that prison functions as a drying-out centre and helps to restore men physically debilitated by drink, undernourishment and exposure to the weather.

Only one phase in the alcoholic's short sentence is looked upon with apprehension: being processed through Reception and enduring the first few days of any sentence, which stand in sharp contrast with the easy-going atmosphere of life on the landings, in the workshop and in the alcoholics' discussion groups. Having endured the police cell, processing through a magistrates' court and transportation to the jail, the alcoholic is often confronted with long hours of waiting in Reception before he receives a meal and is seen by a doctor. Any initial medical examination the prisoner undergoes in Reception is, however, viewed with contempt:

There might be as many as 50 men waiting to be seen by the doctor. When my turn arrived he spent about ten seconds on me. He asked me if there was anything wrong with me but when I pointed out that I was sick from the drink and wanted something to steady me up he just said 'No, if you feel bad tomorrow then ask to go sick.'

. . . the doctor tells you that you're OK and that's it. He doesn't really examine you.

When it came round to seeing the doctor he told me that a friend of mine had died in the hospital wing the day before. I was feeling pretty rough myself, but all the doctor said to me was 'Mathews, your mate is stiff up there – it could be you next time, the state you're in.'

Experiencing withdrawal symptoms during the first few days of a sentence can be particularly frightening:

The first two days your nerves are all to pieces.

Getting over the drink is the worst part of it. The doctor doesn't do anything for you and you spend your time being sick. If you're into DT's they'll put you in the strip cell but sometimes you go through minor DT's in Reception and in your cell. The don't allow you any tablets, so you just live through it.

Only if you're absolutely incapable of propelling yourself about will you end up in the hospital wing. But generally they don't give you anything to help you through [withdrawal symptoms].

'Doing time': the alcoholic awaits his discharge

When alcoholics live on skid row, the meaning that time takes on for them is determined by its unpredictability. Time is puncutated by alternating periods of sobriety and drunkenness, each period varying in duration according to the availability of drink and friends to share a bottle with. In particular, drinking bouts may be interrupted by spells in a police cell or as a result of admission to hospital or a rehabilitation hostel. Only short-term tasks have any relevance for derelict inebriates; where and how to procure the next bottle or planning where to spend the night are important immediate pre-occupations. Little, if any, consideration is given to long-term goals.

The unpredictability of daily life on skid row stands in sharp contrast to 'doing time' in prison. Enforced confinement and the absence of alcohol impose a new routine on skid row men. Once alcoholics have been processed through Reception and any effects of alcohol withdrawal have disappeared, two areas of activity feature largely in their prison lives: working in the Light Textiles workshop and attending group meetings on alcoholism.

The official function behind providing work to prison inmates is to keep men occupied and provide them with an opportunity to learn skills useful to them on discharge. As mentioned above, from the alcoholic's point of view the 'rag shop' is the most convivial environment for mixing with men they are familiar with on skid row. Statements like those below typify the opinion inmates hold of the workshop:

> When it comes to job allocations most of us find ourselves going to the 'rag shop' . . . but if you're in only for 7 to 14 days, well then you don't give a fuck about doing any work – you're only interested in talking with your mates about what is going on around Waterloo, Euston and the East End.

> They call it occupational therapy in the 'rag shop' – actually there's nothing therapeutic at all about it.

> We know that the officers refer to the 'rag shop' as the dumping ground for men who can't do anything else. So, if you don't work hard, the officers in charge don't worry about it.

Going to group discussions on alcoholism is the other main activity which homeless men engage in. Group meetings for the habitual drunken offender are designed to meet the social and personal problems of the inmate by increasing his awareness of alcoholism and preparing him for his return to the outside world. The obstacles the prison welfare officers encounter *vis-à-vis* offering alcoholics treatment and after-care have aready been explored. But how do skid row men themselves view the prison's efforts at rehabilitation? Once again, the short sentence and the numbers of alcoholics in prison are regarded as cancelling any efforts at offering inmates help with their problems. Very little is expected of the services offered:

> There is no rehabilitation in here – it's only on paper . . . In any case, nobody can help alcoholics unless they first want to help themselves.

> Sometimes there are as many as 20 men at a time with a chit to visit Liaison, but when the officer interviews you he ony asks two or three questions about what you will be doing when you get out.

> St. Mungo's have girls who work on their staff sent in here to run the group. They think they can bounce any ball and educate us.

Inmates stated that a prime motivation behind attending group meetings was to obtain free cigarettes from outside experts conducting the sessions. In addition the meetings provided an excuse to escape the monotony of being locked up in a cell.

In theory officers concerned with the welfare and after-care of skid-row alcoholics have two aims in mind: firstly, that while in prison individuals will gain some insight into their predicament and, secondly, that the goal of attaining sobriety can only be achieved on discharge by having alcoholics admitted to a rehabilitation hostel. However, the logic of these two interrelated goals is not always at the centre of the alcoholic's thinking. Although enforced sobriety does sometimes lead alcoholics to appraise their situation with a view to 'staying off the beer', when released, most men inevitably 'break out'. This is how alcoholics put it:

> If I'm in here only for 7 or 14 days all I think about is the money I'm going to be given when I get out. If it's a Saturday they give you the money here in prison because the Social Security offices are closed. As soon as I'm out I make my way straight to Camberwell Green where I meet some of my friends.

> I'm looking forward to a drink when I get out.

> When a man comes out of the nick he feels he deserves a drink.

> When you're in here, especially if it's longer than usual – say three months or over – you have time to think why you're in. You even think you can stay off the beer. But myself, I know I have a craving for drink when I'm on the outside. Once, when I tried to stay dry I found the first week was murder. Trying to fill in time was the biggest problem. If you have a go at sobriety you have to lead an orderly life, sort yourself out and things like that – it's easier to go on the drink.

With the return to street drinking the circuit skid row alcoholics become so familiar with is made complete. The cycle commences once again with the first bottle of cheap wine or cider. Before long the alcoholic is re-arrested and thereby re-enters the penal revolving door – unless he makes his way into the circuit of treatment and social rehabilitation. An analysis of this circuit is the subject of the next chapter.

6
The Rehabilitation Network

Interaction in the world of treatment

This chapter focuses on the relationship between social rehabilitation agencies, their personnel and skid row alcoholics. The institutions of social rehabilitation, especially street contact and residential facilities,[1] are taken as the base through which social workers and alcoholics articulate opinions of each other and of the rehabilitation regimes they operate and participate in.

Contemporary rehabilitation strategies are defined by professionals working with skid row alcoholics as alternatives to the traditional revolving door policy of law enforcement. In theory an interrelated network of rehabilitation services is proposed as a replacement for ineffective penal and correctional approaches to homeless men. The importance of developing a complete, interrelated system of treatment and care is regarded as crucial if rehabilitation is to be effective. Thus the Home Office Report stresses the need for an alternative approach, which will cover the different stages of the rehabilitation process within a co-ordinated network of services.[2]

The objectives and structure of the rehabilitation network

The main problem confronting proponents of long-term rehabilitation is not that law-enforcement agencies continue in practice to handle the majority of skid row alcoholics, in spite of widespread acceptance that such handling is considered inappropriate and expensive. Instead, it is achieving the overriding official objective of the rehabilitation system, which is their main preoccupation. This objective may be spelled out as follows: ensuring the successful recovery of the alcoholic through permanent sobriety and facilitating his re-entry into society. But, since social workers and other professionals are aware that derelict alcoholics have a long-standing attachment to life on skid row and that there is little evidence for their permanent recovery, any rehabilitation process is viewed as being inevitably marked by obstacles and interruptions. The following statement illustrates the difficulty in achieving long-term rehabilitation:

> Treatment really begins with the first attempt at motivation and in a sense all 'treatment' of the alcoholic is no more and no less than the provision of a motive not to drink. Motivation therefore is not a once-for-all but a continuous process in which all treatment agencies have a part to play. The street side centre . . . is perhaps best viewed as the first link in a long chain extending from Skid Row and culminating, eventually, for some period at any rate, in a stable life in the community. It is however a tenuous chain which is apt to break not once but many times, and at varying points. The first link has to be restored and an attempt made to build the chain afresh.[3]

Behind the overriding objective of rehabilitation and the difficulties inherent in it lie two further major considerations. Firstly, there is the need to make contact with, instil motivation in, and sustain a professional–client relationship with, men regarded as living totally outside the boundaries of conventional society. Skid row alcoholics have no family contacts, no steady employment nor a permanent home address. They are consistently defined as socially inadequate, out of touch with reality, isolated and withdrawn. These definitions are frequently invoked by the personnel manning the rehabilitation agencies which, in one way or another, seek to help homeless men. But the social distance between alcoholic and professional is a wide one; it is seen as imperative, therefore, that this gap be closed if the application of rehabilitation techniques is to make any impact.

Secondly, there is the problem of achieving an adequately co-ordinated system of treatment. It is claimed that agencies offering treatment and rehabilitation – street contact services, alcoholic units in hospitals, and residential facilities – work for the most part in an uncoordinated fashion. Either the alcoholic, because of his repeated lapses, uses the available services in an *ad hoc* fashion or, more significantly, a particular service fulfils a particular stage of rehabilitation but any follow-up treatment deemed necessary for the full recuperation of the alcoholic is made impossible because of an incomplete or unco-ordinated rehabilitation network.

The importance of establishing an interrelated rehabilitation network is stressed by most persons responsible for the organisation of alcoholic recovery agencies. The objectives outlined above, and the strategies that go towards attaining them, are reflected in the structure of a rehabilitation system designed to meet the problems of 'putting men back into the community'.

This structure is made up of two basic parts: street contact services and small-scale residential facilities. Hospital-based alcoholism units are sometimes included as part of the structure, but are not always viewed as a necessary part of rehabilitation.[4] In essence the structure of the rehabilitation system consists of a series of tiers through which alcoholics ought to progress from skid row back into the community. Although no single agency on skid row offers a complete, self-contained system of rehabilitation, an ideal model of the system is graphically illustrated in Figure 3.

In theory alcoholics entering the treatment network do so through a street-level contact service and are then referred into an alcoholism treatment facility, usually a residential hostel. The gradual detachment from skid row drinking and a corresponding assimilation into conventional society are represented by the passage of the alcoholic through the different tiers of the network. Each tier ideally represents a progressive stage in the recovery of the homeless alcoholic.

Because the skid row rehabilitation network is organised by a variety of voluntary and statutory agencies working independently of each other, there are a diversity of approaches to making the initial contact with alcoholics. Soup runs or soup kitchens, night shelters and day centres, shop-front offices, and out-patient mental hospital clinics are some of the services making up the first tier of rehabilitation. Each of these services usually operates a walk-in policy whereby men drinking on the row may contact a social worker or other professional. In addition residential facilities with a rehabilitative environment are characterised by a diversity of operational regimes. The assimilation of alcoholics into the community is attempted through short-stay hostels, shelters, half-way hostels, residential crypts and communities, and agency-controlled flatlets or bed-sitters. A variety of agencies, then, use different methods and settings by way of contacting homeless men, instilling motivation in

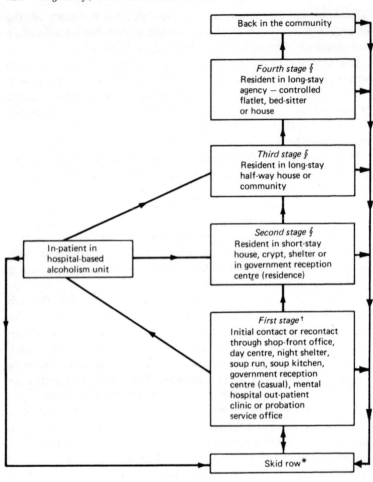

* Homeless, destitute and drinking
† Street-level contact services
§ Residential services

FIGURE 3   *The structure of the rehabilitation network*

them, and developing and sustaining a professional–client relationship.

But this variety is linked by a specific structure and reflects a major theme running through the thinking of rehabilitators. When homeless men are drinking on skid row their social distance from the normal community is such that it requires a careful and methodical transition through a series of rehabilitation stages if alcoholics are to gain enough social skills to be able to avoid drinking, and participate adequately in the community.

One final comment should be made before exploring in detail the views held of this network by rehabilitators and alcoholics. At present the majority of alcoholics on the row are handled by the agencies of law enforcement; comparatively few men make use of street-level contact services and residential facilities with a view to attaining sobriety. Of those that do enter the network, the great majority fail to pass through each of the recovery stages. Very few alcoholics, relatively speaking, successfully achieve a status as recovered alcoholics living in the community independent of skid row agencies. The majority that make use of the rehabilitation network do so by only making contact with the street-level services,[5] while a smaller number will enter the residential stages of rehabilitation. Moreover, since the probability of relapsing into drinking and returning to skid row is high, a diminishing number of individuals are progressively referred through each of the recovery stages. For the most part, then, the skid row man lives in a closed rehabilitation circuit made up of drinking on skid row interspersed with periods of sobriety in a hospital or in one or another residential facility.

The important feature that characterises the residential stages of rehabilitation, at least in theory, is that alcoholics are meant to show increased detachment from the skid row life style as they move through each of the rehabilitation stages. Correspondingly this detachment is meant to be accompanied by a gradual attachment to activities expected of recovering alcoholics: obtaining steady employment and a regular wage-packet, acquiring personal and consumer goods, displaying an interest in leisure activities and, above all, learning to handle the problems of everyday life without resorting to drink. Just as alcoholics at the skid row level are described as social inadequates, so progression through each of the rehabilitation stages is meant to reflect increasing social adequacy.

Moreover the number of professional staff and their degree of care of alcoholics decreases through each of the stages. At the contact stage several professionals may man a street-level service (partly as a reflection of the numbers of homeless men). If a professional–client relationship is forged, an assessment of the client's needs is made and an adequate referral into a residential facility (or hospital) is attempted. Residence in a second-stage facility is often viewed as a temporary expedient: the alcoholic is removed from the street or large skid row institution and is expected not to drink. A close professional–client relationship is maintained and residence at this stage is often regarded as a period when the alcoholic's motivation is tested and assessed with a view to referral to the third stage. Long-stay half-way hostels or residential communities often impose no time limit on the residents' stay. Professionals at this stage include one or two residential social workers or hostel wardens but some facilities operate without any resident staff, although a professional–client relationship may be maintained. Finally, a limited number of rehabilitation agencies have established long-stay bed-sitters or houses with no resident professionals and absolutely minimal attention by them. But the number of alcoholics who are referred to these facilities is small in comparison to men passing through the preceding treatment phases. All the residential stages are governed by the one central rule, which underpins any attempt at rehabilitating alcoholics, namely that residents are not permitted to drink.

The remaining part of this chapter is devoted to a closer exploration of the first and third stages of the rehabilitation system. The selection of these two stages is not entirely arbitrary: street-level services are considered strategically crucial if alcoholics are to be contacted and referred into the residential system, and long-stay half-way hostels or residential communities make up the core of the residential facilities in terms of fulfilling a rehabilitation function.

Street-level contact services

Because the skid row culture is considered as being totally outside society's cultural mainstream, professionals concerned with the welfare and rehabilitation of skid row men often find it necessary to make contact with them by taking their services to skid row. The skid row man needs to be contacted at the level where he is most visible and frequently finds himself – on the street. Thus welfare and rehabilitation agencies promote a variety of street-level contact services, such as shop-front offices, day centres, night shelters, soup runs and soup kitchens located in areas where men tend to congregate. These institutions are designed to function as the initial contact point with homeless, down-and-out men, with a view to providing them with such basic needs as clothing, food and shelter and assessing their need for treatment and care.[6] The principles underlying the work of street-level contact services are summed up in the following comment by an organisation conducting a soup run:

> The soup run is the axis of the Community's work, being the first source of contact on their territory, in their environment, with those living on the streets . . . The soup run contacts between 200 and 500 men and women a night offering help at two levels. On one level is the purely material aspect of providing soup, bread and clothes . . . But on another level we attempt to meet a more acute need: to bring companionship, informal and personal contact to alienated people. It is the regularity and punctuality of the soup run that enables us to work at this level . . . over a period of time, through regular contact, relationships may be formed through which it is possible to offer men a greater degree of support in one of our houses, or in the Night Shelter.[7]

The theme of making contact with and establishing a relationship between professional and homeless man is taken as the most valuable function street-level services fulfil. This strategy is articulated in all the statements made by personnel running such services.

Interaction in a street-level contact service – the case of a shop-front office

In the Home Office Report *Habitual Drunken Offenders* the establishment of shop-front centres in skid row areas is recommended as means of making initial contact with alcoholics. The Report defines such centres in the following terms:

> What is vital . . . is that the centre is known to the vagrant alcoholic population of the area as a place in which there is an ever open door to immediate help *for their drinking problem* . . . The function of the 'shop front' centre therefore is to reach out with a helping hand again and again to attract the man who has not sought help before but also to maintain contact with and tempt back those who have tried before and failed.[8]

Before the Report was published, one rehabilitation agency, the Alcoholics Recovery Project,[9] opened three shop-fronts in London. These centres consist of small offices open daily for two hours and manned by a social worker and a recovered alcoholic working in the capacity of a professional. The objectives of the shop-front offices and the nature of the professional–client relationships that unfold in these offices are analysed in the section below.

The shop-front workers view their assignment[10]

Alcoholics visiting a shop-front office do not necessarily present the same problems and needs. The latter will probably vary mainly according to the length of time they have lived on skid row. Thus one social worker was able to distinguish between three types of men making use of a shop-front office. (a) There is the long-standing alcoholic, with many years' experience of living on skid row, who has achieved a level of drinking and a personal life style permitting him to maintain a degree of self-respect and avoid alcoholic crises. This type of man only tends to request first aid and help with applications for social security benefits. (b) There is the homeless alcoholic who has little or no experience of the skid row culture, is referred to the centre by non-specialist agencies, but is viewed as being in danger of becoming caught up in the penal revolving door. In this case the task is to prevent the alcoholic's socialisation into the skid row life style by offering him a place in the rehabilitation system. (c) Finally comes the hard core of heavy drinking alcoholics, with considerable experience of skid row, who drink in tightly knit drinking schools. Their heavy group drinking produces alcoholic crises, with a consequent need for the social worker to intervene and offer individuals a place in the rehabilitation network.[11] The majority of alcoholics using the office fall within this last category. Here is what one social worker had to say of this group:

> . . . they have accepted the shop-front as somewhere where they will be accepted, where they will be assured of attention without the formal ties of first having to make an appointment. They will have used the office regularly while drinking. In this way it has been possible for us to link them up with relevant agencies at any point of crisis . . . we are able to facilitate [their] recovery . . . Once

recovering, the men are encouraged to cut all ties with the area, but maintain contact with the office.[12]

Since a shop-front office operates without a system of official appointments and pursues an open-door policy, any alcoholic, sober or drunk, is entitiled to make use of its services. In theory, social workers regard an alcoholic coming to the office for the first time as someone who will be requesting help with his drinking problem. Nevertheless, in practice, experience has taught the personnel manning the office that skid row alcoholics may be there for a variety of reasons. The initial task, then, is to separate those men who are thought to be suffering from a drinking crisis from those who use the office as a possible source for hand-outs or a place where they can be temporarily off the streets:

> There is no screening prior to entry, so the man arriving may be drunk or sober. In practice, little interviewing time is devoted to those who are very heavily intoxicated.[13]

> It is useless even to try to talk with a drunken man. The only rule seems to me is to say firmly but kindly 'come and see me when you are sober and we will talk about it then'.[14]

Not all alcoholics are held to want help with their drinking problem. Given the official objectives of the office, it is not surprising that men refer to the problems their drinking is causing, but their real motives need to be probed:

> Firstly, the age old 'testing-out' period by the client of the social worker and the agency has to be endured . . . One learns to pinpoint the true alcoholic, as opposed to the 'dosser' who is trying to get on the band-waggon . . .[15]

> One of the problems I have to face here [in the shop-front] is that when I'm dealing with the genuine cases I'm constantly interrupted by men who are still drinking and who are not concerned with obtaining places in the houses. I'm thinking of introducing a rule that if a man has been drinking on the day he shouldn't be allowed into the office.

Establishing a relationship with the client is the second task that the social worker is confronted with. Any motivation the client has needs to be encouraged. However, there is little point in helping the alcoholic unless, in the first place, he wishes to help himself.

> An alcoholic must be helped in his own time, in his own way, at his own pace. Until a man is ready to come off the drink at his own volition, it is useless to try to force the position, or to persuade him to do something he doesn't wish to do . . . He will be back to square one, and very resentful of the pressurising which occurred.[16]

The strategy is to present the alcoholic with an alternative to the life style he is leading on skid row by outlining the possibilities of treatment and rehabilitation in hospital alcoholic units and half-way houses. A third task of shop-front social workers, therefore, is to make a referral that fits the needs of the individual client.

Because rehabilitation facilities are limited in relation to the number of skid row men coming into contact with street-level services, social workers are sometimes confronted with the problem of not being able to achieve an adequate 'fit' between the alcoholic's needs and the type of hostels available. In particular the winter months are regarded as a time when the demand for hostel beds far exceeds the supply. At critical moments shop-front workers experience the tensions of providing a contact service with no possibility of offering back-up services in a half-way house. Either alcoholics are asked to keep attending the shop-front till a hostel vacancy occurs (sometimes a condition of sobriety is imposed in order to test the client's motivations) or referrals are made to facilities which, in the last analysis, social workers define as inappropriate to long-term sobriety, such as arranging for men to be admitted to a common lodging house, reception centre or mission. For instance:

> We put three or four blokes into a mission hostel out in the countryside. I told them straight that if they just wanted a rest from skippering and drinking, and if they could put up with the Bible classes, then it was a good place to rest and fatten up. They accepted that – you see, winter was coming up. Mind you, one of them stayed quite a long time.

The final important assignment is to recycle men who have lapsed from rehabilitation hostels and returned to skid row. In fact, shop-front offices have partly been established with a view to not losing touch with men who 'break out' drinking from residential facilities. Alcoholics are informed that if they start drinking, their relapse will not be held against them[17] and that they should take the first opportunity to reforge their links with shop-front workers. In view of the high recidivist rate amongst alcoholics, the shop-front social workers' case-load usually includes a high proportion of men who have already passed from street level to residential facilities. One worker commented:

> The work load has doubled as apart from the new cases, people who have done well for several months . . . suddenly appear one morning in the crypt having hit the bottle again, so once more a lot of help, support and time has to be given . . . we try to pin-point the incident where things started to go wrong and alcoholic thinking was triggered off again.[18]

Another social worker had this to say: 'They tend to feel they have let us down if a relapse occurs but frequently they reappear to try another treatment method.[19]

Relapsed alcoholics making a return visit to a shop-front office bring with them reputations acquired during past attempts at sobriety. The shop-front workers' attitude to a client who has 'broken out' is often determined by the number of opportunities he has been given to stay dry, how he has made use of his time in a rehabilitation hostel, and the degree of co-operation he has shown in going along with the rehabilitation plans made for him in the past by the shop-front personnel.

Thus, in some case, men are held to have 'spoiled their copy-book': repeatedly spending only three or four weeks in a rehabilitation hostel, showing no interest in going out to work, and asking to be referred to specific hostels or hospitals while rejecting others out of hand, are among some of the more important reasons given by shop-front social workers for discriminating against relapsed alcoholics. Conversely, men with a record of long-standing sobriety behind them (with many months or even years away from skid row drinking, holding a steady job and living independently of social work support) elicit from shop-front workers special efforts to prevent the client losing the stability and social credit acquired during sobriety.

The alcoholics' perception of the shop-front and its staff

Before examining in some depth how alcoholics look upon the services offered in a shop-front office, we should have some idea how homeless men view the presence of treatment and rehabilitation facilities in general. It would be useful to know their opinion of the counselling professions they come into contact with, and how they regard their alcoholic condition in the light of attempts to bring about in them a state of permanent sobriety.

The establishment of a rehabilitation network has not, as yet, made sufficient impact to alter the institutional profile of skid row. The degree of contact skid row alcoholics have with medical and social-work oriented professionals is at present minimal in comparison with the amount of contact they experience with law-enforcement officers. Nevertheless alcoholics are aware of the emergence of treatment services and the experts that man them.

In general skid row alcoholics view professional counsellors with suspicion and mistrust:

> Most dossers don't want to know about social workers, probation officers, psychiatrists or anybody like that.

> While you're drinking you know that no social worker will want to help you . . . they're not interested.

> If I can't do it on my own [achieve sobriety] I can't see how any social worker is going to help me.

There is a prevalent feeling that experts charged with helping men who stand outside the boundaries of conventional society have little understanding of, and sympathy for, their situation. Closely equated with the above feelings about social workers and doctors is the adoption of a critical stance towards the institutions these professionals represent. Hospitals, rehabilitation establishments and welfare offices are charged with discriminating against the veteran skid row man, especially if he is known to have a drink problem.

Moreover the derelict inebriate defines his personal and social condition by either seeking to deny his deviant role or accepting it as a permanent condition. For example, here is how two men defined their situation:

I've got a regular casual and I'm skippering, but I don't see that as a problem.

One can drink for years, live rough, go in and out of prison, and never think about one's life as a problem – we don't set any panic stations about the way we live.

But more often comments are made about the irreversible state of being an alcoholic. Typical of how many men see their condition are the following remarks:

There is no cure for alcoholism – I've had a go myself – once an alcoholic always an alcoholic.

Leading this kind of life, I know there is little hope of me ever staying sober, getting myself a regular job and a room. Even once he stops drinking an alcoholic can never guarantee he'll not drink again.

When you're drinking heavy the one easy way to stop the sickness [withdrawal symptoms] is to take another drink . . . There's no limit to what an alcoholic will drink.

The skid row alcoholic, then, appreciates that his way of life separates him from the mainstream of conventional life but holds out little hope for any radical change in his outlook. Any sense of personal failure is reinforced by the failure of experts to do anything substantial about his predicament. The inability to shake the physical and psychological grip of alcohol confirms his status as a worthless derelict.

How, therefore, do homeless men who attend a street-level contact service with a treatment and rehabilitation orientation (in this case a shop-front office) view its function? If alcoholics regard their situation with such a degree of fatalism or ennui, why do they then go to such a facility? Does making regular contact with experts intent on helping them in any way alter their perception of social workers?

The significance that alcohol addicts attach to the shop-front depends to a certain extent on their awareness of its official function. Clients visiting the office for the first time, with little or no experience of the skid row rehabilitation loop, may regard it as a potential hand-out centre. On the other hand, they may have been referred to it by other agencies or been informed by skid row men that the office focuses primarily on getting them into hospital or small-scale hostels. In any case at any one time the clientele will consist of a regular set of alcoholics familiar with the shop-front and its allied rehabilitation houses, plus a smaller number of first-time visitors who may be unacquainted with its services.

Reasons for attending the shop-front do not always tally with the primarily rehabilitative endeavours of the social workers. As noted above, shop-fronts have been established in order to forge relationships with men defined as being 'out of touch with reality', gain their trust, carry out an initial assessment, and refer them into the appropriate treatment setting. Some homeless men, however, define the shop-front in a different, more pragmatic, way. From their viewpoint the shop-front has important extra-curricular functions. For instance, alcoholics see the office as a convenient day-time off-the-street refuge offering a couple of hours' shelter; as a place where the social workers will help with sorting out social security benefits, employment cards and clothing grants; as a source of money (either begged or borrowed) from social workers or recovering alcoholics; and, finally, as a place where one may pass the time between drinking bouts and just talk to friends.

But beyond these immediate reasons, and in spite of the prevalent attitudes they hold about their personal condition and the experts charged with their care, many alcoholics using a shop-front do so for the purpose of entering hospitals and rehabilitation houses. Skid row men often experience the debilitating consequences of protracted drinking to a point where they feel the need to stop drinking temporarily. Continuous ingestion of alcohol, coupled with undernourishment, exposure to the weather and irregular sleep, reduces their physical and psychological stamina. A point is reached, in fact, where derelict alcoholics appear to shift their stance:

> When I'm drinking and living rough I don't always feel the need to get off the streets . . . But there comes a time when I feel the need for a break. I was sick of drinking and of the way I was living.

> I was tired of being done by the law . . . the police had it in for me . . . I decided to give it a break.

> Drinking in a school, all you talk about is the drink . . . and all you think about is where the next bottle is going to come from. But then

you start thinking about doing something about it. Your mind is working all the time – you're caught between drinking and thinking you've got to stop it. And then suddenly you refuse the next bottle . . . and you make it down to the shop-front.

I'd been drinking and walking the streets for three nights till I went into the shop-front . . . the social worker realised I was in a bad way and needed a dry-out. He got me into hospital the same day.

In addition, but not so frequently, the need to stop drinking is brought about by somewhat more dramatic circumstances, such as the sudden death of a drinking companion, a feeling that 'the next bottle of "jake" is going to kill me', or the frightening experience of delirium tremens or alcoholic hallucinations.

Men who are seasoned consumers of rehabilitation services soon learn that they are competing for limited resources when they wish to regain access to a treatment establishment. Being admitted to hospital or a half-way house requires overcoming two major obstacles: (1) convincing rehabilitation staff that their needs are real and that they're not 'conning' the system, and (2) successfully detaching themselves from the skid row drinking scene.

So far as the alcoholic is concerned, showing genuine evidence of his need for a hospital or hostel bed is the first hurdle to overcome. Past rehabilitation effort can be a passport to a treatment facility:

I'd been doing well in one of the houses when I suddenly had a slip – having kept off the beer for 13 months I knew that if I went back to the shop-front they'd want to help me.

Displaying adequate motivation also helps:

If you're not prepared to work for your sobriety then the social workers won't give you any help. You've got to show them that you're genuine . . . Not going down the office drunk tells them you're trying.

You figure out ways of trying to get back into line.

It's no use asking to get into a house right away – the social workers won't wear that.

The second major problem for the inebriate is severing his day-to-day connections with the world of skippers and park drinking, as a preliminary step to entering a treatment facility. Alcoholics experience a tension between the drinking orientation of life on the row and the abstaining orientation of the shop-front. Aware that it may take two or three weeks of daily visits before being referred, one man summed up the problem in this way:

> I found it difficult going down the shop-front while at the same time I was living rough. You see, once the office has closed down [the office is open two hours per day] where do you go? You hit the park and you're offered a bottle, or you buy a bottle yourself. Getting steamed up might mean getting knocked off by the law or into a patch of trouble. Then when you don't visit the social worker for several days they think you're not really sincere.

Many of the homeless men who use a shop-front for the purposes it is intended for sooner or later overcome these hurdles and are referred into a treatment establishment. How residents and staff interact in one kind of treatment establishment – a half-way house – is the subject of the next section. Nevertheless, as with all street-level contact services, the shop-front is strategically located in the rehabilitation network at the point closest to the drinking life of the skid row man. Thus, not unexpectedly, when some shop-front clients are rejected or fail to obtain the help they feel they need, the shop-front and its personnel come in for criticism.

> After being told it would be about three weeks before they could get me into a house I didn't bother any more. Some men won't wear it, all this waiting.

> I was asked to stop in the Reception Centre till the social worker got me a hostel bed. I don't think she was trying to help me, if not she wouldn't have sent me there.

> One of the workers at the shop-front is a recovered alcoholic – but he's no better than I am . . . I think it's a waste of time going down there.

These last few remarks epitomise the sense of exploitation and mistrust alcoholics feel for social workers when they are living on skid row. It does not matter whether such feelings arise out of a correct or erroneous appraisal of the social workers' role. Neither is the general feeling altered by the fact that alcoholics do sometimes appreciate individual social workers for their efforts in facilitating their recovery. What is central is that, from his standpoint, the alcoholic believes that he is exploited and therefore views skid row experts with deep suspicion.

Residential services

Merely making contact with men at street level and establishing a relationship with men described as alienated is not considered sufficient. The point is to offer homeless alcoholics an alternative to a social and physical environment defined as inimical to the health and well-being of individuals considered incapable of helping themselves. To this end voluntary rehabilitation agencies have established a chain of residential facilities designed to provide a milieu capable of countering the grip of the skid row life style. Small residential houses for up to twelve homeless men, through which they will graduate away from skid row and possibly back into society, are currently envisaged as the most appropriate rehabilitation setting. The idea is that as residents gain insight into their problems and increase their confidence in handling the tasks and relationships of everyday life (i.e. as they are gradually rehabilitated), they will progress through a series of residential tiers or stages, each characterised by increased autonomy and independence.

Rubington, writing about the half-way house movement for American skid row alcoholics, spelled out the ideological factors linking all small-scale rehabilitation houses. Such houses are explicitly meant to stand in opposition to the institutional life of prisons, mental hospitals and skid row common lodging houses.

The ideology of the half-way house, upon which it bases its hopes for success, can be summarised as follows: As size decreases, residents have more of a chance to get to know one another as complete individuals. As the rules shrink in size and increase in clarity interaction may prove much easier . . . consensus becomes more likely. As status differences between expert and client shrink, communication can proceed more easily, reach its mark, and take effect. Informality, in making for a home-like atmosphere can induce a desire to remain a member of the group, to abide by the rules, and thus be subject to increasing positive influences to change behaviour, the prime objective of the half-way house.[20]

Broadly speaking, in Britain, there are two distinct types of small-scale residential house, with separate structures and operational ideologies. These types of facility are referred to as communities or hostels.[21] A number of organisational and operational factors distinguish the concept of community from that of hostel. For instance, communities possess a higher ratio of social workers to residents; workers invariably live in, eat and share tasks with residents; and there is no difference in income for both workers and homeless men, since the latter receive State benefits and workers receive the equivalent sum from the employing agency. On the other hand, hostels do not necessarily engage a residential social worker or hostel warden; one social worker, usually on a professional salary, may be responsible for more than one establishment; and the social worker/alcoholic relationship is implicitly founded on a caseworking approach to solving the client's problems. Whereas communities house all types of homeless men, hostels exclusively focus their attention on the alcohol addict; this means that the internal status and cultural differences arising on skid row between the alcoholic, the mentally ill, and the young unemployed, when carried into residential facilities, result in differing types of ambience between communities and hostels.

But the major difference between communities and hostels is a strategic one. Communities work on the assumption that the majority of skid row habituees are socially damaged to such an extent that they are defined as irrecoverable in terms of returning them to an independent life in the wider society. Once off skid row they require the protection of a self-contained community, probably for the rest of their lives. Hostels, especially half-way houses, officially strive to return homeless men to a conventional working life, so that they may live in society independent of any social-work assistance. Although the time alcoholics may spend in the third and fourth stages of recovery (in half-way houses and agency-owned long-stay bed-sitters and houses) is often unlimited, there is nevertheless an expectation that eventually the alcoholic will want to formally sever his connections with the rehabilitation system.

As a result of these differences in operational methods and objectives the relationship between skid row men and workers or professionals also differs. Communities are more likely than hostels to ignore the need for structured group meetings or formal casework; personal development is expected to grow through residents and workers living and working together in the residential community. Hostels, on the other hand, occasionally run structured group discussions, some psychotherapeutic in orientation. Moreover social workers are expected to handle formal caseworking relationships on a professional – client basis. A more detailed exploration of a rehabilitation hostel now follows.

Interaction in a residential hostel – the case of a half-way house

Half-way houses are one type of residential facility designed to help skid row alcoholics in their recovery. They are usually situated relatively near to areas frequented by drinking men, although they are designed to provide an alternative to repeated drinking, arrest and imprisonment. Rathcoole House is a twelve-bedded hostel run by the Alcoholics Recovery Project to which men passing through a shop-front office are often referred. Below is a broad description of the house and its regime:

The house is run without resident staff. There is one social worker with specific responsibility for the house and a part-time cook prepares the evening meal during the week-days. At the weekend and at all other times the men prepare their own meals and in addition keep the house clean. Non-residential staffing . . . enables the men to have a greater share in the running of the house, to develop a general sense of what it feels like to live in a non-institutionalised setting and removes any feeling of being constantly supervised . . . there is a weekly meeting attended by the residents and the social worker . . . at which house 'business' is discussed. The meetings act as a forum for the exchange of views and ideas as well as for discussion on the wider problems of coping with sobriety. For the staff, their primary function at these meetings is to focus attention on the implications of decisions taken. The decisions and their consequences are then the responsibility of the residents. Selection of alcoholics for admission to residence is by way of an initial interview with the social worker followed by a report to the House meeting. The residents then decide whether to invite the applicant to visit the house for a meal and to attend a selection meeting. A new resident is elected by a vote of the residents. The only defined rule in the house is that of total sobriety: no resident is allowed to drink and remain in residence.[22]

In addition residents are not expected to take on full-time jobs, at least in the initial weeks of their recovery, and no time limit is imposed on their length of stay. Rathcoole, then, is much in keeping with the description of a half-way outlined by Rubington.[23]

Hostel staff define their assignment

Following the above general description of Rathcoole House an exploration of three crucial areas as perceived by the staff responsible for the rehabilitation of its residents is now offered. Firstly, a more detailed account of the function and climate of the hostel sets the background against which the second area of concern is articulated, namely how the rehabilitation performance of the residents is viewed. Finally, given that the majority of alcoholics passing through Rathcoole eventually relapse and return to skid row drinking,[24] the analysis focuses on how the staff cope with the recurring problem of men 'breaking out'.

In Rathcoole House the rehabilitation policy being pursued is one in which staff maintain a low profile *vis-à-vis* offering residents personal counselling or structured group therapy sessions. The non-directive and low-key efforts of the staff are articulated in a number of ways:

> When I first see a man with a view to admission I explain that the house meetings only deal with domestic issues and that there is no psychotherapy or group therapy. They appreciate that. You see, some of the men will say 'I'm not a nutter, I just drink too much' or 'I haven't come here to have my head sorted out but just to stop drinking'.
>
> I visit the house and attend the weekly meeting as an observer and informal assessor – I try not to intervene.

We've adopted an approach where we have learned to reduce our expectations of what alcoholics can achieve in our houses – we now let them determine their own standards.

The factors that have brought about this policy are several. Following the early introduction of Alcoholics Anonymous meetings, professional psychiatric support, and structured group discussions designed to provide residents with insight into their problems, the staff appreciated that skid row alcoholics generally hold little faith in the advice of professional counsellors. In addition the emphasis on Rathcoole as a non-institutionalised establishment, without residential staff and formal rules (except for the 'no-drink' rule), and giving its residents the opportunity to regard it as their 'home' (each resident is given his own front-door key), ran counter to introducing programmed therapy sessions. Lastly social workers responsible for Rathcoole have learned that open and collective discussions of a therapeutic nature are antithetical to the skid row norm that personal troubles are never raised as a topic of conversation in drinking schools or on skid row generally. Here, then, is how one social worker summed up the atmosphere at Rathcoole:

The prevalent atmosphere is one of selfishness and a denial of involvement, in either the house or the well-being of others. Personal feelings are not expressed – although this may be a reflection of the culture from which they [the residents] come. The residents have increasingly tended to stress sobriety as an end in itself . . . [and] seem to have an expectation of harmony and absence of conflict, therefore [they] do not discuss painful issues, either personal or general.[25]

The climate that pervades Rathcoole as a half-way house has significant implications for how staff accommodate to the official objective that the house is at least an alternative to the penal revolving door and at most a means of bringing about personal change in individuals who will hopefully lead independent lives in the community. Wiseman noted in her study how professionals working with skid row alcoholics undergo a process of reality adjustment in order to justify their work in the face of repeated failure by alcoholics to remain abstinent.[26] Instead of aiming for the complete reintegration of their clients into the wider society, they invoke a set of less ambitious criteria to justify their work with homeless men.

The treatment and rehabilitation revolving door has meant that social workers redefine their objectives to take into account the high relapse rate of skid row men. Official objectives are transmuted into work-a-day, short-term goals:

> We're here not so much to see these men get back into society, as to reduce the chaos in their lives.

> Ideally I would like to feel that men think sobriety has a lot to offer in terms of their future . . . that sobriety is worthwhile . . . But the majority of residents who pass through here are not sincere. For these men this place gives them a chance to build up physically and mentally . . . so that they can cope with their next bout on skid row.

The second important area that staff associated with Rathcoole stressed is the progress (or lack of it) that alcoholic residents make in moving away from the skid row life-way. In spite of the emphasis on self-determination and non-directive social-work intervention, hostel workers, like all other agents of social control, need to define their own role and that of the alcoholics they are handling so that they can make sense of the work they are doing. On the basis of their professional experience with alcoholics resident in houses located at different stages in the overall rehabilitation network (see Figure 3), social work personnel are able to appraise a client's potential or actual progress according to a variety of criteria. Thus the mid-way point that Rathcoole holds in the transition from skid row drinking to an autonomous, sober life in the community provides social workers with a convenient frame of reference by which to judge the rehabilitation performance of its residents.

According to recovery performances there are apparently three types of men who gain admission to Rathcoole. In the first instance there is the skid row alcoholic who has little or no previous experience of small-scale rehabilitation houses. Here is how one worker described these men:

> For those men who are new to the house it is one hell of a strain. They have no experience of what it means to be sober. I give them no more than two months before they go drinking. Usually it's less than that.

The other two types consist of alcoholics referred to as being 'dry drunks' or 'sober drunks'. Precise criteria by which each may be identified are not agreed upon by either professional practitioners or recovered alcoholics, neither is there any clear indication as to when in the recovery process men feel or show that they have graduated from the 'dry' to the 'sober' stage.[27] Nevertheless it is evident that the distinction is an important one; social workers familiar with the recovery prospects of skid row men often use the terms to identify the degree of progress a client has made since he entered a residential service. The following remarks show how some social workers identify the 'dry drunk'.

> I find the men who spend a lot of time romanticizing about their days on skid row as being symptomatic of being dry rather than sober. Especially if that's all they can talk to each other about.

> Real sobriety is kicking all the crutches away. Take Micky, for example. He's got no insight at all into his problem and he's been off the beer a long time now. But he's still got social workers running around after him, writing letters for him when he's trying to get a job . . . He is very dependent.

Residents who gamble heavily, become irritated at any delays in receiving welfare payments, boast about their wage packets and savings, show off new suits and recently acquired personal belongings, are deemed as being 'off the drink but not sober'. Above all, 'dry drunks' are viewed as not having any conception of permanent sobriety. In the words of one social worker:

> The majority of residents after three months seem to get stuck, as if they ran out of energy, ideas, stimulation . . . When I talk to them about it they come out with an excuse like 'You've got to understand us alcoholics, we can't start making long-term plans, if not we'll break out'. They're like a record getting stuck.

In sharp contrast the 'sober drunk' acquires a new personal psychology. Skid row as a frame of reference holds less and less relevance for him; instead his future orientation is directed at interests and activities lying beyond the skid row world. He is usually a man who has had previous experience of hostel life as a 'dry drunk' but then came to realise that returning to skid row holds more problems for him than does long-term sobriety. A Rathcoole social worker recognised the 'sober drunk' in these words:

> The sober drunk is able to handle conflicts and tensions without losing his temper.

> Now and again you get a bloke who tells me about his work and the people he has met. He also shows an interest in what is happening to him and to others in the house.

> This time Joe came in he was different. Previously he'd been a good example of a dry drunk. Now he's started using initiative. First he got himself into a hospital with a structured alcoholism programme and stayed the full 13 weeks. He also kept in touch with me by letter. And once he'd settled in here he started talking about getting a job working with people but without too much stress and responsibility. He now works in an old people's home.

Achieving the state of being a 'sober drunk' within Rathcoole has important implications for how the social worker handles the alcoholic, particularly in view of the fact that the majority of residents are regarded as not progressing beyond the 'dry' stage. 'Sober drunks' show signs of wanting to move into a rehabilitation facility, which both recognises and encourages the process toward permanent sobriety and a life independent of skid row institutions. With the assistance of the social worker he will be referred to a facility located at the next stage of the rehabilitation network, usually a flatlet, bed-sitter or house with minimal or no social-work intervention (the fourth stage in the rehabilitation network – see Figure 3).

A further important dimension underscoring the progress that alcoholics make when resident in rehabilitation establishments is the way in which they organise their sober time.[28] The meaning that time has for alcoholics when drinking on the row differs widely from abstinent periods in a rehabilitation facility. During heavy drinking bouts time can be unstructured and take on limitless dimensions; drinking and getting drunk distorts time to a degree where the past, present and future are blotted out. Any awareness of time rarely extends beyond thinking about where the next bottle of alcohol is going to come from. Sobriety in a rehabilitation hostel, on the other hand, imposes on alcoholics demands to use their time quite differently to the way it is spent on skid row.

In Rathcoole the once-a-week house meeting and the evening meal are the only officially set times that residents do not control. Beyond these two domestic activities, how the recovering alcoholic uses his own time is therefore taken by the social work staff as evidence for judging his rehabilitation performance:

> Going out to work regularly is how most residents take up their time. It's the men who don't work that I'm worried about. They try to fill in their time doing a bit of cleaning, peeling potatoes, running errands or placing bets for those who are out at work. But it's not enough . . . once a man has been hanging around for three or four weeks I begin to urge him to get a job.

> The people who get up late, read the paper, spend their time in the betting shop or watch TV all the time – they're the ones who don't last very long.

Whether residents spend their time constructively or not is sometimes linked to whether they are deemed to be 'dry' or 'sober':

> The man who's come off the drink for the first time, you can almost sense his problem. He goes around lost, asking himself 'What shall I do now?' 'When can I make my breakfast?' 'What time do I stay in bed till?'

> Peter and Joey – they spend *all* their time gambling. They have six years off the beer between them but they haven't begun facing up to the real problems of sobriety yet.

The above examples of time structuring revolve around the problems of developing a daily routine. Reading, watching TV, placing bets, going to work, eating and sleeping can be viewed as making up a short-term, almost automatic, routine. From the point of view of the hostel staff time structuring in the mid-term also acts as a measuring rod by which to assess rehabilitation progress. The first few months of abstinence (between 3 and 6 months) can provide a structured time framework during which both rehabilitator and client can appreciate the latter's almost tangible progress. Attending the shop-front office regularly for the first month, being successfully referred to a hospital or short-stay hostel for the second month, finally being referred into Rathcoole and remaining abstinent for another three months, are viewed as distinct stages in the recovery process. But these time stages are to a large extent determined for the alcoholic by professional counsellors. The importance of short-term and mid-term time structuring insofar as they reflect the alcoholics' orientation to time is that they are taken as evidence of an alcoholic being 'dry' as opposed to 'sober'. 'Real sobriety', from the re-habilitators' viewpoint, is achieved when the alcoholic takes on an awareness of the long-term future and the significance it holds for sobriety. Only a minority of skid row recovering alcoholics are said to view sobriety as a permanent state and thereby move beyond short- and mid-term goals:

> Most of these guys do three months or so in Rathcoole and feel good about it when they compare it with life on the streets. But then they ask themselves 'What now?' and find they've no longer got a goal. You see, real sobriety is a thing that is a long, long way off and it's difficult to define.

The majority of men admitted to Rathcoole, then, 'break out' after a few months, having failed to achieve the status of 'sober drunks'. Relapsing, as a social process, is the third important concern of the rehabilitation staff. Here is how one social worker explained the alcoholics' relapse:

> It's not that skid row calls men back to it as if it were an attractive place but it has more to do with a feeling of dissatisfaction with what they've got. When they ask themselves what has sobriety got to offer the answer is nothing much. They realise that being abstinent is too hard work in return for nothing . . . they get no inner satisfaction . . .
>
> These guys haven't got much of a future, when you think about it. They can never really attain society's norms at the age of 45 – you know, a job, a settled place of their own with a woman. Mostly, these things are ruled out for them. They can't even do what their type would like to do: drink socially in a pub.

From the social worker's standpoint a resident's imminent or actual relapse creates both a critical and delicate situation requiring careful handling.[29] 'Going on the drink' is, of course, a direct threat to the objectives of Rathcoole as a rehabilitation hostel. Relapses are met by automatic expulsion of residents who return having drunk.[30] Although an experienced social worker can occasionally detect behaviour patterns in individuals that tell him about a person's likelihood to drink, there is little that he feels can be done about it:

> The men recognise the signs but they'll cover up in front of a social worker . . . They'll avoid me . . . that's when I get a bit worried . . . There's a kind of restlessness about them, like watching part of a TV programme, going to bed in the afternoon, getting up late, or saying they're going out for a walk when they don't normally do so . . . But it's often very difficult to pick out someone who's going drinking – they just do it . . .
>
> I'll suspect a man who suddenly begins to use a mouth-wash or chews mints . . . But I find myself on very dodgy ground till I find a bottle or smell alcohol. You see, I think it's a bum thing to ask a man 'Listen, have you had a drink?', when I'm not certain he has. It only goes to destroy the element of trust and confidence that I try to encourage. Unless I'm sure . . . I don't confront him because he'll give himself away sooner or later.

The recidivism of skid row alcoholics is a commonplace experience for seasoned workers in the field of rehabilitation. When an individual 'breaks out', the loss is not necessarily viewed as either tragic or permanent. In many cases admission to a half-way house and a subsequent relapse is seen as an integral part of the total skid row life style; the agency merely sustains alcoholics between relapses. Thus social workers responsible for the rehabilitation of alcoholics have limited expectations for the permanent recovery of their clients. This is how one social worker summed it up: 'There's certainly a lot of hopelessness with these guys. Suddenly they will say to themselves "Fuck it!" and go straight into a pub.' With a relapse and return to skid row drinking, then, the cycle on the rehabilitation network is made complete.

Life in a half-way house: a resident's perspective

The type of homeless men who are admitted to Rathcoole are perfectly aware that the function of the house is to provide a setting that will encourage abstinence. Originally, when Rathcoole was first established, a resident was permitted one slip; only on a second relapse was he asked to leave the house. But it was eventually decided by the alcoholics living in at the time that a strict 'no drink' rule should be enforced without second chances being granted. Ever since then the emphasis has been on the house being totally 'dry'. In addition many of the alcoholics appreciate the hostel's generally easy-going atmosphere, the absence of any clear-cut therapeutic programme, and the better amenities than those found in larger skid row institutions.

As was evident from the preceding section, the social-work staff are able to distinguish between 'dry' and 'sober' drunks. One worker pointed out that the prevalent atmosphere in Rathcoole was set by the residents being mainly 'dry' drunks. As a half-way house the establishment has become not so much an alternative to the skid row life-way as an extension to it. Support for this claim is demonstrated by the short periods men remain in the house relative to time spent at other points on the skid row cycle; the interest residents maintain in exchanging information about drinking schools, ways of 'making out', and other events and personalities they encounter on the scene; and the social and psychological stresses endured as the price they pay for self-imposed abstinence.

Two significant dimensions, taken from the alcoholic's perspective, are spelled out below in more detail. To begin with, some of the problems the 'dry' drunk encounters in sustaining his sobriety are explored. Finally, how he regards 'breaking out' – the most commonplace reaction to the stresses and strains of abstinence – concludes this chapter on the relationship between alcoholics and rehabilitators.

For the first few weeks the skid row alcoholic might find himself needing to adjust to the new routine of sober time. More than likely there is a period of settling down after a spell of heavy drinking on the streets or time spent in one or another total institution,[31] such as prison, mental hospital or government reception centre, all of them large establishments with somewhat inflexible regimes and strictly coded rules and regulations. The personal adjustment required, even when the resident has had previous experience of non-institutionalised small-scale half-way houses, is often considerable. Indeed, the first few days' residence are considered by both social workers and alcoholics as critical, particularly if the new arrival has by-passed the hospital stage of treatment or residence in a second-stage facility such as a short-stay house (see Figure 3).[32]

Obtaining a bed in a 'dry' setting would appear to be the first important achievement for the homeless inebriate. This is followed by successfully settling down in a house occupied by up to ten other skid row men, some of whom may have been drinking companions, while others are known but disliked. Getting a job is the third important short-term goal.

As the men explain it:

I'd been living rough all the time so just getting a room was a step up in the world.

When I got into Rathcoole I realised that what I needed was three or four weeks rest so that I could build myself up before looking for a job. There's no need to rush straight into a job. One of the first things is to settle down.

There are problems living with others. For example, there can be a needle match going on all the time between some of the men here. Some fellows don't get on with each other . . . I try to keep myself to myself in the house.

When it comes round looking for a job it'll have to be something easy – a steady inside job. Going straight into labouring would be too hard for me . . . I've only done one day's work in the last two years.

Gathering round oneself the overt symbols of sobriety (living in a house that looks no different to others in the neighbourhood, getting a steady job, opening a personal savings account, buying some clothing) is not necessarily difficult, once the alcoholic has got beyond the initial shaky period of settling in. Much more difficult to handle is the whole question of grappling with the psychological dilemma of being abstinent while at the same time having limited expectations about one's future prospects. Earlier on we learned how skid row alcoholics developed self-images that served to remind them constantly of their poor prospects. Repeatedly they keep hearing about or witness the relapse of other men. Stories about recovered alcoholics with years of sobriety behind them suddenly 'breaking out' underscore the thin dividing line said to exist between sobriety and chronic inebriety. They also learn that experts hold little hope for them as far as a constructive long-term future is concerned.

In this context half-way houses like Rathcoole may be perceived as being only one step removed from the skid row drinking scene. This feeling was expressed in a number of different ways:

> A couple of men I know well broke out soon after I got in here. I was frightened that one of them would come back drunk, maybe with a bottle, and ask me to join him.

> I was doing well till Bob phoned me up from the park to tell me he'd just come out of hospital. That did it!

> You know that just one drink can spoil everything. The thing to do is to get your mind off the drink – but it's hard work.

> When you're in the house the thought of having a drink is never very far away from you . . . I remember once when I had a long week-end in front of us and I walked past a pub with all my savings in my pocket . . . I almost went in.

The proximity of skid row drinking is sometimes brought home in a less challenging fashion. The men in Rathcoole are aware that their geographical distance from the drinking scene does not mean that they have severed their long-standing cultural and psychological links with it. Recovering alcoholics give money to friends on the row, occasionally give food to men who call at the door begging, and generally maintain a close interest in the whereabouts of other men. Associations learned and consolidated on the row are carried into the rehabilitation setting; in some respects, then, only the absence of a bottle distinguishes life in a half-way house from that in a drinking school.[33]

On top of learning how to handle sobriety in the company of men with the same background and experiences the recovering alcoholic has to cope with the pressures of day-to-day contact with the ordinary world. For the most part, life on skid row consists of a cycle of drunk time/institution time; any responsibilities toward the conventional world are absent or suspended. But living in a rehabilitation setting means that the alcoholic is expected to reforge his links with the wider community. In practice this means sorting out insurance and national health cards, maybe receiving medical and dental attention, securing a steady job or arranging to receive social security benefits, learning how to handle money and leisure time responsibly, and maybe even making contact with one's family or relatives. For most of us such tasks are taken for granted. For the recovering alcoholic they represent tests of their endurance in maintaining sobriety.

In particular the tasks necessary in making contact with the conventional world and keeping sober require in many instances the proper organisation of time. This is how some men put it:

It's no good building long-term plans or castles in the air – they'll only crash around you.

Trying to fill in time is the biggest problem.

I feel now that I'm changing I've got to work out a routine for myself – that's why I'm thinking of getting a job. My mistake last time was hanging around the house . . . it got me down.

When sober everyone has to figure out how to spend their time. Some men take to going down to the bookies. Others play snooker, go to the pictures or watch TV. I did my own washing and ironing . . . it helped pass the time.

How to plan time is something that most ordinary citizens achieve without too much difficulty. But in the case of skid row alcoholics the ability can, as Wiseman states, 'easily atrophy from disuse'.[34] Unlike drinking on skid row (where there is an absence of schedule) or life in a total institution (where time is highly structured), time in Rathcoole needs to be structured by the resident himself. To do so successfully does not always come that easy.

The perspective of alcoholics in Rathcoole has so far emphasised the problems they encounter in coping with the process of recovery. Implicit throughout their accounts is an awareness that the dividing line between life on the row and in a half-way house is a very thin one. There usually comes a time when, having endured the stresses and strains of sobriety, the alcoholic 'breaks out', only to return to street drinking. Once again he resumes the life of an urban nomad.

Relapses are frequent occurrences in alcoholism treatment establishments. To staff and other residents it is not always readily apparent that an individual is about to relapse. But even where 'breaking out' is imminent and apparent to others, there is common agreement that there is little that can be done to avoid it. In some instances residents in a half-way house try to conceal from staff and other residents that they have had a slip. Nevertheless the vast majority of alcoholics claim that it is difficult to avoid drinking heavily once the first drink is taken.

On the face of it the physical and social conditions on skid row, coupled with the human degradation experienced there by homeless men, when compared with the propriety and standard of living in non-institutionalised half-way houses, might act as an incentive to remain sober. In fact, however, the psychological reality of remaining sober does not always parallel the man's appreciation of the comforts of a half-way house and the respectability of holding a job, earning a steady income, and looking in physical appearance like any other person in the neighbourhood.

One man's conclusion about how alcoholics feel were revealed as follows:

> An alcoholic is never satisfied, even when sober. He knows he can't do like others – go into a pub and have a couple of pints. He never gets over that.
>
>   An alcoholic is an angry person . . . and he's easily upset. That's why he's always slagging [criticising angrily] the social workers.

Eventually the recovering skid row alcoholic stops trying:

> I don't know, it just came over me. It beat me trying to keep off the drink. You see, the bottle won't leave you . . . it's not always with you but, like the devil, it keeps coming back. Everyone goes through this, whether it's a month, two years, or even twenty years after you stop drinking.

In keeping with the general atmosphere at Rathcoole the perspective in this section has been that of the 'dry' as opposed to the 'sober' alcoholic. Of course, some recovering alcoholics graduate from the 'dry' to the 'sober' state, and thus move beyond the half-way house stage in the rehabilitation network. The meaning that sobriety is given by 'sober' drunks is most probably markedly different from the image conveyed by 'dry' drunks. However, as stated earlier on, all the evidence of social workers in close touch with skid row alcoholics is that half-way houses like Rathcoole are predominantly used by men who express a 'dry drunk' attitude to sobriety. Relapse rather than permanent sobriety is the norm. For most of its residents, then, Rathcoole represents the end point in a recovery process that merely interrupts life on skid row or in the penal revolving door.

7
Social Policy and the Skid Row Alcoholic

The rediscovery of a social problem

In the first chapter skid row was defined in terms of its institutional boundaries. Two themes in particular were explored. Firstly, skid row was seen to consist of a complex of formal institutions that could not be understood as isolated responses to problems of homelessness and chronic drunkenness but needed to be located in the context of the demise and rise of specific control ideologies. Thus the ideological underpinnings of skid row agencies were identified as being either moral, penal, medical or social. Secondly, although the contemporary control structure is composed of institutions that represent all these basic approaches, the impact of contemporary medicine and social work is such that they seek to replace traditional moral and penal approaches. Consequently the formulation of social policy in the field of skid row alcoholism is increasingly directed at the establishment of facilities where individuals are to be offered medical treatment and social rehabilitation as opposed to moral suasion and penal correction. In this chapter the making of social policy is analysed with a view to illustrating how the problem of vagrancy, including that of homeless alcoholics, has been rediscovered.

The Home Office report on habitual drunken offenders

In 1971 the Home Office Working Party published its report *Habitual Drunken Offenders*.[1] The thrust of this document was to recommend that skid row alcoholics would best be treated within the framework of a socio-medical approach to the problem rather than having men repeatedly handled by law-enforcement agencies. Thus the main corpus of its recommendations centred on the provision of an interrelated system of treatment facilities in which the co-ordinated efforts of street-level contact points, detoxification centres, and therapeutic hostels would provide a strategy of care based on the expertise of psychiatry and social work.

Two considerations need to be taken into account if the recommendations are to be understood in the context of the nature of skid row alcoholism as a social problem. In the first place, chronic drunken offenders are viewed against a background in which a constellation of socio-medical factors come together. Single, unemployed, with little if any family contacts, living rough or in large common lodging houses, the skid row drunk is perceived as lacking the social skills with which to survive in conventional society. In addition he is said to be suffering from problem drinking or alcoholism and that this condition needs to be viewed as a disease. This means that with the skid row alcoholic both a social and medical condition are telescoped into one. Thus social policy is based on a response that claims to attack both these interrelated factors simultaneously. Secondly, having accepted alcoholism as a disease entity and defined the incumbent as socially inadequate, it becomes patently illogical to handle men by having them continuously arrested, fined and imprisoned. The revolving door policy is held to be ineffective and costly in deterring and correcting individuals habitually arrested for public drunkenness. Furthermore the impact of psychiatry in advancing the claim that the addictions can only be adequately controlled through treatment programmes provides the kind of ideological climate for proposing that skid row alcoholics be added to the list of other petty and recidivist offenders deemed to be in need of medical treatment and social rehabilitation.

The rationale for shifting the deviant status of the alcoholic from 'criminal' to 'ill' is made apparent in the Home Office Report. The provision of 'more rational and effective methods of treating him' (the habitual drunken offender) are justified along two dimensions:

One is the deleterious effect upon the habitual drunken offenders themselves of a perpetuation of the present situation [law enforcement] . . . the phenomenon . . . is merely part of the wider problem of alcoholism, which is now widely accepted as a disease . . . The habitual drunken offender on Skid Row has reached a state of despair and himself feels so often that he is at the point of no return. The combination of alcohol addiction and acute

social deprivations are crippling . . . The second factor is the effect
upon the rest of the community, which is also great. If it is only
considered economically its cost in terms both of the loss of
productive labour and of the burden it places on the police, courts
and prisons, quite apart from the community services of many
kinds, must be considerable.[2]

Thus the direction British policy is taking in the control of skid row
alcoholism, as crystallised in the Home Office Report, is widely
accepted in principle by both government departments and the voluntary agencies working in the field. After all, the handling of public
drunks through detoxification centres rather than police cells is
already practised in some American and Canadian cities, although
these are not always backed up by community-based rehabilitation
facilities. The demonstrable failure of the penal 'revolving door'
control strategy has been made apparent by Pittman's policy-
oriented study of the St Louis chronic drunken offender.[3]

The shift from penal to socio-medical control of homeless alcoholics, then, has been achieved at an ideological level. This shift has
been facilitated by the power of psychiatry to redefine habitual
drunkenness as a medical condition, by the limited introduction
across the Atlantic of medically oriented facilities to handle chronic
public drunks as an alternative to arrest, and by the failure of law-
enforcement agencies to deter public drunks from committing further
similar offences. However, two specific questions need exploring in
order to explain this redefinition. In the first place, what social forces
have determined this ideological redefinition in view of the apparent
historical disappearance of widespread vagrancy and destitution?
Secondly, why is it that in spite of this ideological shift, the vast
majority of homeless alcoholics continue in practice to be handled by
the law?

The withering away of vagrancy and the destitute poor

The existence of vagrancy and destitution on a large scale goes back
at least to early Tudor times. The role that the state then played in the
control of chronic poverty and pauperism reflected the urgency with
which it regarded the problem. Jordan writes in his *Philanthropy in
England*:

The most immediate and pressing concern of government . . . for something more than a century (1520–1640) was with the problem of vagrancy. There is no doubt whatever that vagabondage was widespread, that it was organised, and that it imposed on rural and village communities burdens and dangers with which they could not cope.[4]

There is no scope in this report for an extensive historical survey of vagrancy and government attempts to contain or eradicate the problem. Instead the central question being asked here is why has the state at the present moment chosen to re-enter the debate about the control of vagrancy and the single homeless when the magnitude of the problem is vastly reduced compared with previous periods? This question becomes especially pertinent in view of the effect the development of organised trade unionism and state welfare provision has had in removing from the social scene the worst effects of casual employment and disreputable poverty.

In an historical essay on the attrition of skid row in the United States Rooney argues that the contemporary forces of technological innovation and large-scale industralisation require a stable, skilled or semi-skilled labour force. In contrast, the period leading up to industrial expansion required an unskilled, often highly mobile, army of workers engaged in agricultural harvesting, mining, and construction. These workers used skid row as an area where they could spend periods of unemployment. Thus skid row was regarded as an economic institution, providing an easy-to-hire, highly mobile industrial work force. Today, in contrast with previous ages, skid row takes on a new function:

Since World War II welfare institutions have played a relatively greater role in drawing men to skid row. From its origin the skid row area has served several functions, but the relative importance of each function has changed. Skid row no longer is mainly a base of operation for seasonal workers; instead, it serves as a haven for dropouts from the working class. As a result of these changes the range of personality traits found among the skid row population has narrowed. The exodus of most of the actively militant migratory workers has left behind weak, passive men, of whom approximately one third are alcoholics.[5]

The extensive provision of common lodging houses and casual wards in Britain during the nineteenth century fulfilled a similar function to American skid row areas, since they were established to house a population of chronically poor and intermittently employed casual and unskilled labour. At the time moral weakness coupled with chronic unemployment were regarded as inseparable, and in need of a solution.

Generally speaking, the *raison d'être* behind the rapid expansion of common lodging houses during the middle and latter half of the nineteenth century was expressed in terms of a policy of 'housing the houseless poor', who, owing to economic forces, consisted mainly of individuals temporarily or permanently separated from their family households. But the raising of living standards, especially after the First World War, reversed a rising trend in men, women and children sleeping rough or in lodging houses. Common lodging houses, as a conception in housing the chronically poor, began to disappear. Women and children were no longer to be found among the down-and-out. Casual wards also closed down. Poor Law philosophy, whether reflected in central and local government casual ward provision or in the quasi-religious approach of the Salvation and Church Armies, was gradually replaced by the ideology and apparatus of the modern welfare state. Problems of vagrancy and destitution came to be associated with a past era. It was argued that the remaining sectors of the outcast working class would eventually wither away altogether with advances in full employment and welfare provisions.

Skid row and the single homeless – a rediscovery

The starting point for the rediscovery of skid row by the state during the early 1960s can be traced to two interrelated factors: the apparent rise in the number of persons sleeping rough in London and the creation of a new voluntary social-work movement drawing attention to the welfare state's inadequate provision for the single homeless population. Large commercial, voluntary and local authority common lodging houses were, of course, already providing accommodation for the destitute and casual poor. But with the establishment of small hostels or half-way houses the concepts of community-based therapy and rehabilitation gained credibility as alternative solutions to the problem. The voluntary social-work movement altered radically the strategy and *modus operandi* of how to tackle the problem of vagrancy and casual poverty; for the size and character of their facilities were aimed to avoid the institutional-isation inherent in large common lodging houses. But it was the argument that the number of persons sleeping rough had increased which triggered off and sustained the rediscovery of skid row as a social problem. This section analyses some of the forces behind this rediscovery.

Homeless Single Persons Report

Welfare legislation after the Second World war, designed to eradicate the inequities of a competitive *laissez-faire* economy, failed to abolish the existence of vagrancy and the casual poor, although the extent of the problem had been markedly reduced from a peak in the years of the depression. Thus, significantly, the 1966 National Assistance Board's Report, *Homeless Single Persons*,[6] moved beyond its usual survey of the population using government reception centres, to include persons sleeping rough and living in common lodging houses, hostels and shelters. This more inclusive list was not the product of an accidental whim by the National Assistance Board; as the publication points out:

> In 1964 and 1965 a number of voluntary bodies expressed concern both to the Government and to Government Departments about what they regarded as the *increasing problem* of the misfits and the drifters of society, particularly those who habitually live in lodging-houses and hostels or sleep rough. This concern was not in itself by any means new, but it was clear that *the problem was attracting increased public attention*, and discussions were held among the Government Departments most concerned . . . [my emphasis].[7]

It is quite clear from the evidence produced in the NAB survey that the overwhelming bulk of accommodation for persons defined by legislation as 'without a settled way of life' was provided by commercial or voluntary establishments, and not by the welfare state. Indeed, apart from the dwindling number of government reception centres, the state did not directly make any housing provision for homeless men.

Although the survey did not set out to 'provide answers to the problems of homelessness, vagrancy and social inadequacy', it did briefly stress the need for small-scale therapeutic hostels to handle the problem more adequately:

> . . . thus many people with characteristics associated with instability and rootlessness were found to be living together under the same roof and in circumstances which could well make it difficult for individual help to be given. It seems, therefore, that consideration may need to be given both to whether or not there is going to be sufficient accommodation and to the advisability and practicability . . . of having smaller hostels where more individual attention can be given to what are essentially individual personal problems.[8]

The basis for this claim lay in the conclusion that almost two-thirds of the men in the survey were in skid row institutions of 100 beds or more.

The policy implications of the survey not only clearly pointed in the direction of small hostels as a solution to the problem but also underscored a shift in the explanation of why men were on skid row in the first place. The forces of economic fluctuation were no longer held to be of any real significance; instead problems of personality and social adjustment were primarily held responsible for the persistence of a hard core of skid row men.

Two further factors need reviewing in order to complete the picture as to why the single homeless re-emerged as a social problem. The first is the implementation of the Mental Health Act, 1959, and its implications for the after-care of the mentally abnormal offender; and the second the post-war trend in the closure of reception centres and common lodging houses, and the reduction of cheap rented accommodation in producing pressure on the remaining accommodation for homeless men.

The Mental Health Act, 1959

The powerful claim of psychiatry to control deviant behaviour has meant that an increasing range of behaviours formerly dealt with by the law are now handled through psychiatric treatment. One of the main principles on which the 1959 Mental Health Act is founded is that treatment, both in hospital and through after-care, should be given to the mentally abnormal offender. The trend for discharging mental patients into the community had already started before the introduction of the Act, particularly as a result of the advent of tranquillisers in the treatment of the mentally ill. In addition the assumption behind the rapid discharge of patients was that the function of in-patient treatment should be diminished in favour of community care, especially in hostels, thus avoiding the institutionalising effects of long-term hospitalisation.

However, one of the consequences of the Mental Health Act was to produce a steep rise in the patients admitted to hospital from skid row, especially under Parts IV and V of the Act, which gave powers for petty offenders to be referred by law-enforcement agencies for treatment to mental hospitals instead of the former observation wards. The feature distinguishing the skid row, mentally ill offender from others admitted to hospital under the Act is his numerous readmissions to hospital and repeated arrests for typical skid row misdemeanours.

Crucial to an explanation of the rediscovery of skid row as a social problem is the functioning of the Act in relation to its intention of having the rehabilitation of patients completed in community hostels. Rollin, in his study, sums up the problem created by the failure to provide adequate after-care facilities once the Act had reached the statute books:

So with almost reckless enthusiasm the gates of the mental hospitals were flung open and a horde of mental cripples, unable to survive in society without very considerable support, were discharged only to find that this support either did not exist or was hopelessly inadequate . . . Some . . . stole food from shops or stalls in open markets, or broke into houses or buildings, or into locked cars to find shelter . . . it followed not infrequently that on the very day of their discharge, they exchanged a hospital bed for a prison cell.

The ping-pong sequence now begins, or in many cases, is continued . . . the 'open door', a concomitant of the progressive hospital, is thus in effect transmuted into the 'revolving door'.[9]

Rollin's assessment, although it fails to introduce the role that the institutions on skid row play in sustaining the revolving door, touches upon the essence of the social control process as it affects the homeless man on the row. What Rollin failed to stress was that, in the main, the reception centre, the common lodging house, the soup kitchen and the hand-out, the skippers and the parks, become the locations homeless men frequent between prison and the hospital. However, it is quite clear from his account that Rollin's mentally abnormal offender and the habitual drunken offender described in this report are both the target of the same institutional skid row complex. The only factor that distinguishes alcoholics from the mentally ill is the relatively greater frequency with which alcoholics are imprisoned as opposed to being hospitalised.[10]

The significance of the 1959 Mental Health Act, in terms of the argument in this section, is that it immediately preceded, and appears to have had a direct influence on, the pressure brought by voluntary agencies on the government to broaden its quinquennial survey of reception centres to include other facilities and situations in which destitute men found themselves.[11] It was argued by the voluntary agencies that many of the persons living rough and in skid row institutions were those very persons who were being discharged from mental hospitals without having a fixed address to return to. Confining the study to the reception centre population would only serve to underestimate the total single homeless population.

The decreasing availability of traditional skid row accommodation

In addition to the negative effects of the 1959 Mental Health Act apropos the control of the homeless, mentally abnormal offender the demand for beds in common lodging houses, reception centres and private, small-scale cheap rented accommodation has recently exceeded the supply. During the last five years or so, particularly during the winter months, the number of men turned back from these facilities is reported as having increased. Although the evidence for this trend is often based on personal reports by establishment managers, it has played a crucial role in upholding the belief that the number of persons sleeping rough has increased dramatically. There are, however, three interrelated developments that have produced a shrinkage of the accommodation market on skid row – the closure of commercial and voluntary common lodging houses, the closure of government-run reception centres, and a decrease in the number of small private lodgings catering for single working men.

Since the end of the Second World War the government has pursued a policy of reducing its network of reception centres (the old casual wards) throughout England and Wales. Two reasons have underscored this policy. Firstly, most centres were under-used immediately after the end of the war. Secondly, the state took on the explicit policy – it became a statutory duty – of influencing persons 'to lead more settled lives'. The traditional policy of having reception centres within walking distance of each other, therefore, became antithetical to the new resettlement policy pursued by the National Assistance Board.

Of the seventeen centres left by 1970, the Camberwell Reception Centre provided accommodation for over half the total reception-centre population in England and Wales. The role that this centre has played in highlighting the rediscovery of the problem has been crucial, since it has been the sharp rise in homeless men using it that has served as an indicator of the effects of the Mental Health Act and the reduction in both cheap skid row and non-skid row lodging house accommodation. Indeed, the particular attraction of London for vagrants, casual workers and other homeless men has prevented the Camberwell Reception Centre from becoming under-used to the extent that other centres have. Indeed, in 1972 three smaller overspill centres were opened in London.

Secondly, the closure of voluntary and commercial common lodging houses in London is taken as further evidence that the problem of single homelessness is growing worse. This trend is invoked as an argument for drawing attention to the problem. The two following statements adequately represent the argument that there is a crisis in accommodation. One agency states:

> The trend over the last ten years has been a reduction in the amount of cheap lodgings available and a rise in the number of people sleeping rough . . . The largest single factor has been the closure or 'up-grading' of large, commercially run hostels. For example, Rowton Hotels provided 4,536 beds in London in 1960, compared with 2,180 beds in 1972 . . . In London, Brandon gives a figure of 4,708 beds in 1972 with 6,415 in 1960 [for local authority registered common lodging houses].[12]

The Campaign for the Homeless and Rootless argues similarly:

> Data collected by St. Mungo Community and St. George's Mission in East London from their soup runs in London support the view that there has been an increase in the numbers of people sleeping rough . . . One reason for this increase . . . has been the dramatic decline in the number of beds provided in common-lodging houses . . . The trend looks as though it will accelerate over the coming decade . . . Pressure has therefore been building up on the place of last resort – the [Camberwell] Reception Centre.[13]

Finally, a further source of pressure on the existing skid row accomodation is seen to come from the reduction in small, private lodgings catering for six to twenty working men. Although these are not strictly part of the skid row institutional complex, Beresford and Diamond have argued that the chronic reduction in this type of cheap accomodation has created pressure on the remaining, larger skid row establishments.[14] Their argument is built on a domino theory, namely that shortage in this relatively more expensive sector of the total cheap accommodation market increases pressure on the less expensive sector, with the eventual consequence that the weakest and worst off are forced out on to the streets.

Although the evidence used for supporting the thesis that the problem of skid row accommodation has grown worse is only partial[15] its impact on the rediscovery of skid row has been real. The strategic importance of the argument has been in its power to call for the expansion in the number of much smaller hostels with a rehabilitation orientation.

Social policy and the new voluntary movement

Social problems in our society do not receive equal amounts of attention from the mass media and the apparatus of the welfare state. Neither is public awareness of specific social problems a function of the rise and fall of official statistics used to measure the problem. Instead the possibility of generating a moral panic,[16] which serves to increase such awareness, is partly a reflection of the problem's relative position in a hierarchy of competing priorities. Other social issues jostle for the attention of the media and the distribution of resources by the welfare state. It is the task of moral entrepreneurs to legitimise their activities by engaging in publicity and securing recognition for their efforts, so that the significance attached to a social problem is closely allied to the political impact made by groups engaged in expanding or innovating facilities for its control.

Quite clearly some forms of deviancy elicit greater degrees of moral indignation than do others. For example, the widespread acceptance of alcohol as a legitimate drug in most industrial societies is probably a significant factor in explaining why alcohol addiction does not generate a campaign of moral indignation akin to that directed against youth cultures using illegal drugs. In particular derelict alcoholics, despite their high public visibility, maintain a low profile in the media and collective consciousness of the public. Unlike other drug cultures, the skid row life style is not articulated as an expressive or hedonistic philosophy; consequently it fails to threaten social conventions and rules openly, in the way that some drug cultures do.

In addition, historically, the same problem may vary in terms of its political, moral and social impact and in the amount of resources deployed to contain or eradicate it. This has been the case with vagrancy, destitution and single homelessness. Consequently legislative and social policy has not been the product of unconnected social forces, but has emerged as a result of these fluctuations at specific periods in time.[17]

I have already intimated that the modern welfare state has not undertaken direct responsibility for the long-term rehabilitation of vagrants. The reason for this has been the assumption that widespread vagrancy has virtually disappeared and that its remnants would wither away with advances in provision by the state. Consequently the remaining hard core of persons who over time have been variously described as tramps, vagrants, itinerants and wayfarers came to be viewed as having a low priority in relation to other demands placed on the state.

The rediscovery of vagrants – now relabelled single homeless persons – has been mainly the result of political pressure exercised by voluntary agencies working in direct contact with the problem. These agencies have consistently defined their task as one in which they were rescuing the 'social casualties' of a welfare system that had failed to incorporate them within its provisions. Although the roots of voluntary and philanthropic work with the casual and destitute poor precede the establishment of the modern welfare state, the operational strategies of psychiatry and contemporary social work are relatively recent. Alcoholism units, the proposed detoxification centres, medical treatment, and the establishment of half-way houses, reflect the application of contemporary social control methods to a problem that has been reconceptualised in the rhetoric of treatment and rehabilitation.

Although the major impetus for the after-care of skid row men comes from a complex of voluntary agencies, these agencies have tended to pursue a political strategy that seeks to increase the concern and responsibility of the state for the single homeless person. This strategy is held to be consistent with a view that the long-term solution for persons defined as 'rootless and adrift in society' can only be achieved by the provision of small residential facilities to remove individuals from life on the streets and in common lodging houses, prison and mental hospitals. The effectiveness of a political strategy directed at central and local government has sharpened through the Campaign for the Homeless and Rootless (CHAR), a national umbrella agency representing the interests of voluntary organisations working directly with single homeless persons.

Analysis of the policies that CHAR has pursued not only reflects the trend to redefine skid row as a problem requiring medical and social welfare solutions, but has helped crystallise the rediscovery of vagrancy and destitution. This has been achieved by pursuing a policy that promotes public awareness of the problem and seeks to locate responsibility for the single homeless within the welfare state system. Both central and local government have therefore become major target points that CHAR has pressurised in order to achieve its aims. CHAR's campaign charters states:

> Acts of Parliament have long existed to enable central and local government to provide for the single homeless, but their needs are given a very low priority. Most local authorities do not use their powers, weak as they are. Most local authorities do not want the homeless and rootless in their area, so they make no provision for them. Central government departments, though increasingly aware of this growing social group, fail to provide sufficient finance for local authorities to do their job. The general public know little of the acute poverty of these people and invariably want to push them out of their locality. The burden of caring for and housing the

homeless and rootless is almost entirely carried by charities and voluntary bodies. The grants they receive from the statutory authorities, while vastly improved, still leave them with a heavy task of fund raising. Many exist on a shoestring.

CHAR has been established because charitable bodies can no longer carry this burden alone. Central and local government must fulfil their responsibilities instead of avoiding them. Only a vast increase in statutory planning, housing and finance can avert a worsening situation for the single homeless.[18]

In its objectives CHAR explicitly directs its policy towards the decriminalisation of vagrancy and habitual drunkenness, demands that the welfare state, both at central and local level, guarantees single homeless persons adequate housing, social benefits and medical care, and calls for an end to the economic exploitation of skid row men through improvements in casual work, pay and conditions. In spelling out these objectives CHAR has located the problem of single homelessness squarely within a policy framework that has shaped, and is reflected in, the recommendations made in recent government reports and circulars.

Government social policy and the single homeless[19]

The state has three formal and direct methods of responding to the problems presented by the single homeless. These are exercised through the institutions of criminal law, mental health and social welfare. Police, courts and prisons, mental hospitals, and welfare assistance, coupled with rehabilitation in reception centres, constitute the official response to skid row. However, the function that these institutions play in the long-term correction and treatment of skid row alcoholics is currently held to be ineffective. Most official investigations and the argument advanced by voluntary agencies reinforce the view that individuals on skid row are being repeatedly recycled through the same institutional complex. Therefore, it is argued, alcoholics are in need of long-term care and support in small, non-institutionalised hostels and communities. For instance, the Final Report of the Joint Working Party on *Homelessness in London* concludes with the view that alcoholics, among others, require a new approach:

Single persons needing care and attention appear to us to be a social services responsibility and we recognise that there is an unmet need for social support and residential care for the socially inadequate, alcoholics, the mentally handicapped, the mentally ill and others. We recommend that Borough Councils should review and expand their social services programmes for all these groups.[20]

The thrust of these recommendations is in accord with the official decriminalisation of habitual drunken offenders. The 1967 and 1972 Criminal Justice Acts give powers to the police and courts to refer men for treatment in rehabilitation hostels and detoxification centres where they exist. But these practical alternatives to prosecution and sentencing have so far remained academic, in spite of legislation. Voluntary agencies, as innovators in therapeutic community and half-way hostel movement, have been frustrated at the time central and local government is taking to translate intention into practice.[21]

An awareness by the welfare state that it is playing a peripheral role in the definition and control of single homelessness, and that it needs to increase its legislative and financial commitment to the problem, has been brought about, in the main, by the political impact of voluntary agencies working with homeless men. As already indicated, the scope of the government's 1965 survey on single homeless persons was influenced by the pressure of voluntary agencies. This impact has been consolidated as a result of the political role performed by CHAR, which has attempted to channel the demands of voluntary agencies and has sought to establish a bridging point between agencies in face-to-face contact with the problem and the policy-making function of the welfare state. One of the main arguments on which CHAR and voluntary agencies have based their demand for the increased intervention of the welfare state (beyond the provision of government reception centres) has been the claim that the size of the problem in London and elsewhere has dramatically increased in the last few years. Thus the Department of Health and Social Security (DHSS) in its document 'Homeless Single Persons in Need of Care and Support', which has been circulated to local authorities, acknowledges this claim.[22]

The circular considers in some detail the policy that local authorities might take in assessing the extent of need in their area, and recommends a strategy in keeping with the mainstream of rehabilitation theory in the field of the single homeless. Local authority social service departments are asked to embark on a programme of experimental action, which will encompass:

> . . . ways in which more help can be given by the social services to single adults who are without a permanent home and who, because of personality disorders and failure to accept secure acceptance in society, are in need of long-term accommodation and support . . . There is a need if possible to modify [their] pattern of aimless and rootless existence and so bring benefit both to the individual and the community.[23]

The main practical recommendation is to establish 'modest experimental schemes . . . of rehabilitation' in which 'the accommodation should be as non-institutionalised as possible', governed by a flexible regime, with a minimum of rules for residents, and providing 'a genuinely homely environment'.[24]

Following the above circular, the DHSS issued a second policy statement entitled 'Community Services for Alcoholics'.[25] This document covered all types of alcoholics and alcoholism facilities, but certain important sections were devoted to the problem of the skid row alcoholic. The advice to local authority social services departments contained in 'Homeless Single Persons in Need of Care and Support' was generally reiterated when reference was made to the specific problems attached to vagrant alcoholics. The circular explains:

> The rootless or vagrant alcoholic, whether or not he is an habitual drunken offender, may need a special approach. There is a degree of overlap between the subculture of the homeless or vagrant alcoholic and that of single homeless people to whose needs attention was drawn in Circular 37/72 ['Homeless Single Persons in Need of Care and Support'] and the type of residential care these alcoholics may be able to accept is likely to be similar to that described in that circular.[26]

The sections that focus on vagrant alcoholics also replicate the central recommendations advanced in the Home Office Report *Habitual Drunken Offenders*, with its emphasis on street-contact points (shop-front offices), detoxification centres, and back-up community hostels.

Both circulars are linked by a common concern for the long-term rehabilitation of individuals defined as 'homeless inadequates . . . . without a settled way of life'. Firstly, their recommendations take into account the theoretical arguments advanced by medicine and social work. The solution offered by local authorities to problems of homelessness and vagrancy no longer lie in the housing of the destitute poor in large common lodging houses, but in the application of treatment and rehabilitation techniques within small therapeutic communities or half-way houses. Secondly, the circulars acknowledge the innovatory role played by voluntary agencies in promoting a social rehabilitation strategy; local authorities are urged to support or work in close co-operation with voluntary agencies providing specialist facilities for skid row men.[27]

Skid row and the politics of welfare

The central concern of this chapter has been the rediscovery of vagrancy as a social problem. The analysis has focused on three factors behind this discovery. In the first place, the redefinition of vagrancy along lines in which medical and social-work definitions predominate has resulted in social control methods coming into line with methods advocated for a widening range of deviant behaviour. Secondly, on the basis of the reduction in the number of traditional institutions housing skid row men (such as common lodging houses and reception centres), plus the unintended consequences of mental health legislation, voluntary agencies have argued that there has been a dramatic increase in the number of persons sleeping rough. Finally, the voluntary movement has exercised a significant political influence on central government in terms of the government's policy statements and reports. Government policy is helping to legitimise the redefinition of the problem.

Thus the rediscovery of the vagrant, now labelled the single homeless, cannot be understood as an accident of history, divorced from specific interrelated social forces. Moreover a sociological explanation of this rediscovery over the past 10 years needs to go beyond merely investigating why individuals become alcoholic and gravitate to skid row. The construction of social policy has arisen out of such wider forces as those explored above and in the introductory chapter of this book.

In addition increased awareness of the problem is a reflection of the success the rhetoric of psychiatry and social work has had in its redefinition. The rediscovery of skid row, then, has also been a function of the power of these two professions in claiming that they are able to provide answers to a problem the penal system and, to some extent, a quasi-religious moral framework have failed to resolve.

One further issue needs exploring in relation to the rediscovery of vagrancy and the formulation of contemporary social policy: what has prevented the problem from being tackled within the framework of already existing welfare state provision and why are homeless men still, in practice, mainly the responsibility of a fragmented voluntary movement? It is clear that, despite the single homeless problem receiving renewed attention, there is little evidence that central government and local authority housing and social services departments are implementing recommended policies. It would appear that a basic reason for homeless men falling through the net of the welfare state is their low social status: skid row men remain part of the disreputable, and therefore undeserving, poor.

As Matza points out, the disreputable poor, of whom skid row men can be said to constitute the most visible sector, have always been the target of a set of attitudes that serve to mark them off from the deserving or honest poor.[28] In spite of identical class origins to the vast majority of the working class, skid row men are socially divorced from their class roots by not only economic considerations but, more important, by a clear set of moral, political and social attitudes. This separation, for instance, is brought out in a document on London's skid row:

> The division between [the] vagrant class and the lower working class is just as real . . . as that between the working classes and the middle classes . . . [Vagrants are] persons possessing certain common social characteristics which are taken to qualify them for intimate, equal status relationships with one another, [but] which restrict their interaction with members of other social classes.[29]

In the contemporary response to skid row the terms by which the phenomenon is identified – habitual drunken offenders, homeless alcoholics, single homeless persons – allude mostly to moral rather than economic factors. Concepts of unemployment and poverty are not considered central to an understanding of the problem. Instead notions of moral defectiveness, such as drunkenness, begging and vagrancy, are claimed as more relevant.

This distinction between moral and economic attributes is crucial to grasping the politics of welfare and the context in which social policy has been formulated *vis-à-vis* homeless alcoholics. This chapter has demonstrated how skid row and its inhabitants are not a central concern of the modern welfare state; indeed, the social rehabilitation control of vagrants has remained the monopoly of voluntary agencies. However, these agencies have increasingly pressed the state to include the problem in its policies on homelessness and social welfare. It is probably the fact that skid row men are essentially defined as part of the disreputable poor that has hindered their transfer from the category of undeserving to deserving poor. An exploration of this distinction follows.

The division between deserving and undeserving poor is not merely the result of the welfare state's concern with establishing a set of priorities as to which social problems should take precedence over issues such as vagrancy and homeless alcoholism. Although priorities are established and single homeless persons are considered a 'political lightweight' in competition with other social issues, there are long-standing historical reasons for the distinction being carried over into our contemporary setting. The idle poor have for a long time been ideologically and administratively separated from the labouring poor; poverty due to moral laxity has not been considered as deserving as poverty due to economic forces.[30]

The roots of charitable work with the undeserving poor precede, of course, the establishment of the modern welfare state. But charitable welfare and state aid stem from quite distinct ideological origins. As far as the Victorians were concerned, their preoccupation with the undeserving poor was based on philanthropic movements aiming at the reform of the individual. Organised charity during the nineteenth century was primarily based on the assumption that moral pauperism was the great evil that needed attacking. On the other hand, the genesis of state aid stood in sharp contrast to the individualist philosophy of charitable aid. State aid was the product of collectivist movements such as trade unionism and Fabian socialism; their target was the amelioration of poverty wrought by the inequities of a competitive market economy. Questions of moral pauperism did not arise to explain the existence of the deserving poor. It was the poverty of the labouring, not the idle, poor the modern welfare state based its approach on. Woodward sums up the contrast between the two welfare perspectives as follows:

> Hence the modern social reformers have concentrated on the factors that determine the flow of economic wealth into the cups of the poor: such as the business cycle, the distribution of wealth, the incidence of taxation . . . We worry more about unemployment than indolence, and more about the propensity to consume than frugality. We seek salvation in structural changes rather than moral regeneration.[31]

With the ascendancy of state aid philosophy, designed to eradicate economic poverty, the problems presented by the undeserving poor became relatively unimportant.

The connection between these developments and the late attention the problem of vagrancy has received from the modern welfare state can now be made apparent. Insofar as skid row is incidental to the implementation of welfare state policy, it is so because the control of the disreputable poor, including vagrants and habitual drunkards, has been and remains the province of charitable voluntary agencies working within a philanthropic tradition. It is only recently that this tradition is being modified by the attempt of the new voluntary movement to sanction its strategies of rehabilitation with the assistance of central and local government. However, in practice the distinction between the deserving and undeserving poor is still real. Men on skid row are considered less than worthy of access to the existing health and welfare system. Consequently, in advocating a social policy towards single homelessness, the new voluntary movement is confronted with overcoming the resistance of the welfare state – a resistance based on historical legacy – to implement the policies outlined in the Home Office's *Habitual Drunken Offenders* and in government circulars.

Concretely, in the making of social policy the new voluntary movement claims that solutions to the problem of skid row drunkenness are hindered by the reluctance of any one specific department within the apparatus of the welfare state to accept formal responsibility for implementing policy. Two reasons are advanced for this reluctance. Firstly, since the components of the skid row alcoholic are defined as consisting of homelessness, criminality, disease, and social disaffiliation, bureaucratic responsibility for him is held to be divided between the housing, penal, health and social welfare departments of central government. Secondly, at local government level, not only is this division of responsibility replicated but the argument is often advanced by local authority officials that homeless men, including alcoholics, do not contribute to rates and taxes and are not ordinarily resident within local authority boundaries.

Pittman, in a policy statement on American alcoholic offenders, wrote:

> The major problem confronting us in dealing with the chronic drunkenness offender . . . is the lack of a focus of community, State and Federal responsibility for this problem group. Many conventional social and medical agencies state that the problem is not their responsibility. These offenders are on skid row: therefore they are considered to be the responsibility of the Salvation Army or the Volunteers of America. The police frequently say it is the responsibility of the courts; the courts counter with the responsibility of the penal institutions; and the latter counter-attack with the responsibility of health and mental hygiene agencies. The net result is that no suitable institution or person assumes responsibility for the social problems of these men. Thus America continues to clutter its courts and jails with individuals whose 'crime' is a physical and social illness.[32]

The significance of Pittman's remark is that it clearly illustrates the dilemma faced by the new voluntary movement in handling skid row alcoholics. More important, it demonstrates why one traditional model of social control – law enforcement – continues, in practice, to operate in spite of the claim that alternative medical and social-work approaches would be more appropriate.

Thus a dominant theme, which voluntary agencies advance, is the need for one centralised, co-ordinating government team responsible for the general implementation of social policy. This call for centralisation is a direct outcome of the rediscovery and increased awareness of skid row as a social problem but is made against a background in which the policy intentions of central government are held not to be consistent with practice.

Skid row men – including homeless alcoholics – are therefore perceived as remaining for the most part outside the machinery of the welfare state. Local government authorities are charged with not including the problem in their welfare planning proposals. Central government legislation and circulars are viewed as ineffective in not making implementation of policy a mandatory duty on local authorities. The Campaign for the Homeless and Rootless (CHAR) is thus seeking to reinforce the new strategy of locating the problem squarely within the framework of state aid. A recent CHAR report on homeless alcoholics reflects this strategy:

> ... the age-old provision of lodging house, prison, reception centres and park benches continues ... Despite reports, legislation, circulars and good intentions, on almost all sides, the homeless alcoholic is still in a situation where neither his homelessness nor his alcoholism is ever satisfactorily tackled, never mind both problems together.
>
> There is clearly a gap of despairing size yawning between the intent of provision and reality ... The absence of any new major provision in the field ... is due to the undecided issue of who should take responsibility for making the provision required.[33]

The report continues:

> The Government has committed itself to find a way of dealing constructively with the vagrant alcoholic ... CHAR therefore wishes to put one clear proposal to the Secretary of State for Social Services: that she establish forthwith a three-man team charged with the sole full-time objective of implementing the major recommendations of the 1971 Habitual Drunken Offender Report.[34]

Implicit in the strategy is the aim to shift the status of the skid row alcoholic from someone who has been consistently defined and reacted to as part of the disreputable, and therefore undeserving, poor to someone deserving the attention of the welfare state. But, in keeping with some of the basic definitions imputed to individuals who live on skid row, the homeless alcoholic remains the outsider *par excellence*; for, whether he be the object of moral reform, penal correction, medical treatment, or social rehabilitation, the vagrant alcoholic appears to resist personal change. His one commitment is to the skid row way of life.

8
Vagrant Alcoholics and their Guardians

Skid row as social interaction

This study has explored skid row alcoholism as a social problem within a framework that radically departs from most contemporary research into deviant behaviour. Most criminological and deviancy research focuses exclusively on deviant individuals, particularly with the aim of discovering and isolating variables in their personal histories that predispose them toward breaking society's conventional rules. Thus, once answers to the aetiological puzzle as to why homeless alcoholics take on deviant drinking are provided by studies with a correctional bias, the ground is laid for tackling the problem, especially by advocating the treatment or rehabilitation of the alcoholic at an individual level. In order to achieve these correctional objectives a complex of institutions is established. Each of these institutions reflects particular ideas as to how getting men out of skid row and back into society might best be achieved. The nature of these institutions – whether officially based on penal, religious, or socio-medical approaches to the problem – and the role they play in the deviant phenomenon are often taken for granted and therefore remain unexplored.

In contrast, this investigation has stressed a number of alternative dimensions. The deviant act, as opposed to the personality structure of the individual alcoholic, has informed my analysis. Crucial to this emphasis has been the attempt to locate the deviant act within the wider context of the ideological and institutional structure of skid row, and to understand the meaning alcoholics give to surviving on the row, the definitions both alcoholics and agents of social control have of each other, and the direction social control policy is taking in containing the problem. In short, the skid row phenomenon as a whole becomes the object of analysis. The assumption has been that the deviant act can only be made comprehensible in relation to the efforts of specific social control agents and the establishments they represent.

Social interaction – an organising perspective

A sociology of the homeless alcoholic analysed within this framework requires a specific perspective – a point of view – if any coherence is to be given to what otherwise would be a complex collection of facts and opinions about skid row. The perspective adopted throughout this report[1] has assumed that the social organisation of skid row, both in terms of the deviant act and reaction to it, consists of patterned and interrelated lines of action. The meanings that drinking on the row and living in its satellite institutions have for alcoholics and control agents result in regular styles of acting toward the situations both parties encounter. On this basis skid row as a social phenomenon takes on a life of its own. Alcoholics learn how to confront problems of addiction, homelessness and chronic poverty; agents of social control attempt to meet the problem by agreeing upon common strategies directed at the successful re-entry of alcoholics into the community.

Both parties adopt various functions and roles in relation to each other; they create informal and formal institutions through which they handle the problems they meet. Thus derelict alcoholics develop and maintain a set survival strategy through the creation of such informal institutions as skippering, begging, thieving, doing casual work, and obtaining state and charitable aid in the form of money, clothing and food. Drinking schools, as the most important informal skid row institutions, enable homeless alcoholics to meet their primary need for alcohol. Agents of social control, on the other hand, establish and perpetuate correctional strategies, which aim by different methods to achieve long-term sobriety in alcoholics and a return to conventional society. These strategies are crystallised in a variety of formal skid row institutions. Among the more important are religious-based missions; the police, courts and prisons; mental hospitals and alcoholism units; and small-scale social rehabilitation houses. Moreover these institutions, as Chapters 5 and 6, on the penal revolving door and social rehabilitation circuit, illustrated, make up the scenarios for the face-to-face interaction of alcoholics and their guardians. Within these settings participants take on particular roles and formulate opinions on how to handle the situations that unfold within them.

The relationship between alcoholics and their guardians does not remain static. Human experience is such that the process of defining this relationship is ever-changing. Personnel manning the skid row institutions and the inmates towards which their expertise is directed each learn through interaction with others how to define, interpret, and act towards the situation they find themselves in. Homeless men acquire a particular status and identity through their socialisation into skid row institutions. They continuously take account of renewed attempts by society to bring them under its control; but, because the majority of veteran homeless men fail to move out of the institutional skid row orbit, in effect a symbiotic relationship has developed between social control agents and their charges. A partnership, mutually beneficial to both sides, has been established in spite of the different meanings each ascribe to the same objective phenomenon. In exploring this relationship one clear message has emerged: the institutions of control would appear to attract alcoholics into this orbit in such a way that their escape becomes increasingly difficult.

Subculture, deviant identity and social control

The sociological perspective sketched out in the preceding section enables a particular approach to be taken towards researching social phenomena. In the interactionist perspective the researcher's major preoccupation lies with the application of a specific set of guiding concepts, which facilitate a plan of research action. Implicit throughout this study has been the use of concepts such as 'self', 'interaction', 'definition of the situation', 'meaning', 'signifcant others', and 'socialisation'.[2] These concepts have been used to analyse the data and thereby render possible the developmentof a systematic image of the skid row world.

A useful way of understanding the relevance of these concepts would be to relate them to concrete questions about the organisation of skid row. Thus this book, among other questions, has attempted to give answers to the following. How do alcoholics and skid row personnel view each other and what consequences do these views have for their respective identities? How do participants in the skid row life-way and in its formal institutions behave towards each other? Do alcoholics and agents of social control define the problem in similar terms, or do their definitions conflict? What is the structure of skid row in terms of the relationship between different methods and institutions of control? What impact does repeated interaction with the agents of law enforcement, religious missions and social rehabilitation have on the alcoholic's commitment to a life on skid row?

In addition to the guiding concepts implicit in the interactionist perspective three desciptive concepts are used here to analyse the data collected. They are 'subculture', 'deviant identity' and 'social control'.

Subculture

The term subculture directs attention to the existence of a particular social structure, which permits individuals who are poverty-stricken, homeless and alcoholic to make specific forms of adaption to their physical, social and economic environment. Rubington and Weinberg, both sociologists who have adapted an interactionist perspective to the study of deviancy, offer the following definition of a subculture:

> A subculture is apt to come into being when a category of persons find themselves suffering a common fate. It is essential, however, for them to be in contact with one another and to find out in the course of communication that they do in fact have common interests. These interests arise generally from their social situation because they face more or less the same dilemma.[3]

In order for subcultures to develop a degree of organisation is required by the incumbents. The existence of deviant beliefs, values, and norms make for social organisation. In turn the social organisation is used by members of the subculture to control its members, through the socialisation process inherent in it. Another sociologist re-emphasises the above definition by asserting that a subculture 'is continuously being created, re-created, and modified whenever individuals sense in one another like needs, generated by like circumstances, not shared generally in the larger social system'.[4]

The accounts given by homeless alcoholics of how they manage to survive in a hostile world, the manner in which they collectively organise their drinking activities, and their response to society's attempt to bring them into line, have been explored in detail. The subculture of the derelict inebriate is characterised by chronic poverty, homelessness and alcohol addiction. None of these inter-related problems weigh down on skid row men in such a way that they are rendered totally helpless and isolated. Instead a workable social organisation has been created, interpreted, and given meaning by men who have turned both the informal and formal institutions of the row to their advantage.

The skid row subculture, then, functions as a social system through which homeless men are able to cushion the problems they are confronted with. To the outsider, in particular to individuals who have a vested interest in rescuing alcoholics from skid row, the subculture is by definition pathological, bizarre, and meaningless. But by spending time within the skid row community as a participant observer,[5] one comes up with a new interpretation. The world of skid row takes on a new dimension when its inhabitants are permitted to 'tell it as it is'. For the homeless alcoholic the precepts of life on the row are internalised and transmitted. The new arrival on skid row, with what is probably a serious drink problem already, undergoes a process of socialisation in which his developing self-image and membership of the deviant subculture are gradually consolidated. The consequences of participation in the subculture have important implications for the alcoholic's identity.

Deviant identity

Participation in the skid row subculture, including repeated in-teraction with a variety of control agents entrusted with altering the skid row alcoholic's attitudes and behaviour, results in the alcoholic assuming an identity in accord with his personal condition and status as an outsider. The notion of deviant identity is important in understanding the nature of the relationship between the alcoholic and his benefactors. As Brittan states in his discussion on the interpersonal negotiation of identity:

The key term is identity. Who am I? is the fundamental question posed and the answers given are very often couched in the language of social labels . . . Identities are bargained for, and once established are put on the market again at a higher price. This means that identity is not considered to be a fixed quality. It has to be constantly confirmed in a complex matrix of social exchange. Thus identity becomes a mask behind which the 'individual' temporarily finds some stability and satisfaction.[6]

This definition has the value of indicating that any one individual takes on a variety of identities according to the different social situations he finds himself in. This leads Brittan to ask whether a real identity lies behind the variety of masks we project through participation in a multiplicity of formal and informal institutions.[7] He argues that identities are not internalised in some hit-or-miss fashion but, as in the case of deviant identities, are assumed against a backcloth in which socially enforced rules and norms are enacted through official agencies empowered with the social control of deviancy.

The importance of introducing the role of official agencies into any discussion of deviant identity is that it facilitates the formulation of a more adequate definition of subculture than that offered above; for if deviant identities are to a degree the product of interaction between rule-breakers and rule-enforcers, then the creation of a social organisation by which deviants are able to meet their problems will have to take into account the official intervention of law-enforcement and rehabilitation agencies. Any account of the skid row subculture needs to account for differences in reaction to homeless alcoholics and their impact on the deviant's identity. Identities are articulated and acted out within the institutional contexts of the skid row phenomenon. Subcultures, then, are not exclusively the product of 'persons who find themselves suffering a common fate' but are also the creation of specific control strategies directed at the subcultures' incumbents.

Social control

The notions of subculture and deviant identity have been spelled out. Their interrelation has been made apparent insofar as any subcultural organisation provides the basis for its members to answer the fundamental question 'Who am I?' Deviant identities are made more readily apparent if learned and reinforced through participation in the subculture. But crucial to the recognition of a deviant identity, whether acquired through the processes of subcultural association or not, is a prior awareness by the individual that he may be subject to a variety of social control forces that may serve to change his status from that of normal to deviant.

Alcoholics on skid row are primarily engaged in a form of action that is hurting no one but the agent himself. Nevertheless they are seldom free from outside interference and control. The nature of social reaction to homeless alcoholics has therefore received as much detailed attention in this book as the persons to whom the reaction is directed at. There has been a need to understand as much about the factors determining social control as to understand the structure and form of the deviant enterprise.

Two important factors may be advanced as explanation for the social reaction to homeless alcoholics: moral indignation and humanitarianism.[8] Young, writing about moral indignation in relation to drugtaking, invokes the analysis of A. K. Cohen:

> The dedicated pursuit of culturally approved goals, eschewing of interdicted but tantalizing goals, the adherence to normatively sanctioned means – these imply a certain self-restraint, effort, discipline, inhibition. What is the effect of others who, though their activities do not manifestly damage our own interests, are morally undisciplined, who give themselves up to idleness, self-indulgence, or forbidden vices? What effect does the propinquity of the wicked have on the peace of mind of the virtuous?[9]

For Young the significance of Cohen's statement is that it alludes to deviancy not as an act which has an inherent universal meaning but that it needs to be understood against a framework of widely accepted norms and rules that constitute the base from which social reaction will spring. For instance, even with deviant activities not directly affecting persons other than those who engage in the activity – what Schur[10] called 'crimes without victims' (such as drug addiction, abortion, homosexuality) – there is a tendency to see them as challenging the rules of conventional society.

Once such a threat is perceived, that is, once there is a social problem to be resolved, then moral entrepreneurs will seek to institutionalise their sense of indignation by promoting and legitimising methods of social control designed to eradicate or contain the problem. These methods are often promoted in the language of humanitarianism, whether they be articulated by law-enforcement agents or therapists and social rehabilitators. As Young points out:

> Humanitarianism occurs where powerful groups seek to change the behaviour of others. They act, overtly at least, in the better interests of the socially inferior group they define as a social problem. The group thus designated may or may not accept this designation . . . Now humanitarianism is, I would argue, an exceedingly suspect motive; for it is often – though not necessarily – a rationalisation behind which is concealed either a conflict of interests or moral indignation . . . Moreover, unlike in the Middle Ages, we are loath, because of an ubiquitous liberalism, to condemn another man merely because he acts differently from us, providing that he does not harm others. Moral indignation, then, the intervention into the affairs of others because we think them wicked, must necessarily be replaced by humanitarianism which, utilizing the language of therapy and healing, intervenes in what it perceives as the best interests and well-being of the individuals involved.[11]

The forces of social control hold a central position in this analysis of the skid row phenomenon in that they help to determine the subculture's official institutional matrix. Society, its response to the problem mediated through the establishment of social control agencies, seeks to contain what it defines as deviant drinking. The definitions ascribed to the deviant serve as a basis for classifying, stereotyping, and socially differentiating; encounters with official social reaction punish at the same time as they set apart. Even the social action of agencies broadly concerned with the welfare and rehabilitation of the homeless alcoholic reflect forces that typify and differentiate individuals in terms of their deviancy. Thus courts and prisons, common lodging houses and reception centres, mental hospitals and rehabilitation hostels, are all settings that separate and sustain the development of a subculture.

Skid row and the alcoholic: the co-existence of social control and deviance

The role that skid row institutions play in stimulating the development of a deviant subculture is quite clear in the case of the homeless alcoholic. Furthermore it should be apparent from the discussion in this chapter that the alcoholic's definition of his situation and his participation in the skid row life-way are interrelated phenomena. Thus the terms subculture, deviant identity and social control, although they can be separated out analytically, in practice are indissolubly wedded when applied to an analysis of the problem.

Skid row consists of an interrelated set of institutions which, together, form a unique social system. Homeless alcoholics are dependent on these institutions for their survival; but within the orbit of the institutional circuit single men suffer a form of stigmatisation that labels them as complete outcasts. The definition that distinguishes skid row from other deviant social systems, both among its residents and in the rest of society, is its reputation for being known as 'the last resting place for social misfits, the "mile of forgotten men", the "bottom of the barrel"'.[12] As a total system it effectively segregates its members from conventional society. It matters little that in Britain there is no special area, no urban reservation, for society's outcasts, that can be easily identified. For what is important is the existence of a continuous sociological and psychological territory which homeless men inhabit and which they rarely leave once immersed in its culture.

Society does not confront the twin problems of alcoholism and homelessness in any one single fashion. Traditional methods of control are being challenged by methods held to be in line with contemporary socio-medical thinking on issues of alcohol abuse and disaffiliation. But the replacement of outmoded institutional care has proved to be, for the time being, mostly an academic issue. The most obvious and common form of regulating derelict inebriates continues to be through the agencies of law enforcement; and common lodging houses, reception centres, hand-outs, plus open spaces, derelict buildings, drinking schools and other informal institutions remain at the hub of the skid row way of life. On the other hand, because of their small number and novelty, medical units and small-scale social rehabilitation hostels for the homeless alcoholic remain, so far, recovery stations located on the fringes of skid row. Their introduction, however, is functioning to expand, not constrict, the traditional institutional system 'of control. Increased numbers of derelict inebriates, in addition to their usual identities as drunken offenders, prison inmates and lodging house dossers, will begin to acquire self-images as psychiatric patients and social-work clients, with the establishment of treatment-oriented services.

The identity – the self-image – of homeless alcoholics is conceived of two distinct processes: (i) the identification emerging through interaction with like-minded individuals; (ii) the identification arising in reaction to attempts by social control agents to bring alcoholics back into line. Both these processes are mutually dependent on each other. Homeless alcoholics are situated in a specific social milieu by virtue of belonging to a certain category of deviants; consequently they join together to carve out a common identity, based on their struggle to survive the efforts of destitution, alcohol addiction, and stigmatisation.

When law-enforcement officers, mission directors, psychiatrists and social workers describe skid row alcoholics as social inadequates, they are doing so from the standpoint of their own expectations and culture. To them the fact that alcoholics are in a perpetual orbit of public and institutional life is sufficient evidence of their inadequacy. The measuring rod by which agency personnel judge alcoholics is not the skills they develop to survive on the row but their departure and social distance from the values and behaviour of conventional society. In other words, the term social inadequacy denies the authenticity of the alcoholic's interpretation of the world he inhabits; such a term only reflects the perspective of those who come into contact with men on the row with the object of controlling or reforming their behaviour. On the other hand, to alcoholics the criteria by which they judge themselves are not based on their inability to re-enter the community as sober citizens, hold down regular jobs, develop leisure interests, and take on responsibility for home and family. These aspects of participation in the conventional institutions of society are not touched upon in everyday conversation among homeless men. Instead, what is of more relevance is their ability to overcome the difficulties of surviving in a world that is essentially hostile to the habitual public drunk.

It is not surprising, therefore, that the needs of alcoholics do not necessarily correspond with the professional aims of those persons charged with their care. As Brittan puts it:

It is a commonplace of interaction theory that individuals in an interaction episode each define the situation from different or slightly different perspectives. It is also a commonplace that the way each actor defines the situation varies from situation to situation, and from time to time.[13]

Although the overriding factor binding men on the row to the personnel manning the skid row complex is their mutual interest in problems associated with destitution and alcohol addiction, there is wide divergence of opinion as to how deviants and control agents define and approach the problem. This divergence has been uncovered in the preceding chapters: dependent on the situational context different mental frameworks and lines of action are constructed by either side. Wiseman arrives at somewhat similar conclusions in her American study of the relationship between down-and-out alcoholics and deviancy managers:

> Rather than being bound together by their mutual goals, however, Skid Row alcoholics and agents of social control are hostile toward each other, existing in what might be described as a constant state of outrage, distrust and disappointment . . . In the case of the agents of social control and the Pacific City Skid Row alcoholic, the class and status difference between them set the tune or style of emotional interaction expected by each during . . . interaction. In general, agents of social control are middle-class and have absorbed middle-class professional ideas as to the proprieties to be observed in the giver–receiver relationship. These ideas, somewhat naturally, are not always in agreement with those of the Skid Row alcoholic man, who is predominantly of lower class origins.[14]

Skid row drinking: a collective solution to a social problem

It will be evident from the perspective adopted in this report that an understanding of skid row alcoholism in the context of the relationship between deviancy and its management is considered of more central interest than studies of the psychotropic effect of alcohol on individuals, or the teasing out of factors in the personal biography of alcoholics as evidence for the claim that they are suffering from some form of individual pathology. To have accepted either one, or both, of these latter approaches, would have been 'to lay causal blame on the individual or drug *in a vacuum*'[15] Young explains in his book on the social meaning of drug use:

> It is necessary . . . to examine the complex of relationships the individual finds himself in primarily at the moment and in his near and relevant past. We must ask: what problems are thrown up by this human matrix, rather than what are the inherent qualities of the drug involved or the essential nature of the man's personality emanating from his far distant childhood experience. And to explain the man's intimate relationships we must then turn our attention to the wider society in which they occur.[16]

This book does not entirely round off the analysis by adhering to Young's exhortation that the study of drug use should include 'attention to the wider society' in which the social problem is located.[17] Instead the main thrust of my analysis has centred on the immediate relationships between alcoholics and social control agents, and the institutions they occur within.

The direction that contemporary social policy is taking toward the homeless alcoholic is mainly cast in the rhetoric of medicine and social work, with its emphasis on individualising the problem for the alcohol addict. However, there is little, if any, substantial evidence from participating in the skid row subculture that there is widespread acceptance by alcoholics of the alcoholic 'sick role' expounded by the medical profession. Neither do homeless men identify with the strategy that lies behind psychiatrists, social work counsellors and prison welfare officers enquiring into individuals' family history, schooling and occupational record, experience of institutional life or the amount of alcohol they consume.

Far from developing an isolated solution to an individual problem, while on skid row alcoholics engage in a collective response to their immediate predicament. Although alcoholics are aware of the central role that alcohol plays in undermining their physical and psychological health, the interpretation they attach to their life style is made in terms of their low status and the concomitant social relationships that arise from it. Bahr is correct when he asserts:

> The primary problem of the skid row man is not alcoholism. Nor is it advanced age, physical disability and moral inferiority. Instead

the primary problem is that the combined weight of stigmatization which accompanies many different kinds of human defectiveness is focused upon a few men in a distinctive neighbourhood. Disease, dirt and drunkenness are elements of the stereotype of the skid row man. Poverty, sloth and irresponsibility mark skid row and it does not matter that some of those characteristics are only in the beholders' eye. The skid row man himself is one of the beholders, and his stereotypes about the row and its men are just as harsh as those of more respectable citizens. Skid row is where the degenerates, the dregs and the defective settle, and the resident must fight a continual battle to maintain enough self-esteem to live.[18]

Homeless men, then, interpret their condition in the light of society's reaction to them. The struggle to maintain self-esteem, however, is one which alcoholics gradually lose. Repeated arrests and incarceration, or the repeated failure to attain sobriety, confirm their defectiveness. Paradoxically habitual intoxication both confirms the alcoholic's low status and acts as a solution to the hardships of living on skid row.

Thus the significance that life on skid row holds for alcoholics, shaped by society's reaction, can be considered the major stumbling block to their recovery, whether the impetus behind an attempt at such recovery emanates from the alcoholic himself or the expert. Heavy drinking in the context of skid row social relationships simultaneously divorces alcoholics from the normal community and consolidates their identification with the skid row world. Homeless alcoholics are not socially isolated, as is commonly supposed, but have constructed a web of relationships that are socially meaningful to them. They find in others common problems with which they are able to identify. Nevertheless it would be incorrect to claim that alcoholics find skid row attractive; they are frequently critical of life on the row, of other men they encounter there, and in particular of the institutions and personnel that attempt to alter their status. Rather, in the absence of any acceptable alternatives, alcoholics are drawn to the social organisation of life on the row—a life that provides them with a set of survival strategies of their own making.

9
Research Perspective and Method

An outline and critical commentary

A symbolic interactionist account of skid row, and skid row alcoholism and its intersection with social control agents, their institutions and ideological premises, has now been completed. The purpose in this chapter is four-fold. First the methodological perspective of symbolic interactionism needs to be set out; it has been the interactionist perspective that has guided the research project, allowing for a focus and orientation towards the phenomenon, and giving shape to an otherwise disparate and amorphous collection of data, experiences and observations. Secondly, the appeal of symbolic interactionism for the study needs to be critically located and set against recent developments in the theorisation of deviancy and crime. Deviancy theory has finally emerged from a long intellectual and methodological slumber, partly as a result of the introduction into crime and deviancy research of assumptions and orientations that have seriously challenged dominant structural functionalist, positivist, and even interactionist perspectives. Thirdly, participant observation, as the principal research technique used in this study, will be looked at in terms of its application to the skid row phenomenon. There are close methodological links between the demands made by symbolic interactionism as a perspective in sociology and the requirements of participant observation as a research technique generating specific types of information. Fourthly, by way of keeping the theoretical and methodological debate open, and also by way of indicating that the social reality of skid row and social control presented in this book is only partial, a critical and brief analysis of the shortcomings of the interactionist perspective adopted will be offered.

The methodological perspective of symbolic interactionism

Herbert Blumer has probably done more than any other sociologist to set out systematically the parameters of symbolic interactionism as a methodological perspective in the human sciences.[1] Sociology is indebted to Blumer for having provided the major thrust in clarifying such a methodological position with which to grasp social reality. The position is outlined below; for the moment the intellectual roots of symbolic interactionism are traced through the philosophical work of William James and John Dewey, and through the sociological advances on philosophical pragmatism made by Charles Horton Cooley, W. I. Thomas, and George Herbert Mead.[2]

Symbolic interactionism as one strand of social behaviourism began to take shape in America around the turn of the century, primarily under the influence of philosophical pragmatism. Both William James and John Dewey had been heavily influenced by the philosophical idealism of Hegel, but had sought to transform this influence by attempting a reconciliation of idealism with science in which individuals were viewed as constantly constructing the environment as well as being determined by it. In the end neo-Hegelian philosophy takes a back seat to pragmatism in terms of its impact on symbolic interactionism. For the interactionists the accent is placed on the notions of 'meaning' and 'attitude', with their point of gravity focussed on the concepts of 'self' and 'personality'. Thus both pragmatism, and the interactionist perspective derived from it, were heavily socio-psychological in their orientation.

William James

For James man was possessed of plasticity. James explored the concept of habit as a central dimension in the process of socialisation undergone by human beings. But habit was not viewed as an immutable force, for the essential quality of man's plasticity was that it permitted man to yield to outside influences while at the same time not yielding completely. Against this claim, consciousness was reconceptualised as a process, not as a fixed property. Consciousness is to be understood as a stream of thought, as subjective life. Through a reconsideration of the importance of habit, and a view of consciousness as a process, James opened new possibilities for a sociological reconceptualisation of the self. Insofar as one of the properties of consciousness is that it demands a degree of awareness of the person's self, then that person appears in two ways – 'partly known and partly knower, partly object and partly subject'.

John Dewey

The task of reconciling idealism and science was carried forward by John Dewey, who made the transition from German idealism to pragmatism under the influence of James. Dewey held at the centre of his thinking the importance of intelligence and mental activity *as a process*; his conception of the individual is one in which man is in continuous process of development, simultaneously constrained by and reformulating his environment, growing within a complex of interactions and relationships. Through the social process the individual is made into an image of his fellows, his uniqueness being reduced while at the same time extending the limits of possible development.

Charles Horton Cooley

The specifically sociological extension of the philosophical pragmatism of Dewey and James begins with the writings of Charles Horton Cooley, who asserted that the image people have of one another 'are the solid facts of society'. Society is a mental phenomenon, a relation between personal ideas. Cooley applied to society the approach that William James had applied to the self; thus Cooley's notion of self corresponded closely with James' notion of the social self.

The self consists of things the individual conceives as belonging peculiarly to himself; the core of the self is formed by an instinctive self-feeling. Imagination and habit, operating on an insticitive self-feeling, create the social self. Cooley's famous 'looking-glass self' was his particular form of what William James called the social self. The general argument, of course, is that the social self arises reflectively in terms of reactions to the opinion of others on the self.

Cooley moved beyond his concept of the 'looking-glass self' to the development of a general theory of society in terms of an explanation of groups and social organisation. His contribution to a theory of groups and group behaviour consisted of a re-evaluation of the structure and dynamics of what subsequently came to be known in social psychology and sociology as primary groups, particularly by exploring the relationship existing between primary groups and the social self. For Cooley the primary group is a fundamental institution in forming the social nature and ideals of the individual. Ideals such as those that make up the reflexive self and are produced by the primary group constitute the unity and structure of the social mind. Social organisation, then, constitutes both the unity and structure of group life and the individual self.

W. I. Thomas

Thomas' central contribution to the interactionist position was made in conjunction with Florian Znaniecki in their massive work *The Polish Peasant in America and Europe*.[3] It is in the theoretical sections of this work that we find the fullest statement of their orientation. For Thomas and Znaniecki the purpose of sociology was seen as one of tracing the dependence of individuals on social life and culture, and the dependence of social life and culture on individuals. The subject matter of sociology consists of the study of attitudes, values and processes of consciousness, as determined by the objective conditions of the actors' immediate environment (the social and physical ecology of the city), pre-existing attitudes in the community, and the definition of the situation constructed by actors in confronting specific circumstances.

   In *The Unadjusted Girl*[4] Thomas made his analysis of attitudes and values secondary to his concern with the notion of the definition of the situation:

> 'Preliminary to any self-determined act of behaviour there is always a . . . *definition of the situation* . . . gradually a whole life-policy and the personality of the individual himself follow from a series of such definitions.[5]

For actors the necessity to resolve the tension arising out of conflicting definitions of the situation is forever present. There is 'always a rivalry between the spontaneous definition of the situation made by the member of an organised society and the definitions which his society has provided for him'.[6]

There is a certain parallelism between Thomas and Cooley, in terms of Thomas' postulates about the relationship between the individual, on the one hand, and culture and social life, on the other, and Cooley's thinking on the interconnectedness of the self in relation to primary groups and social organisation. The objective cultural elements of social life are made up of attitudes and values; attitudes are the component parts of the process of individual consciousness, and determine real or possible activity in the social world; values are the objects in the world to which attitudes are addressed. The individual's attitudes and values – in their objective manifestation constituted as social institutions and social organisation – are always reflected in concrete, practical situations. Thus:

> The situation is the set of values and attitudes with which the individual or the group has to deal in a process of activity and with regard to which this activity is planned and its results appreciated. Every concrete activity consists in the solution of a situation which involves three kinds of data: (1) the objective conditions under which the individual or society has to act and which at the given moment affect the conscious status of the individual or the group; (2) the pre-existing attitudes of the individual or the group; and (3) the definition of the situation by the individual or group as a more or less clear conception of the conditions of consciousness and of attitudes.[7]

The individual, then, is the product of interaction. To become a social personality the individual must learn the meaning social objects possess and also learn how to adapt himself to the demands which puts upon him. Since meanings imply conscious thought – he must do this by conscious reflection, and not by a mere instinctive adaptation of reflexes. The thrust of Thomas' argument here suggests another area of parallel development in Thomas' and Cooley's thinking. Just as for Cooley an analysis of the self through the construction of social organisation and institutions was a step forward from his notion of personal ideas, so for Thomas and Znaniecki their analysis moved from the concepts of attitudes and values to that of the definition of the situation.

George Herbert Mead

Through the work of G. H. Mead the inner structure of symbolic interactionism was reconstituted to a higher level of theoretical sophistication. Mead proposed to start the analysis of social life with an observable activity – the dynamic, continuing social process and the social acts that are its component parts or elements – and then to treat the 'mind' and 'society' as discriminations arising within this process.

Thomas and Znaniecki had taken attitudes, values and the definition of the situation as conceptual king-pins in their theoretical framework for *The Polish Peasant*. Mead was influenced by these ideas, for he took the notion of attitudes as central to his analysis of social life, but the notion was given a more precise significance. For Mead attitudes have the simultaneous character of representing both a state of introspection and the starting point for purposive human behaviour – the human act. The way in which human acts are socially constituted is to be understood in terms of the attitudes held by actors.

Social interaction implies that the actions of one person are in part the basis of the action of another. Meaning and mind have their origins in the social act and are made possible – in fact, necessitated – by language. The mind arises in the social process; when this occurs, the individual becomes self-conscious and can therefore be said to have a mind. It is by means of reflexiveness – the turning back of experience undergone by the individual upon himself – that the whole social process is thus brought into the experience of individuals taking part in it. Reflexiveness is essential, within the social process, for the development of mind.

For the individual the attitudes of other actors are internalized. Mead asserts: 'The organized community or social group which gives to the individual his unity of self may be called the 'generalized other'. The attitude of the generalized other is the attitude of the whole community'.[8] Through the generalized other the community exercises control over the conduct of its individual members. The two stages of the development of the self are thus (1) the organisation of particular attitudes of other individuals towards one's self and (2) the organisation of the social attitudes of the generalised other towards one's self. The self reaches full development by organising individual attitudes and generalising them. But just as the self arises as one kind of organisation, so society appears, in Mead's words, as another:

> There are what I have termed 'generalized social attitudes' which make an organized self possible. In the community there are certain ways of acting under situations which are essentially identical . . . There are . . . whole series of such common responses in the community in which we live, and such responses are what we term 'institutions' . . . Thus the institutions of society are organized forms of group or social activity – forms so organized that the individual members of society can act adequately and socially by taking the attitude of others toward these activities.[9]

In short, for Mead institutions are to society what the mind is to the self.

Herbert Blumer

The teachings of Cooley, Thomas and Mead took forward, sociologically speaking, the philosophical pragmatism of James and Dewey. Their conceptual frameworks acted as guidelines to a significant body of empirical work carried out by the Chicago School of Sociology during the inter-war years – work focusing on the sociology of urban life, particularly on the social problems and social disorganisation of 'zones of transition' in Chicago and other American cities.

The Chicago sociologists were intent on discovering the laws of social life in order to predict and ultimately control the problems of urban existence. An enormous amount of empirical research on urban life, race relations, delinquency, divorce, social disorganisation, mass communications and other fields was turned out within the confines of an emergent, somewhat loosely defined theory of symbolic interactionism. The ghetto, the Gold Coast, the slum; the jack-roller, the hobo, the hotel dweller; the gang, the suicide, the delinquent – all provided concrete material for research by the Chicago sociologists.

But before moving on to examine their impact on new deviancy theory following the Second World War, we need to examine the work of Herbert Blumer in some detail. For Blumer the central thrust of symbolic interactionism lies in three basic premises:[10] (1) human beings act towards things on the basis of meanings that the things have for them; (2) the meaning of such things is derived from, or arises out of, the social interaction that human beings have with their fellows; and (3) meanings are handled, and modified through, an interpretive process used by persons in dealings with the things they encounter. Against the background of these three premises a cardinal principle of symbolic interaction is that any empirically oriented scheme of human society, however derived, must respect the fact that in the first and last instances human society consists of people engaging in action.

Symbolic interactionism sees human society as people engaged in living. Such living is a process of regular activity in which participants develop lines of action in the concrete situations they encounter. Actors are caught up in a process of interaction, in which they have to fit their developing actions to one another. This process of interaction consists of making indications to others of what to do and in interpreting the indications made by others. The process of interaction should be seen in the differentiated character it necessarily has by virtue of the fact that people cluster in different groups, belong to different associations, and occupy different positions in the social structure. People accordingly approach each other differently, live in different worlds, and guide themselves by different sets of meanings. Whether one is dealing with a family, a boys' gang, an industrial corporation, or a political party, one must see the activities of the collectivity through a process of designation and interpretation. In so many words Blumer summarises his remarks on the nature of symbolic interactionism.

What are the methodological implications of the perspective for the researcher? Firstly, the investigator wanting to understand the concrete action of people must attempt to see the world as the actors see it. The researcher must place himself in the role of others. To identify objects of central concern one must have a body of relevant observations. These observations are rarely those yielded by questionnaires, polls, scales and surveys, since through these research tools investigations often fail to guard against the imposition of their own pre-established images of phenomena. Secondly, action needs to be seen as a formative process in its own right, not as a mechanical response to outside forces, which determine it. The form of social interaction is a matter for empirical discovery, not a matter to be fixed in advance. Social action is multitudinous; it varies according to situations. Third, insofar as social acts are constructed through a process in which actors note, interpret, and assess situations confronting them, it is imperative for the observer to analyse social action as a process continuously being constructed and reconstructed. Finally, the complex interlinkage of acts that comprise organisations, institutions, divisions of labour, and suchlike, need to be moving, not static, affairs. Moreover institutional arrangements need to be viewed as arrangements of people who are interlinked in their respective actions. The point of view of symbolic interactionism is that it is participants who have to be seen, studied, and explained as they handle real-life situations.

New deviancy theory and the interactionist perspective

Attention has been drawn to the impact that the development of a specific sociological perspective, namely symbolic interactionism, has had on the study of human behaviour, particularly in the area of deviance and social disorganisation. The multitude of empirical studies conducted by the Chicago School of Sociology during the 1920s and 1930s bears testimony to the forceful appeal that the perspective has had for sociologists wishing to unravel and grasp the intricacies and social constructions of specific social phenomena prevalent in inner-city zones of transition. However, theoretical and empirical work on the sociology of deviance and crime, as promoted and applied by the original Chicago sociologists, did not withstand the thrust of both positivisim and structural functionalism, as alternative paradigms assuming intellectual dominance over the interactionist perspective.

Two interrelated weaknesses in the original interactionist perspective marked its relative demise as a useful framework through which to study deviancy. Firstly, the original Chicago studies, although emphasising the internal structure and organisation of deviant enterprises and thereby granting them an authenticity hitherto neglected or ignored, failed to appreciate fully the close connections between deviancy and social control. In short, the emphasis was placed on the social organisation of deviancy and the deviant act at the expense of grasping the role, function and consequences of the control culture and its institutional arrangements. Secondly, the very absence of a significant political sociology of social problems, a neglect of the power of social control agents and their institutions to manage and shape the career of deviant actors and their individual or collective life-styles, resulted in the original Chicago variant of the interactionist perspective failing to locate its theoretical work and empirical findings in the context of a theory of the wider society and its structural components. It was precisely the ability to fulfil this requirement, among others, that enabled structural functionalism to locate crime and deviancy within an analysis of assumptions about the nature of the American social order taken as a whole. In particular the work of R. K. Merton, and modifications made by his successors[11] to his original work, resulted in fresh orientations being taken to crime, delinquency and subcultural theory.

A new generation of interactionists, emerging after the end of the Second World War, gave the perspective a new lease of life by shifting attention to the impact that moral entrepreneurs and social control agents have on deviancy. The central axiom around which the new deviancy theorists centred their attention is contained in the following statement by Becker:

> Social groups create deviance by making the rules whose infraction constitutes deviance, and by applying those rules to particular people and labelling them as outsiders. From this point of view, deviance is not a quality of the act the person commits, but rather a consequence of the application by others of rules and sanctions to an 'offender'. The deviant is one to whom the label has successfully been applied; deviant behaviour is behaviour that people so label.[12]

Here we have a sociological orientation to social problems directly springing from the labelling perspective developed by Edwin Lemert in his *Social Pathology* and subsequently taken up in his *Human Deviance, Social Problems and Social Control.*[13] Adopting Lemert's analytical distinction between primary and secondary deviation, new deviancy theorists begin to shift the focus of their enquiries away from deviants to the crimogenic function of social control agents, and their institutional and ideological bases.

The significance of interactionism for deviancy theorists of the postwar school, both in the United States of America and later on in Great Britain, lay in its critique of those criminological orthodoxies represented by the positivist and structural functionalist schools. Cohen[14] has demonstrated how criminologists in Great Britain have remained locked in an approach to crime distinguished by its interdisciplinary stance, pragmatism, positivism and correctionalism. Positivist criminology has taken on one of the main features characteristic of an applied social science discipline, namely its insulation from mainstream sociological theorising. The new deviancy theorists, recognising the intellectual poverty of positivist criminological work, embraced a perspective that rejected the individualism, scientism, absolutism, correctionalism and pathologising of the deviant subject embraced by such an approach. Thus, for example, Box, in an evaluation of Matza's contribution to the new deviancy theory, sums up the interactionist perspective on crime and deviancy in the following terms: 'The perspective has shifted from one which viewed [deviance] as a simple pathology in need of correction, to another which views it as complex diversity we should appreciate.'[15]

Similarly the politically conservative implications of structural functionalist analysis on poverty, inequality and crime, in spite of its efforts to understand these issues at a societal level, led the new deviancy theorist to reject this approach. The rejection sprang from an identification with the victims of a unequal society and a critique of the unintended negative impact of social control agents to stigmatise the underprivileged and oppressed sectors of society. Structural functionalists did not make this critical point. Instead they viewed poverty and crime as dysfunctional to the general social order. Social control to the functionalists took on the purpose of bringing the disadvantaged and disaffected into the consensual fold.

Symbolic interactionism has helped shape the work of the new deviancy theorists by pointing them in the direction of exploring and analysing issues on crime, deviancy and delinquency in terms of four major dimensions: the continuity between criminology and mainstream sociology; the significance of social control; a naturalistic appreciation of deviant phenomena; and the political implications of studying deviance for the criminologist. In what follows I wish to outline the importance of these dimensions for the new deviancy perspective.

The continuity between criminology and mainstream sociology

The founding fathers of sociology – Pareto, Weber, Durkheim, Marx, and Parsons – are all concerned, in their own particular fashion, with seeking answers to one of the central questions posed by the arrival of a highly complex, industrial social system in the western world. The question, simply stated, is: how is order and social control arranged and maintained, given the radical transformation of society from a pre-industrial to a highly differentiated industrial society? All the above sociologists, with the exception of Marx, appreciated the importance of elaborating a theory of society in terms of the problems posed by the necessity to understand how complex industrial societies are *integrated*. Marx, with his interest in class conflict, social change, power, and the contradictions inherent in class-divided societies, made the problem of societal integration peripheral to his analysis. Yet it remains that he was concerned with the development of a comprehensive theory of society; in doing so he developed a theory of the domination of the ruling class over the proletariat, which, without systematically using the term, amounts to a theory of social control. For sure, each of these sociologists analysed specific social, political and economic issues with an eye for fine empirical detail, but all their empircal work was carried out in terms of its relevance to constructing a theory of man and society. Focusing on particular aspects of industrial society did not result, for them, in what subsequently became, in the historical development of sociology, a set of isolated and unconnected specialisms, divorced from a theory of society.

Criminology, at least a major sector of it, has developed into just one of those very isolated sub-disciplines of sociology. Mainstream, orthodox criminology has been marked by an almost complete dissociation with sociological theory; there has been a general distrust of theory or some master conception of crime and deviancy in relation to the wider society. The major part of the intellectual production of criminologists, particularly in Britain, has centred on an eclectic positivism, reducing crime to an assorted collection of statistically correlated 'facts' designed to produce a basis from which reformers could devise policies and implement recommendations for the control of crime and deviance.

At an intellectual level the emergence of a new deviancy theory is a response to the isolation of criminology from the concerns of mainstream sociology. The interactionist perspective, in spite of its theoretical limitations, contains within it the elements of a political sociology of crime and deviance, because it has raised questions as to the diversity of values and beliefs, the exercise of power and control, the nature of law and order, and the impact of social reaction, in relation to deviant phenomena. In short, the new deviancy theory moves towards a stance in which its empirical forms strive towards reforging the links between criminology and some of the major conceptual concerns of mainstream sociology.

The significance of social control

One major consequence of the new deviancy school of thought has been to turn mainstream criminology on its head. For mainstream criminology the function, purpose and impact of rule and law creation and enforcement has remained unproblematic. The interactionist perspective has, instead, produced studies focusing on the origins and nature of social control, particularly in terms of analysing its impact and effect upon the creation and transformation of deviancy. Interactionist criminology has inverted the common-sense assumption that deviancy leads to social control by asserting that much the most fruitful line of enquiry would be to investigate the proposition that social control is a basis on which deviancy is generated and sustained.[16]

This focus on the impact of social control on deviants stresses the relevance of sociologically explaining how social control serves to alter the form and content of the deviant enterprise. The interactionists' awareness of the part played by social control agencies and their personnel in stereotyping and classifying deviants constitutes the very point of departure for an imminent political analysis of social control ideologies, strategies and techniques. Plummer captures the significance of the concept of social control for the new deviancy theorists in the following comment:

It is this awareness of the role that 'reactions' play in 'creating' deviancy, that has led to an increasing concern with the political nature of deviancy. Deviancy becomes one form of conflict situation in which norms and laws are seen as the product of economic, moral and political conflicts, and encounters between 'deviants' and 'controllers' are 'exchanges' between groups with differential access to power.[17]

Of equal significance to the effect that formal and external social control processes have on deviants in confirming their identity by bringing them into the orbit of medical, social-work, or law-enforcement agencies, is the role that informal and internalised forms of social control play in facilitating an appreciation by the deviant actor of his own predicament. For example, it does not require the intervention of the police or social workers to make an alcoholic aware of his deviant identity. In keeping with the methodological position of symbolic interactionism it is sufficient for the deviant actor to develop an appreciation of his outsider status by indicating to himself who he is in the context of a generalised awareness of societal hostility.

The naturalistic appreciation of deviant phenomena

> The major theme in Matza's work . . . is *naturalism*: the constant attempt to remain true to the phenomenon one is studying. His objection to other theories of deviance is that they distort the essence of deviant reality – that in the process of explaining deviancy they provide accounts of deviance that just do not tally with what the deviants themselves would recognize or give as motivational accounts for their own actions. In one important sense, then, Matza's work is an attempt to re-address and redirect criminologists and sociologists to the central question of the relationship between beliefs and action.[18]

Taylor, Walton and Young, in the above comment, correctly pinpoint the major contribution Matza makes to criminology in terms of replacing a correctionalist by an appreciative stance towards deviant beliefs and action. The naturalistic perspective outlined by Matza,[19] in one way or another applied by both the original Chicago School of Sociologists and the second generation post-Chicagoans, rests on a straightforward methodological axiom – 'tell it like it is'.

Matza's distinction between appreciative and correctional research is developed in *Becoming Deviant*:

Appreciation [of deviant beliefs and actions] is especially difficult when the subject of enquiry consists of enterprises that violate cherished and widely shared standards of conduct and morality. Almost by definition, such phenomena are commonly unappreciated; indeed, they are condemned. Accordingly, the purpose of much research on deviation has been to assist established society ultimately to rid itself of such troublesome activities. The goal of ridding ourselves of the deviant phenomenon, however Utopian, stands in sharp contrast to an appreciative perspective and may be referred as correctional.[20]

This distinction between correctional and appreciative investigation serves as a convenient watershed separating a positivist criminology (overwhelmingly concerned with questions of causation and aetiology) from the interactionist perspective (focusing on natural phenomena in which an appreciative and empathetic stance by the researcher is an important tool of enquiry). Polsky, in his 'Research Method, Morality, and Criminology',[21] adopts a sympathetic position to Matza's distinction between correctional and appreciative criminology, beseeching sociologists to sever their connections with social control agencies if they wish to embark on appreciative studies and avoid becoming corrupted by the ideology and practical aims of such agencies.

Now I would argue that a naturalistic appreciation of deviant phenomena is not necessarily, by definition, subverted by either adopting a research interest in social control agencies (indeed, this study has applied an appreciative stance towards both deviants and social control agents and their institutions) or by receiving the material support of control agencies to conduct research among deviants within a naturalistic perspective. And, somewhat appropriately, given the subject matter of this book, Matza cites Nels Anderson's *The Hobo* (a classic work in the tradition of the early Chicago sociologists) as an example of how the tension between correctional and appreciative perspectives can be resolved. Matza points out that Anderson's study was

. . . supported and partly financed by municipal agencies and commissions that were interested in ameliorating the grievous conditions associated with vice, alcohol, wandering, vagrancy, and begging [but which nevertheless] conveyed an inside, or interior view of the phenomenon and in which the hobo's own perspective was made prominent by Anderson's analysis.[22]

A naturalistic theory on the social reality of deviant action and social control, in which the analysis emanates from the world-views of protagonists engaged in that reality, forces the sociologist to treat deviance and social control as a subjective process. Most orthodox accounts of deviance (issues of social control for the most part being ignored) assume that societal norms are part of an absolute reality, objectively given, and consequentially unproblematic. Both positivist and structural functionalist theories of deviance, particularly the former, are constructed around notions as to the pathology and inauthenticity of the deviant person. Any conception of deviance as a socially constructed and meaningful enterprise, developed and articulated against a backdrop of the power of control agencies to shape deviance, is made impossible by sociologists avoiding the problematic of social control. The interactionist perspective takes up this very lacuna in our knowledge and understanding of deviancy by grasping social reality in terms of the consciousness of both deviants and social control agents as arising through concrete and specific situated interactions.

In his preliminary comments to a study of homosexuality Plummer summarises a set of consequences flowing from the interactionist perspective he adopts. These consequences reveal the separation that the interactionist perspective achieves from orthodox approaches to crime and deviancy. Adopting a naturalistic stance, that is, grasping deviance as subjective reality, has resulted in the following outcomes: first, it has thrown up a series of studies that serve to locate the world of deviancy as it is phenomenally experienced by the deviant in his natural environment; second, it has attempted, similarly, to locate the subjective reality of agents of control by demonstrating the emergence and consequence of 'deviancy typifications' through an appreciation of the routine and concrete actions and meanings directed at deviants by law-enforcement, treatment, and rehabilitation agents; third, it has treated deviancy as inherently meaningful, not as a set of 'meaningless irrationalities', as is commonly assumed; fourth, a naturalistic stance has resulted in the emergence of studies of deviancy as a form of stigma symbol producing profound changes in identity for labelled deviants; fifth, the subject areas on which the interactionists now focus go beyond conventional categories of crime through an understanding of deviance as a process that emerges within a wide variety of situations not coming to the attention of official control agents; finally, the relativisation of deviancy has resulted in issues about the 'value-freedom' and 'value-commitment' of sociologists engaged in deviancy research being raised, forcing them to examine how their values enter into what traditionally was taken to be the objective analysis of social problems.[23]

The political implications of studying deviance for the criminologist

Raising the problem of values within criminology, deviancy theory, and the sociology of social problems merges with an important process, which has become increasingly apparent in recent years – the politicising of crime, the criminal and the criminologist.[24] This politicisation flows from the challenge to traditional perspectives on crime offered, in the first instance, by the new deviancy theorists and, more recently, by neo-Marxist theorising on crime, law and morality.

There is no scope here to explore the full course, and its ramifications, of the politicising process that crime, the criminal and the criminologist are undergoing. Suffice it to say that the interactionist perspective has served as a useful and convenient point of departure for criminologists to reintroduce politics and power into their analyses by bringing into focus the nature of the relationship between deviancy and social control. The criminologist has been forced to turn his analytical skills partly on himself, and critically explore his own political position in relation to the organised power of social control agents, the relative powerlessness of some deviant individuals and groups, and the increasing politicization of others.

The most significant political implication for criminologists adopting an interactionist perspective has been the granting of authenticity to the deviant enterprise while simultaneously offering a critique of social control ideologies and practice in terms such that much deviancy is viewed as the product of social control. Contained within this axiom is the critical question, originally put by Howard Becker, as to whose side are criminologists on.[25] In much interactionist work there is an implicit allegiance of the criminologist toward deviants and criminals, while agents of social control are taken as the *bêtes noires*, if not generating crime, at least sustaining and amplifying it.

Thus one significant contribution of the interactionist perspective to deviancy theorising has been its capacity to open up a debate on the political nature of crime and the role of the criminologist. However, the shortcomings of the perspective, outlined in greater detail in the final section of this chapter, are that, as far as its political implications are concerned, much interactionist work engages in a false romanticisation of criminalised or stigmatised groups and misdirects its political critique at middle-range social control agencies at the expense of ignoring society's master institutions and the wider social structure.

Participant observation as a research technique

It was no intellectual accident that Herbert Blumer wrote the foreword[26] to Severyn T. Bruyn's *The Human Perspective in Sociology: the Methodology of Participant Observation*.[27] Bruyn's account of the method of participant observation is one of the most thoughtful and careful discussions on the subject. Blumer writes:

> His [Bruyn's] approach might be said to stem from the proposition that the cardinal requirement of an empirical science is to respect the nature of its subject matter. In place of applying to human life an imported scheme of scientific procedure, he stresses the need of recognising in the first instance the peculiar character of human beings, their behaviour, and their group life. And he persistently develops the thesis that scientific study in these areas must be grounded in an appreciation of this peculiar character . . . Professor Bruyn has used the concept of 'participant observation' to cover his extensive discussion and systematic analysis because the concept brings neatly into flow the position of the scholar and researcher who proposes to study human group life. The concept signifies the relation which the human observer of human beings cannot escape – having to participate in some fashion in the experience and action of those he observes.[28]

Such a statement has a major affinity with the methodological position of symbolic interactionism. To begin with, participant observation demands of the observer that he immerses himself in the phenomenon under study to the point where any preconceptions are suspended in favour of grasping the perspective, the central meanings, constructed by his subjects. Definitions of the situation constructed, sustained, and transformed by the protagonists in any regular human activity (if we are to capture their form and content adequately) can only be grasped by using the technique of participant observation.

The origins of a participant observer approach to research are to be traced back through the early anthropological field studies around the turn of the century. This research strategy demands systematic, qualitative analytic descriptions and explanations 'of the symbolic modes of life among distinct human groups'.[29] Much of the work of the Chicago sociologists represents the careful analysis of social phenomenon flowing from the direct participation and observation of sociologists in the world around them. Without exception, the work of investigators such as Robert Park and Ernest Burgess revealed the possibility of conducting sociological research without reducing observations to measurable indices or relying on the results of statistical analyses as a basis for theorising about the development of urban life.

The method of the participant observer entails a specific approach by the investigator in order to acquire knowledge. The objective of systematic investigation using participant observation is to capture the experience, thoughts and feelings which are in the minds of the subjects studied. Herbert Blumer has brought this approach into focus when he asserts:

> To catch the process, the student must take the role of the acting unit whose behaviour he is studying. Since the interpretation is being made by the acting unit in terms of objects designated and appraised, meanings acquired, and decisions made, the process has to be seen from the standpoint of the acting unit. To try to catch the interpretive process by remaining aloof as a so-called 'objective' observer and refusing to take the role of the acting unit is to risk the worst kind of subjectivism – the objective observer is likely to fill in the process of interpretation with his own surmises in place of catching the process as it occurs in the experience of the acting unit which uses it.[30]

Bruyn has usefully reduced the framework of participant observation to three basic rules or axioms, the first two of which contain a corollary.[31] These rules and corollaries indicate the specific stance adopted by observers of human life in their attempt to appreciate how actors construct, sustain and develop meaningful attitudes and behaviour. In short the rules and their corrolaries state:

Axiom 1: The participant observer shares in the life activities and sentiments of people in fact-to-face relationships. The corollary to this axiom is that the participant observer requires to be both detached and part of what is going on. He is deliberately and systematically sharing in the life and everyday activities of actors, and in doing so is transformed by being one of his subjects (taking on the role of the actors under study), but simultaneously expects that some part of him, the investigator, remains unchanged and detached.

Axiom 2: The participant observer is a normal part of the culture and the life of the people under observation. This methodological rule has as its corollary the view that the scientific role of the student is interdependent with the social role in the culture of the observed. The significance of this axiom and its corollary are two-fold. In the first instance the observer takes on a role congruent with the roles of the people being researched; he needs to merge himself in the culture under study in such a way that he becomes a part of that culture. Secondly, in seeking to apprehend, record, interpret, and conceptualise the social facts and meanings of his subjects the observer will become aware that his scientific role coincides in many ways with his social role as participant; his social role interpenetrates with, and is an indispensable part of, the scientific process.

Axiom 3: The role of the participant observer reflects the social process of living in society. George Herbert Mead stressed the importance of viewing men as compelled to engage in social interaction and symbolic communication with one another to be members of society. To do this men engage in the process of role-taking; all people take on the roles of significant others in order to engage in meaningful action. The process of role-taking is essential to the method of the participant observer; it is through such a process that a basis for knowing man in his essence becomes possible.

The skid row phenomenon and participant observation

The choice of participant observation as the main research technique in this study was made during the very earliest stages of the research enterprise. This choice was no accident; it follows on from the specific perspective and methodological considerations outlined so far. No technique of social enquiry is atheoretical. Theory, methodology and the tools of investigation are themselves interacting pieces in the research process; the manner in which the data is sought, collected, and analysed is symbolic of the researchers underlying perspective. The intent of participant observation is to record the experiences of those observed through their symbolic and behavioural worlds. To adopt this research technique implies a commitment by the observer to the basic principles of symbolic interactionism.

Participant observation may be most profitably treated as a method of qualitative analysis that requires observer submersion in the everyday life of the protagonists in the phenomenon under study. A number of assumptions underscore the technique. Firstly, as has already been indicated, the investigator shares as intimately as possible in the life and activity of the subjects observed. Secondly, direct participation in the symbolic and behavioural world is necessary: the observer learns the language, etiquette, and habits of the research subjects while at the same time guarding against the danger of 'going native'. That danger places the observer in the position of submerging himself in the phenomenon studied at the expense of abandoning his research objectives; he finds himself defending rather than actually analysing the values of his subjects. To avoid this danger the researcher not only keep notes of his observations but makes a careful record of any shifts in his own perspective. Thirdly, there is a continuous attempt to carve out a role as observer and participant *within* the context of interaction situations being observed. The student must attempt to persuade those he is studying to accept him, and to question and observe them. On the whole the observer should avoid wherever possible presenting himself as something he is not; in particular any attempt to pass as a deviant or as someone concerned with their correction should be resisted, especially when the researcher is interested in developing and sustaining a close yet simultaneously distanced relationship with his subjects.

On the basis of these assumptions the participant observer makes his presence as an investigator known, allows relationships to develop over time, and thereby overcomes any original superficiality and hostility inherent in the original stages of contact. He has his role as observer sanctioned by the subjects studied, and moves from the status of being a provisional member to that of categorical member. Increasing rapport is established throughout the different stages.

One of the first problems of conducting fieldwork among skid row men is the relative dispersal of skid row institutions throughout the inner zones of large cities in Britain. With the possible exception of the Grassmarket area in Edinburgh and to some extent the East End of London there is not, unlike in the United States, an ecological area containing the majority of skid row institutions. We cannot talk validly of specific skid row areas in British towns and cities. A second problem is that, although skid row men share with the dominant culture many of its symbolic characteristics – language, for instance, which presented no problem apart from understanding the linguistic and symbolic formations specific to the culture of homeless alcoholics – the skid row man may be regarded as the deviant *par excellence* by virtue of his total immersion in a life style that places him completely outside orthodox, conventional life styles. This means that the researcher, if he is to obtain an adequate analytic description of the phenomenon, must move freely among homeless alcoholics in the different situations they encounter as part of their daily routine. A third major problem, which soon became apparent in this particular research exercise, was the necessity to study in depth both the culture of homeless alcoholics and the different ideological and practical orientations of social control agents and their institutional arrangements in confronting the problems presented by habitual public drunkenness, vagrancy, homelessness and chronic poverty. I have dealt with these problems elsewhere;[32] however, some of the major research problems and the tactics employed in overcoming them, particularly in gaining access and sustaining a close relationship with the world of skid row alcoholics and their guardians, now need outlining.

Observing the world of the skid row alcoholic

The first stage of the research act consisted of two interdependent phases: firstly, an extensive reading of the literature, both American and British, on skid row, vagrancy and alcoholism; and, secondly, an attempt to gain a flavour of the institutional matrix making up skid row by carrying out occasional visits to hostels, soup runs and kitchens, magistrate's courts, common lodging houses, parks and other open spaces frequented by alcoholics. I was usually accompanied by a recovered skid row alcoholic familiar with many of the situations and personalities encountered during these visits, thus developing, from the outset, an insider's perspective. This stage served as an invaluable point of departure, by which I was able to appreciate the breadth of the phenomenon I was undertaking to study. Informal and open-ended conversations were held with alcoholics and professionals working in the field throughout this stage; moreover the recovered skid row alcoholic acting as an interpreter of my original observations offered a detailed biographical account of his own acculturation into the skid row world, thus sensitising me to some of the major issues I would need to explore during the main stage of my fieldwork.

Since there was no one specific skid row area in London where fieldwork could be anchored, a deliberate choice as to where to begin had to be made. In the event, partly by accident and partly as a result of a rational decision, I decided that gaining entrée into a drinking school would offer me the best point of departure for obtaining an insider's view of the skid row world. The decision was rational insofar as it soon became apparent that drinking schools were the one regular institutional arrangement created by skid row men themselves through which they acted collectively. I assumed that not only was it essential to obtain information about the structure and meaning of drinking schools, but that through them I would be able to collect information about many other aspects of the skid row culture, including definitions of alcoholics themselves and the plethora of social control agents they came into daily contact with. The decision was partly accidental, since, fortuitously, I was introduced to a skid row alcoholic drinking in a park, and he had at one time been a client of the social worker making the introduction. For a period of close on 3 months during the first stage I made a point of occasionally seeking out this alcoholic, exchanging a few words with him and giving him enough money to buy a bottle of cider for himself and his drinking companions. I thus developed a relationship with him, hoping that he would act as the bridge allowing me permanent entry into the drinking school he frequented.

The handling of this first stage of the research process was in keeping with the recommendations of sociologists experienced in fieldwork. For instance, Anselm Strauss and his colleagues write:

> A . . . characteristic of fieldwork is its temporally developing character. The fieldworker usually does not enter the field with the specific hypotheses and a pre-determined research design. To be sure he does have general problems in mind, as well as a theoretical framework that directs him to certain events in the field . . . The initial phase of fieldwork is a period of general observation: specific problems and foci have not yet been determined. The fieldworker is guided mainly by sensitivities to data derived both from his professional background and from his general notions about the nature of his research problem. As he surveys the field initially, he is continuously 'testing' – either implicitly or explicitly – the relevance of a large number of hypotheses, hunches and guesses. Many preconceptions fall by the wayside during this initial period, as the observer struggles to ascertain the meaning of events and to place them in some initial order.[33]

Direct participation in the events under observation are virtually non-existent at this stage; at most the researcher intervenes by the occasional comment or question directed at his subjects. As Polsky points out in his essay 'Research Method, Morality and Criminology', it is incumbent upon the participant observer to maintain a relatively low profile during the early steps of the fieldwork process, using his eyes and ears rather than doing too much talking.[34]

I began full-time fieldwork after the first phase of nine months' preliminary investigation, during which I explored the literature; made the initial contact with skid row institutions, their professional personnel and some of the alcoholics using them; and drew up a formal research proposal. My intensive period of fieldwork research – the second stage of the study – commenced with me joining my original skid row contact and his regular drinking companions in a park in South London for several hours on a daily basis. An immediate problem needed to be confronted: my association with a social-work agency by the alcoholics in the drinking school resulted in them imputing a social-work role to my presence among them; this in turn made it imperative that I divulge my true identity, as a research sociologist, at the earliest possible moment.[35] Once I sensed that sufficient rapport between the alcoholics and myself had been achieved (within the first couple of weeks), I took the opportunity to explain the exact purpose of my regular presence with the drinking school to my initial field contact. My main strategy was to explain that, as far as doctors, social workers, probation officers, law-enforcement personnel and others working with homeless alcoholics were concerned, their images of the alcoholics' life style was heavily distorted by having only partial glimpses of their situation, viewing them as patients, social-work clients or offenders, without appreciating their predicament and their view of the world around them.[36] In short, an account of their experiences and viewpoint was badly needed if professionals were in any way to balance the distorted images of alcoholics they held as a result of being locked into particular professional ideologies and practices.

Such an explanation for my presence appeared to be accepted without further questioning. Undoubtedly, contributing my share to the finances of the drinking school made my regular contact with its core members an attractive proposition to them. In addition my participation in the daily routine of public drinking – occasional begging, informing the drinking school of the presence of a policeman on his beat making 'the run' to an off-licence for cider or cheap wine, and generally sharing in the conversation about skid row life, its institutions, and specific professionals and alcoholics working and living in them – contributed to my general acceptance by the core members of the drinking school.[37]

The initial assumption that the drinking school would not only reveal its inner logic but in addition throw up a great deal of information about other aspects and institutions on skid row was soon borne out by the data collected. However, one of the requirements of participant observation is that, wherever possible, the investigator must follow up leads picked up in the course of carrying out fieldwork by exploring for himself the descriptions and explanations offered of events and situations. Information gathered from participants in a drinking school about their views on common lodging houses, shelters and skippers, police cells, law courts and prisons, rehabilitation hostels and hospitals, needed following up by actual visits to these places. Consequently, after approximately six months of participant observation in a drinking school, I began to collect data on other skid row institutions by observing and participating in their daily routines.

Polsky refers to the methodological process of gradually expanding and deepening one's experience and awareness of the phenomenon under study as 'snowballing'.[38] The point is not to check out all institutions, behaviour, attitudes and beliefs thrown up by participants during the initial stage of fieldwork, by exploring a statistically random sample of such institutions, behaviour and attitudes. For sure the frequency and distribution of pehnomena – their idiosyncratic or regular appearance – serve as an indicator of what needs pursuing or not in greater depth. But it is the *central meaning patterns* that need their reliability and validity tested; the phenomenological essence of human action only emerges by pursuing in depth specific leads rather than statistically spreading one's participation and observation across a representative number of events, situations, and individuals.

An indication of the locales, institutions, numbers of alcoholics, and the time spent on skid row is included in Tables 1–4. The information in these tables illustrates where and over how long participant observation was conducted. Notes on some of the methodological problems I encountered in different locales and institutions (see pp. 222–7) reveal how, at different stages of the research process, the participant observer needs to modify his approach, sometimes shifting his role to that of the full participant, at other times taking up the stance of a distanced observer with little, if any, active participation in the environment or situation under study.[39]

Summary tables of observations on deviant culture

TABLE 1   *Formal fieldwork period on deviant culture*

(i)	Overall time span conducting fieldwork among skid row alcoholics	13 Sep 1971–25 Oct 1972–407 days
(ii)	Total number of days on which observations were made and recorded among skid row alcoholics	133 days
(iii)	Total number of hours spent on skid row among skid row alcoholics	363 hours

TABLE 2 *Category and number of locales in which fieldwork was conducted, and number of alcoholics interviewed or observed*

(i)	Category of locales and institutions in which fieldwork was conducted	Number of locales and institutions
	(a) Public and open spaces	17
	(b) Formal institutions	36
	(c) Informal institutions	23
	(d) Other	24

(ii)	Number of alcoholics interviewed or observed during fieldwork	85 identified
		156 not identified

TABLE 3 *Summary of observations by type and number of locales or institutions, number of observations, and alcoholics interviewed or observed in them (For reference to column numbers see foot of table, overleaf)*

Column 1	Column 2	Column 3	Column 4	
			(i)	*(ii)*
(i) Public and open spaces				
(a) Parks and open spaces	15	88	37	66
(b) Main railway stations	2	20	20	29
(ii) Formal institutions				
(a) Police stations	2	3	10	6
(b) Law courts				
Magistrate's courts	2	18	74	28
Crown courts	1	2	2	0
(c) Prisons	2	14	8	16
(d) Common lodging houses	2	22	22	n.c.
(e) Missions	5	11	8	n.c.
(f) Day centres	1	5	2	n.c.
(g) Hand-out centres				
Soup kitchens	2	6	4	n.c.
Soup runs	3	8	7	n.c.
(h) Hospitals				
Mental	4	6	6	12
General	1	1	3	0
(i) Shop-fronts	3	22	18	n.c.
(j) Rehabilitation hostels	6	16	31	0
(k) Social security offices	1	2	3	n.c.
(l) Alcoholics Anonymous	1	1	1	16

Table 3 *(continued)*

Column 1	Column 2	Column 3	Column 4 (i)	Column 4 (ii)
(iii) Informal institutions				
(a) Drinking schools				
In parks/open spaces	8	74	57	62
In common lodging houses	3	9	15	0
In social security offices	1	1	4	0
In skippers	1	1	2	0
(b) Skippers				
In derelict buildings	3	3	4	0
In parks/open spaces	6	8	n.c.	n.c.
In underground car park	1	1	1	n.c.
(c) Street casual work 'agencies'	2	2	n.c.	n.c.
(iv) Other institutions				
(a) Cafés	6	18	n.c.	n.c.
(b) Tea-stalls	4	12	n.c.	n.c.
(c) Off-licences	6	13	n.c.	n.c.
(d) Public houses	6	26	16	n.c.
(e) Betting shops	2	6	n.c.	n.c.

Notes Column 1: Type of locale or institution in which observations were made
Column 2: Number of locales or institutions observed
Column 3: Number of occasions on which observations were made
Column 4: Number of alcoholics interviewed or observed
(i) Number of alcoholics identified by name
(ii) Number of alcoholics not identified by name
n.c.: Not counted

Table 4   *Number of references made by alcoholics included in fieldwork notes according to specific indexed aspects of deviant culture*

Indexed aspects of deviant culture	Number of references in fieldwork notes
(i) Strategies of survival	
(a) General	30
(b) Money	
Begging	102
Social security benefits	24
Work	30
Thieving	31

Tᴀʙʟᴇ 4 *(continued)*

Indexed aspects of deviant culture	Number of references in fieldwork notes
(c) Shelter	
Skippers	67
Formal institutions	131
(d) Food/clothing	22
(ii) Drinking	
(a) Drinking schools	272
(b) Alcohol, consumption and effects	206
(c) Public houses	41
(d) Off-licences	6
(iii) Encounters with law-enforcements agencies	
(a) Alcoholic–police encounters	186
(b) Alcoholic–law court encounters	130
(c) Alcoholic–prison encounters	102
(iv) Encounters with rehabilitation agencies	
(a) Alcoholic–religious mission encounters	120
(b) Alcoholic–reception centre encounters	21
(c) Alcoholic–shop-front/rehabilitation hostel encounters	73
(d) Alcoholic–hospital (alcoholism unit) encounters	34
(e) Alcoholic–Alcoholics Anonymous encounters	14
(v) Self-definitions by alcoholics	
(a) Status comments	243
(b) Life events leading to skid row	40
(c) Rehabilitation aspirations	31
(vi) Miscellaneous	
(a) Conversation topics on skid row	44
(b) Public attitude toward alcoholics	36
(c) Gambling	4
(d) Geographical mobility	23
(e) Weather conditions	12

Observing the world of the social control agents

The technical problems of approaching social control agents concerned with skid row and, more specifically, the correction of skid row alcoholics, were not as complex as the problems of gaining entrée and immersing myself in the culture of the homeless alcoholic. Firstly, the educational, class, and cultural background of researchers is often relatively close to that of professionals engaged in 'deviancy work'. Secondly, in the case of this particular study, my association with a particular social control agency was turned to advantage insofar as I was able to use the credentials of the agency as a passport to many agency meetings where professionals with different interests and orientations towards homelessness, vagrancy, public drunkenness and alcoholism discussed issues in handling the problem. Thirdly, using single and multiple-agency meetings as a source of observation enabled me to gather information about the beliefs and actions of professionals, which served to highlight both the similarities and differences arising amongst them, over and against the ideological frameworks within which they define the skid row problem and any action advocated towards it. Fourthly, during fieldwork among alcoholics in face-to-face encounters with correctional agents I was able to observe simultaneously both the perspective of alcoholics and agents of social control. Finally, unlike skid row alcoholics, agents of social control often articulate their ideological and practical prescriptions for dealing with the skid row phenomenon by documenting their distinct approaches to problems of correction and control in memoranda, case records, reports and books. Thus the world-views of social control personnel and their institutions were also appreciated as a form of subjective reality – the naturalistic method proved to be equally valid in studying mission workers, psychiatrists and nurses, social workers, law-enforcement agents, and other professional workers.

There is, of course, no total separation between, on the one hand, studying the perspective of vagrant alcoholics and, on the other, appreciating the stance taken up by control agencies. Observations among alcoholics led to investigations that required testing among professionals and vice versa. This enabled the construction of a composite picture – reflected throughout this work – in which the presence or absence of a 'fit' between both sides of the deviancy/correctional enterprise was revealed. Accordingly an ideological and orientational tension became apparent between alcoholics and professionals, underlining the symbiotic relationship both sides have developed through repeated encounters.

The stages of the research act described in the preceding section on observing the world of the skid row alcoholic are equally relevant to conducting an appreciative study of social control agents. Reviewing the literature, visiting formal skid row agencies and talking with the personnel manning them, all acted as sensitising components in the study, guiding me towards appropriate areas of enquiry.[40] For the major part of the study the perspective offered by skid row alcoholics was used as the research base-line from which to offer an analytical description of how correctional agents approach them, since it was assumed at the outset, given the premises of symbolic interactionism, that there would exist areas of both conflict and congruence between skid row men and their guardians. However, I also assumed that deviant/control agent encounters would only offer a partial view of the concerns taken up by professionals working in the field; in addition broader theoretical and policy-making concerns would preoccupy social workers, psychiatrists, law-enforcement agents and, especially, service administrators. These moral – entrepreneurial concerns, taking the social control agencies over and beyond face-to-face encounters with alcoholics, were more than adequately revealed through observing multi-agency discussions and analysing documentary evidence focusing on future policy towards the vagrancy problem.

Summary tables of observations on social control culture

TABLE 5   *Formal fieldwork period on social control culture*

(i)	Overall time span conducting fieldwork among agents of social control	13 Sep 1971–25 Oct 1972–407 days
(ii)	Total number of days on which observations were made and recorded among agents of social control	77 days
(iii)	Total number of hours spent with agents of social control	198 hours

TABLE 6   *Category and number of institutions in which fieldwork was conducted or information obtained on, and number of agents of social control interviewed or observed*

(i) Category of institutions in which fieldwork was conducted or information obtained on	Number of institutions
(a) Police stations	2
(b) Magistrate's courts	2
(c) Prisons	1
(d) Common loding houses	1
(e) Missions	1
(f) Day centres	1
(g) Hand-out centres	2
(h) Mental hospitals	1
(i) Shop-fronts	3
(j) Rehabilitation hostels	3
(k) Social security offices	1
(ii) Total number of social control agents interviewed or observed during fieldwork	103

TABLE 7   *Summary of observations by category of institution and occupational status of social control agents, and number of social control agents and occasions on which interviewed or observed (For reference to column numbers see foot of table, on next page)*

Column 1	Column 2	Column 3
Police		
(a) Police patrolmen	5	7
(b) Police station officers	6	12
(c) Police superintendents	4	6
Magistrate's courts		
(a) Stipendiary magistrates	6	20
(b) Clerks of the courts	4	4
(c) Police court jailers	2	2
(d) Police officers	6	4
(e) Probation officers	6	9

TABLE 7 *(continued)*

Column 1	Column 2	Column 3
Prisons		
(a) Deputy governors	1	3
(b) Prison officers	7	12
(c) Prison welfare officers	7	11
(d) Reception officers	4	14
(e) Probation officers	2	2
(f) Prison padre	1	1
Common lodging houses		
(a) Directors	2	5
(b) Staff	1	3
Missions		
(a) Staff	1	3
Day Centres		
(a) Directors	2	3
(b) Social workers	1	5
Hand-out centres		
(a) Staff	1	1
Mental hospitals		
(a) Psychiatrists	8	10
(b) Nurses/sisters	3	4
(c) Psychiatric social workers	1	3
Shop-fronts		
(a) Social workers	3	35
Rehabilitation hostels		
(a) Directors	5	21
(b) Social workers	9	29
(c) General practitioners	3	7
Social security offices		
(a) Managers	3	4
Other	16	22

Notes Column 1: Category of institution and occupational status of social control agents
Column 2: Number of social control agents interviewed or observed
Column 3: Number of occasions on which social control agents interviewed or observed

TABLE 8   *Number of references made by agents of social control included in fieldwork notes according to specific indexed aspects of social control culture*

Indexed aspects of social control culture	Number of references in fieldwork notes
Problem definition – general	208
Future policy recommendations	140
Alcoholism defined	18
Typifications of alcoholics	119
Attitude of public to alcoholics	13
Police–alcoholic encounters	134
Magistrate's court–alcoholic encounters	70
Prison–alcoholic encounters	148
Common-lodging house–alcoholic encounters	49
Mental hospital–alcoholic encounters	56
Rehabilitation project–alcoholic encounters	262
Social security office–alcoholic encounters	22

Tables 5–8 summarise the type and number of agencies, where observations were conducted, the kind of personnel recorded or interviewed, and the number of occasions on which each type of correctional agent was interviewed or observed. An indication is also given of the main preoccupations social control agents raised in either face-to-face encounters with alcoholics or in both intra-agency and inter-agency policy discussions.

Validity and reliability of the data collected

A criticism often levelled at the use of qualitative data in sociological research is the difficulty in testing the validity and reliability of the data, given the open-ended, relatively unstructured method by which information is gathered in participant observation studies. Since the main concern of the investigator is to record the subjective interpretations of actors rather than to develop, in advance, measurable indicators allowing for the precise quantification of attitudes and behaviours, the critics of phenomenologically oriented research claim that the perspective is at best not sociology, and at worst not scientific.[41]

In participant observation studies, however, the problem of

validity is not whether operationalised concepts are valid represen-
tations of the phenomenon under study from an objective or
scientific point of view. Instead the interactionist perspective, and the
methodological stance of participant observation, demand that the
investigator accurately represents the actors' social worlds as they
themselves perceive it. Fundamentally the problem of validity in
qualitative research centres on whether the social actors under study
build the concepts and constructs of their daily social reality out of
the same experiences and observations the investigator has gathered,
and with the same general forms emerging.[42]

To test the validity of the data collected in this study the following
procedures were employed. Firstly, a sociological informant – a
recovered skid row alcoholic acting as an amateur sociologist – was
used to read the raw data out of which the analysis emerged, at
regular intervals, with the purpose of critically commenting on the
observations made. The informant's comments were not only
incorporated into the raw data, but acted as pointers to further
investigation on specific aspects of the skid row alcoholics' culture,
while occasionally drawing attention to those original observations
which he felt constituted misinterpretations of idiosyncratic beliefs or
events among alcoholics. Thus, with the passage of time, observations were sharpened by concentrating on specific aspects of the
skid row life-way, while other, more exceptional statements and
actions were discarded or ignored as irrelevant to the core meanings
of life on the row. Secondly, an alcoholic still drinking on skid row,
once he was fully informed.as to my research role and having
developed a particularly close rapport with me, fulfilled much the
same role as that of the first sociological informant, but with the
added advantage that he was able to comment on observations made
in the field which he often had participated in or was aware of by
virtue of his intimate acquaintance with either the situations and
institutions or the actors in them. Finally, on a number of occasions
informal and open-ended discussions were held between two or more
alcoholics and myself as to some of the observations and conclusions
arising out of conducting fieldwork in its natural milieu. All these
procedures put together served to test the validity of participant
observation data – that is, they tested whether the data collected
represented what it purported to represent.

The problem of reliability refers to the consistency of the data
obtained. The researcher needs to satisfy himself that the successive

gathering of data, using participant observation, would result in common patterns of behaviour and meaning emerging from his observations. Problems of reliability are closely interwoven with validity problems, since any lack of reliability automatically lessens the validity of the data obtained.

In order to overcome problems of reliability in orthodox sociological research investigators have developed adequate statistical sampling techniques designed to make observations that are taken as representative of the universe of beliefs, behaviour and situations under study. As indicated earlier, symbolic interactionism and participant observation do not require the researcher to pursue statistically accurate sampling techniques. Rather, by using a 'snowballing' technique, he collects specific aspects of human behaviour in such a way that observations are continuously tested through the immersion of the investigator, in this case, in the social world of alcoholics and correctional agents, each informant and situation studied acting as a test of the consistency of previous observations and as a sensitiser to an appreciation of the essential nature of future observations.[43] Thus, although drinking schools were selected as the starting point for fieldwork, it was assumed that, through participation in drinking schools, the information collected would force the investigation into other areas and institutions, and could be tested there for its reliability.

The procedure, then, to test the reliability of the data consisted of cross-checking it by collecting information in and about several situations or institutions simultaneously. Comparative data was obtained, and this data resulted in the elimination of that which was seldom observed or recorded. Both informants acted as guides to the reliability of the information collected during fieldwork. Finally, regular indexing of the raw data revealed what the central concerns of both alcoholics and agents of social control were, the frequency with which beliefs and behaviour were repeated becoming apparent as the fieldwork process unfolded and increasing immersion into the skid row scene was achieved.

An indication of the types of validity and reliability checks used in this study are contained in Tables 9 and 10. In addition Tables 4 and 8 summarise the number of references made in the fieldwork notes according to specific indexed aspects of both the deviant and control cultures.

TABLE 9 *Summary of in-depth interviews with alcoholics to test validity and reliability of data on deviant culture*

	Interviews	Number of alcoholics	Number of occasions interviewed
(i)	Interviews with main informant (recovered alcoholic)	1	24
(ii)	Interviews with other informants (recovered alcoholics)	3	3
(iii)	Interviews with group of alcoholics (resident in rehabilitation hostels)	8	1
(iv)	Interviews with in-the-field alcoholics (living on skid row)	2	13

TABLE 10 *Number of references made by main informant (one recovered alcoholic) to test validity and reliability of data included in fieldwork notes, according to specific indexed aspects of deviant culture*

Indexed aspects of deviant culture	Number of references in fieldwork notes
(i) Strategies of survival	
(a) General	3
(b) Money	
Begging	6
Social security benefits	5
Work	5
Thieving	2
(c) Shelter	
Skippers	6
Formal institutions	32
(d) Food/clothing	2
(ii) Drinking	
(a) Drinking schools	31
(b) Alcohol, consumption and effects	21
(c) Public houses	2
(d) Off-licences	0
(iii) Encounters with law-enforcement agencies	
(a) Alcoholic–police encounters	25
(b) Alcoholic–law court encounters	9
(c) Alcoholic–prison encounters	34

TABLE 10 *(continued)*

Indexed aspects of deviant culture	Number of references in fieldwork notes
(iv) Encounters with rehabilitation agencies	
(a) Alcoholic–religious mission encounters	14
(b) Alcoholic–reception centre encounters	0
(c) Alcoholic–shop-front/rehabilitation hostel encounters	21
(d) Alcoholic–hospital (alcoholism unit) encouters	6
(e) Alcoholic – Alcoholics Anonymous encounters	1
(v) Self-definitions by alcoholics	
(a) Status comments	65
(b) Life events leading to skid row	11
(c) Rehabilitation aspirations	5
(vi) Miscellaneous	
(a) Conversation topics on skid row	3
(b) Public attitude toward alcoholics	5
(c) Gambling	0
(d) Geographical mobility	13
(e) Weather conditions	0

Notes on the role of the researcher in conducting fieldwork

The participant observer is a normal part of the culture and the life of the people under observation.[44]

The scientific role of the participant observer is interdependent with his social role in the culture observed.[45]

Record how the observer experienced and encountered social openings and barriers in seeking accurate interpretations of privately held social meanings.[46]

Record how the observer encountered psychological barriers and openings in seeking accurate interpretations of social meanings.[47]

It is through the first two axioms and both the following methodological prescriptions that Severyn Bruyn urges the participant observer to appreciate his own role throughout the research act. A significant proportion of my own raw material consisted of entries relating to problems I encountered in conducting fieldwork observations.[48] I wish to conclude this analysis of participant observation as a research technique by referring to some of the observations I made of myself as a researcher, particularly in relation to fieldwork among skid row alcoholics.

Reference has already been made to the preliminary phase of the literature review and making my acquaintance with the skid row and social control culture before commencing full-time fieldwork. In addition I have alluded to the procedures by which I was able to gain entry into a drinking school and the approach I employed in grasping the perspective of social control agents and their institutions, at the level of face-to-face encounters and in their formulation of problem definitions and policy-making. However, once my immersion into the culture of control agents and alcoholics had been achieved, the day-to-day activity of participant observation often threw up problems as to how I could adequately handle my research role. An account of some of the difficulties encountered follows; in particular the dialectical tension between the roles of investigator-as-participant and investigator-as-observer are explored, since the role adopted fluctuated according to the exigencies of the differing situations being researched.

Broadly speaking, fieldwork in drinking schools required full participation if I was to obtain adequate information on the structure, and behavioural and meaning patterns of drinking on skid row. Full participation, while at the same time retaining a detached observational role, required that I engage in the drinking activities of homeless alcoholics. Quite clearly, becoming drunk would present a major obstacle to maintaining a realistic appreciation of events around me. Consequently the amount of alcohol I consumed was carefully restricted by taking limited sips from cider and cheap wine bottles. In addition evidence that the effects of alcohol consumption were resulting in my inability to sustain my observational role, at the expense of becoming exclusively a participant, forced me on many occasions to withdraw from the drinking scene. This withdrawal was facilitated by core members of the school knowing that I was conducting research or by making a suitable excuse. Since at no point did I make any written notes while in the field, it became imperative that I noted my observations at the first possible opportunity, usually on returning home.

In any case, repeated and often prolonged visits to specific drinking schools or skid row locales and institutions, hanging around with the same alcoholics, internalising the subtle rules and norms of the skid row life style, conducting fieldwork during the day or night, begging, living in common lodging houses, sleeping in a derelict house with other alcoholics, warning alcoholics of the approach of police patrolmen, being arrested, all served to confirm that I had become a categorical member of skid row.

In spite of all this I repeatedly encountered a number of tactical difficulties in the field. These arose out of the ever-present psychological tension existing for the researcher of maintaining a balance between participation and observation, and the requirement to move freely from one situation, locale or institution to another.[49] Each new observational setting demanded a renewed attempt to establish myself as a participant observer, either by divulging my true research role, or successfully blending into specific social milieus by 'passing' as a skid row man, for instance in common lodging houses, certain parks, open spaces, railway stations, police stations, magistrate's courts, and other locales.

My commitment to the participant observer perspective and my allegiance to skid row alcoholics struggling to maintain some sort of existence as alcohol-addicted, homeless, poverty-stricken, unemployed men, placed me in a situation where I was continuously on the fringes of petty criminal behaviour, and thus the object of police attention.[50] Furthermore I occasionally had to guard against the real possibility that I might be jack-rolled by men who had learned of my true identity but did not accept my categorical membership of the skid row scene, or to maintain a certain alertness given that I could become the unwitting victim of a drunken brawl in which bottles were often used as weapons. The consequence of confronting these types of situation was to produce a degree of psychological stress that shifted my attention to preserving my own safety or my true identity as a sociologist at the expense of exploring and understanding the natural events unfolding around me.

Earlier I referred to the problem of 'going native',[51] that is, taking on a role where participating in the skid row life-way replaces, unconsciously, the deliberate purpose of fieldwork, namely to study the human behaviour and social environment of one's research subjects objectively. Fieldwork notes revealed two occasions when 'going native' became apparent. First, a stage was arrived at when I noted that my participation in one drinking school took on the character of moving along with the flow of events without any methodical attempt to sustain an observational role; it soon became apparent that I was failing to recollect and make written notes on my daily observations, and instead enjoying the experience of hanging around the skid row scene. Secondly, the psychological impact of living in large common lodging houses was such that I was influenced more by an outsiders' perspective on these human warehouses than by the inner perspective of the inmates forced to use lodging houses. The human degradation, misery and alienation that pervade common lodging houses, coupled with the appalling physical conditions, stood in such sharp contrast to my own private domestic living standards that, somewhat paradoxically, I immediately noted it was this very contrast, and the impact it had on me psychologically, that resulted in me adopting a stance that appeared to reflect the position taken up by the great majority of inmates. Unwittingly the stance I adopted was, in keeping with many of the inmates, to remain isolated and passive, without developing any substantive relationship with any of the common lodging house users. In other words, I rapidly got sucked into the atmosphere of the two lodging houses I lived in, failing for the most part to obtain any in-depth information of why and how alcoholics, and other inmates, come to use and view these institutions. Occasionally I was able to strike up perfunctory conversations with a limited number of alcoholics in common lodging houses but, in the event, I had to rely on comments made about lodging houses by alcoholics I met in other research situations and locales.

The significance of these remarks as to the psychological barriers encountered in 'going native' lie in the importance of the participant observer appreciating this shift in his fieldwork sufficiently early to meet the problem. On both occasions I deliberately removed myself from the skid row scene for several days, in order to reflect upon the process of 'going native' and to reapproach fieldwork with a renewed commitment to the research process.

Conducting fieldwork in other formal skid row institutions (police stations, magistrate's courts, prison, hospital-based alcoholism units, shop-fronts, and rehabilitation hostels) required a particular research approach. In the main information collected on these institutions was, in the first instance, derived from listening to alcoholics talking about them while drinking on skid row. However, I followed up the comments offered by conducting direct observational work within these institutions, usually by setting up open-ended informal interviews rather than adopting a participatory role. It was felt this would prove the most fruitful method of investigation given the limitations on research time and the difficulties of gaining access to and developing in-depth relationships in every one of the varied institutional settings alcoholics find themselves in. Thus I did not attempt to duplicate the processes undergone by alcoholics passing through police stations, courts, prisons, alcoholism units and rehabilitation facilities by adopting the identity of a homeless man.[52] Instead I made repeated visits to these correctional agencies, hanging around in them, observing how homeless alcoholics conducted themselves, and, where possible, engaging alcoholics, either singly or in groups, in conversations designed to tease out the meanings given to the institutions and the personnel manning them.

By way of concluding this section some brief comments on my research role *vis-à-vis* social control agents are appropriate. The central role adopted in order to grasp the perspective of correctional agents was that of observer, as opposed to participant. In other words, at no stage in the fieldwork did I take on, or even approximate, the role of social worker, psychiatrist, law-enforcement officer, mission worker, etc. Instead comments about the roles these 'deviancy workers' play, the definitions they impute to the skid row problem, their understanding of the ideological and practical problems they encounter in handling the problem, both through their daily routines and in terms of developing long-term policy strategies, were noted by observing face-to-face encounters between deviants and social control agents, attending multi-agency meetings, or holding unstructured and informal interviews. The assumption underlying these approaches to studying social control agents is that, by definition, the cultural gap between the research sociologist and the staff manning skid row institutions is nowhere as wide as exists between the deviant culture and the investigator. Consequently the social and psychological barriers and tensions encountered, and to a large extent transcended, in carrying out fieldwork among homeless men, were absent when observing or talking to social workers, police and prison officers, magistrates, and other correctional personnel.

However, two different kinds of problem emerged while I was researching the social control scene. Firstly, there was the need to avoid colluding with the stereotypes constructed by correctional agents in the event of their seeking from the researcher statements that would bolster their own partial definitions of homeless alcoholics. Rather, the task of the sociologist is to unpack the elements making up the stereotyped vision held by agents of social control, not to defend them. Secondly, in view of my association with a correctional agency and the inside knowledge I was gaining of the alcoholics' perspective, requests were sometimes put to me at multi-agency meetings on my own views as to how the problems of vagrancy, alcoholism, and destitution could best be tackled. Two dangers flow from granting these requests: one, it was entirely feasible I would align myself with the ideological orientations of the agency employing me, and therefore would take a partisan view of the problem; two, my intervention in discussions about skid row and its problems could potentially alter the flow and direction of the discussion along lines that otherwise would not have naturally occurred. Consequently I needed to remain on guard against such demands being put to me, by either stating explicitly that my research role would be distorted, or by deflecting the request in terms of turning it back on the persons making it, hoping thereby to probe deeper into the issues raised.

New deviancy theory and interactionism: some methodological limitations outlined

The central argument running throughout this book, demonstrated empirically, has been that in order to move towards a fuller understanding of skid row alcoholism, a symbolic interactionist perspective has to be applied to the phenomena. But do the requirements of the perspective allow for an adequate and full scientific understanding and explanation of deviancy and social control? Are there any theoretical and methodological weaknesses in the approach adopted that might push our grasp of skid row and reaction to it beyond our present level of understanding? By way of concluding this chapter I wish briefly to identify some limitations which, if adequately met, would result in a fuller appreciation of the social reality of skid row, alcoholism, and social control.

Quite clearly, to raise the issues or questions in the foregoing paragraph would necessitate another full-length work. A useful summary and critique of some limitations contained within symbolic interactionism has been spelled out by Lichtman.[53] His critique is used here as a basis for suggesting the direction in which further research might profitably be pursued. An outline of the advances made by the new deviancy theory, particularly in relation to mainstream, orthodox criminology, has already been made (see pp. 193–202). For Lichtman the central propositions and mood of symbolic interactionism provide the social scientist with a framework for analysing social reality, which can be taken as a major intellectual advance over 'the banal perversity' of positivism. However, by attempting to move beyond an interactionist perspective, but not abandoning it, Lichtman claims there are elements in the position that could be incorporated in a Marxist perspective, although the interactionist view is inadequate as it stands. Lichtman itemises six deficiencies in symbolic interactionism:

> (i) . . . it is overly subjective and voluntaristic, (ii) lacks an awareness of historical concreteness, (iii) is naive in its account of mutual typifications and (iv) ultimately abandons the sense of human beings in struggle with an alien reality which they both master and to which they are subordinate. (v) It is a view which tends to dissolve the concept of 'ideology' or 'false consciousness' and (vi) leaves us, often against the will of its advocates, without a critical posture toward the present inhuman reality.[54]

I intend to relate each of these deficiencies critically to the development of new deviancy theory with special reference to the interactionist position.

Symbolic interactionism is overly subjective and voluntaristic

Matza's advocacy of naturalism as a perspective forces us to investigate social reality in terms of the subjective definitions offered by actors engaged in carving out suitable action with which to accommodate to their social predicament; it makes for a conception of man viewed as possessed of a free will, able to challenge and transcend the problems he encounters, purposive in his essentially human enterprise. However, interactionism, insofar as it incorporates a naturalistic perspective on the world, overstretches itself on this point at the expense of ignoring some critical factors that serve to temper its notion of man as voluntaristic and purposive. As Taylor, Walton and Young point out:

> Unless we are careful, therefore, the naturalistic perspective can lead . . . into a position where the only true account of how the deviant phenomenon comes into being, and what its real nature is, can be given by the deviants [and the correctional agents] themselves.[55]

Indeed, the naturalistic stance abandons any notion that human beings are also constrained by historically and structurally objective forces, such as power, class and class interests, inequality, and ideology. For sure, insofar as such forces are viewed as constraining factors on human action, they temper the voluntarism that informs the naturalistic perspective, by introducing overriding deterministic elements into the analysis. However, the relationship between a view of man as, on the one hand, a self-willed purposive creature and, on the other, a creature determined by forces beyond his immediate control needs to be grasped dialectically. In short, a synthesis of the more fruitful dimensions of the interactionist position and of Marxist materialism would serve to transcend the limitations contained within the former perspective.

Symbolic interactionism lacks an awareness of historical concreteness

Where is the historical element in the interactionist framework? Precisely nowhere. Blumer, in his seminal essay entitled 'The Methodological Position of Symbolic Interactionism',[56] intimates that historical analysis is imperative to the perspective, but the comment is made as if by way of an afterthought, and then only in terms of the subjectivist methods he directs social scientist towards. Blumer argues:

> The other point is a reminder of the need to recognise that joint action is temporally linked with previous joint action. One shuts a major door to the understanding of joint action if one ignores this connection . . . The designations and interpretations through which people form and maintain their organised relations are always in degree a carry-over from their past. To ignore this carry-

over sets a genuine risk for the scholar. On this point the methodolgical posture of symbolic interactionism is to pay heed to the historical linkage of what is being studied.[57]

Although Blumer correctly berates organisational theorists and system analysts for ignoring a historical dimension to their work, it is precisely this very methodological criticism that may be levelled at the interactionists. Moreover the implications of following Blumer's prescription lie not in pursuing a historically materialist methodology, in which the objective forces of power interests and the social relationships of production are dialectically interlinked, but rather in understanding human action as a process, biography, and moral career of concrete human actors unaware fully of their location in the wider social structure or the implications of finding themselves acting in the context of specific socio-historical formations.

A fusion of Marxist historical materialism – by engaging in a Marxist historiography – with an application of interactionist premises to historical and contemporary date would permit investigators to transcend the bourgeois distinction between history and sociology as two unconnected disciplines, moving our enquiries to a higher plane.[58]

Symbolic interactionism is naive in its account of mutual typifications[59]

The tendency within the symbolic interactionist perspective is to regard the construction of social reality in terms of an infinite number of true definitions of interactive situations offered by actors engaged in conscious, purposive human action. Two consequences flow from the foregoing. Firstly, it makes for a relativist conception of human nature: what is held true for one person may not be true for another. Secondly, and more importantly, it anchors the analysis of social action, in the first and last instance, in the concrete human actor as the only faithful and true beholder of what constitutes social reality. This does not mean that the world is reduced to an indefinite number of unconnected definitions; quite the contrary, since the social nature of interaction results in actors constructing largely overlapping typifications of their immediate, tacit situations. But, in locating these mutual typifications within the consciousness of actors (subjective reality) and the structure of institutional arrangements (objective reality), the interactionist perspective fails to explain how one conception of social reality comes to dominate the social perspective of an individual or group of persons, given an inequitable social structure (in terms of power, wealth, classes and interests).

All this is not to deny the importance and value that mutual typifications have in our understanding of social reality. But are they sufficient for explaining social reality? Lichtman points to a Marxist methodology for overcoming this inherent limitation to the interactionist perspective. He argues:

> How is the meaningful interpretation of action constituted? Democratically? Hardly. *The channelling of interpreted meaning is class structured. It is formed through lived engagement in the predominant class-controlled institutions of the society.* What of the character of those institutions which more specifically pattern the development of socially shared meaning – mass media, schools, etc.? They too are under the predominant control of that class of men who exercise hegemony over the means of production, distribution, exchange and consumption upon which society vitally depends. The definition of activity, the shared description of an act and the very meaning of the function of acting, are largely shaped through the nature of productive power.[60]

Symbolic interactionism abandons the sense of human beings in struggle

On first appearances the claim by Lichtman that the interactionist perspective rejects any notion of men engaging in a struggle to overcome their immediate situation would appear incorrect. For, after all, I have indicated that the interactionist position grants man the capacity to act in a willed, meaningful and purposive way; he is not the passive victim of external exigencies, bending one way or another to forces beyond his control, but rather moulds them to his advantage.

How are we to reconcile, therefore, this latter claim with the criticism offered by Lichtman? A closer inspection of Lichtman's argument reveals the answer. Human activities become possible only through our belief in their possibility, but others remain beyond the limits of our consciousness, given the hegemonic control determined by the ownership of the means of production, communication, and education in a given class structure. As Lichtman concludes, 'this is the point that is totally ignored by symbolic interactionism'.[61]

Once again it is not a question of abandoning the advances of the interactionist view in favour of a Marxist methodology. Instead a synthesis of both paradigms is required, such that, if most people find it difficult or impossible most of the time to alter or control social institutions experienced as impenetrable, nevertheless the concrete means by which human beings can act to transcend this impenetrable reality become apparent in a revolutionary process.[62]

Symbolic interactionism tends to dissolve the concept of ideology or false consciousness

Consciousness and mind are central concepts for Mead's social philosophy. Blumer has spelt out the sociological implications of Mead's thought on these two concepts for symbolic interactionism;[63] only consciousness and mind from an interactionist standpoint are not rooted in the material mode of production or related to the historically specific forms of social relationships arising out of the mode of production. Instead human beings are said to 'possess minds and consciousness as original "givens", that they live in worlds of pre-existing and self-constituted objects, that their behaviour consists of responses to such objects, and that group life consists of the association of such reacting human organisms'.[64]

The standpoint of interactionism stresses that mind is a conscious active process; human behaviour is to be grasped through subjective intentionality. But human action cannot be simply equated with the interpretations and meaning imputed to it by actors. Neither can human action be regarded independently of its constitutive meanings. We need to go beyond the tension inherent in both these views. But how? We must capture the relationship between the specific importance of economic life, the predominantly historical function of social classes, and the notion of consciousness.[65] There is no scope here to examine in any detail the relevance of such a relationship, particularly in terms of how it transforms the idealistic stance of interactionism towards its own conception of human consciousness. Suffice it to say that the meaning that consciousness holds for historical materialism and symbolic interactionism reveals the limitations of the latter's perspective on the concept, especially since consciousness for the interactionists is held as having primacy over, and is disjointed from, the material infrastructure of human society. A full theory of social reality, premised on a dialectically materialist methodology, would not deny the influence of ideology or consciousness; furthermore it would combat 'every effort to separate them from the rest of concrete social life and to attribute to these factors an *autonomous* and *imminent* evolution with respect to what are customarily called infrastructures'.[66]

Having tentatively outlined the interconnections between consciousness and its material infrastructures, one must say a word as to the implications of a materialist conceptualisation of consciousness in terms of its distinction between false and true or potential consciousness, and the 'given' consciousness of the interactionist position. The materialist distinction between true and false consciousness is not made within the idealism of the interactionist framework. If consciousness is taken as 'given', then the conservative implications of W. I. Thomas' axiom that a situation is real if it is real in its consequences becomes apparent. But, as Taylor, Walton and Young have indicated,[67] it does not always follow that situations defined as real are necessarily real in their consequences, for we may come to realise certain definitions – emanating as they do from the dialectical relationship between conflicting material interests and consciousness – as false. The end result of such an appreciation is the possibility of man consciously seeking to transcend false definitions by struggling to overcome and replace them with a true definition. Goldmann draws our attention to this possibility in arguing for the centrality of the notion of potential consciousness as the principal instrument of scientific thinking in the human sciences. For Goldmann,

> *Man is defined by his possibilities*, by his tendency to enter into community with other men and to establish an equilibrium with nature. Authentic community and universal truth express these possibilities *over an extremely long historical period.* 'Class-for-itself' (as opposed to class-in-itself) and the maximum of potential consciousness express possibilities on the level of thought and action *within a given social structure.*[68]

Symbolic interactionism leaves us without a critical posture toward the present inhuman reality

This is the last of Lichtman's criticisms levelled at the interactionist standpoint. I have noted that much of deviancy and social control research after the Second World War embodies a critique of middle-range social control agencies, imputing to them, by virtue of their relative power in the control of deviant phenomena, a crimogenic impetus, unwittingly serving to stigmatise and sustain the deviant or criminal identity of persons coming within the orbit of correctional strategies and tactics (see pp. 193–202). Insofar as this critique is offered, the interactionists do develop a critical posture towards certain components of the control structure. However, interactionism stops short of a materialist critique of the social structure, taken as a whole, and within which the agencies of control, engaged as they are in deviancy management at a face-to-face level, do not constitute the locus of power and control within the total social structure.[69]

The above critique of the symbolic interactionist perspective offered by Lichtman is a substantive one, which cannot be ignored. Moreover, if Lichtman's critique is to be taken seriously, my application of the perspective to the skid row phenomenon and the analytical description that flowed from it limits the scope of this study.

Does it, though, altogether invalidate the work presented here? No, for every work of sociological research is itself located socially and historically within a specific intellectual climate. Earlier in this chapter I outlined the emergence of the new deviancy theory in the light of four major issues: the continuity between criminology and mainstream sociology, the significance of social control, the need for a naturalistic appreciation of the phenomena, and the political implications of studying deviance for the criminologist.

This study has been no exception. Work commenced on it early in 1971, by which time symposiums organised by the National Deviancy Conference in Britain had established a significant challenge to orthodox criminology. The Conference had successfully promoted and developed new deviancy theory to the point where crime, deviancy and social problems were being re-examined within the domain assumptions of this perspective.[70]

But the intellectual and political enthusiasm that both drew inspiration from, and gave theoretical coherence to, the activities of deviants during the late 1960s and 1970s began to wane. Lichtman's essay offers a useful checklist to explain some of the misgivings new deviancy theorists began to have for the theoretical and empirical work they were conducting. In practical and political terms the challenge that organised deviants, blacks, women, welfare claimants, prisoners and others were making on both sides of the Atlantic, needed to be grasped not in terms of expressive politics and an analysis of everyday life and subjective meanings: instead the historical and structural relationships of these groups to the dominant mode of production, the ideological hegemony of the ruling class, the role of the state and of law, were recognised as essential elements in an analysis that would take theory beyond the limitations of naturalism and a political critique of middle-range social control agents. Moreover the importance attached to the above politically marginal groupings (with the exception of women) by social theorists interested in the radical politics of the period was substantially blunted by the deepening crisis in capitalism during the mid-1970s.

These events and doubts, intellectually and politically, led to the emergence of an important debate among radical criminologists, a debate that adopted an imminent Marxist problematic over issues of crime, social control and law.[71] Marxist theorising and method were invoked by way of transcending the advances and limitations contained within the interactionist-oriented deviancy theory.

Now the debate in Britain surrounding the emergence of a Marxist criminology has proved to be complex and open-ended.[72] Indeed, the question has been posed by Hirst as to whether a Marxist criminology is possible in the first place.[73] He has argued that the objects of criminology and Marxism are incompatible. The object of study, conceptual structure and purpose of Marxism are, for Hirst, quite distinct from the paradigm put forward by British criminologists aspiring to a Marxist perspective. Firstly, the central object of study for Marxism is the capitalist mode of production. Secondly, the Marxist conceptual structure (the mode of production, class struggle, the state, ideology, etc.) specifies the objects of Marxist theory. Thirdly, the entire thrust of Marxism is in the direction of a specific purpose: the proletarian revolution and the overthrow of the bourgeois ruling class and its social order. For Hirst none of these elements are contained or are possible in a Marxist criminology.

But what exactly is the paradigm Hirst takes issue with? It is not easy to identify, since Hirst does not concretely specify which theorists in criminology he is directing his remarks at. But the debate has been with Taylor, Walton and Young, and therefore it coud be assumed that it is *The New Criminology* that in the first instance initiates the debate. The paradigm advanced in *The New Criminology* calls for 'the possibility of building links between the insights of interactionist theory, and other approaches sensitive to men's subjective world, and the theories of social structure implicit in orthodox marxism'.[74] The paradigm would include and distinguish between the role of the social structure in generating and sustaining the values and opportunities leading to crime, the social and psychological processes mediating between the social structure and the individual criminal, the interactionist context of the crime itself, and the concomitant social, psychological and structural aspects of societal reaction to crime and deviancy. The whole of this paradigm, of course, would be informed by a historical analysis; and the method of enquiry would be dialectical materialism. Here we have, then, a critique of criminological perspectives, including interactionism, closely resembling the synthesis of Marxism and interactionism advanced by Lichtman.

But subsequent to the debate between Hirst and Taylor, Walton and Young, the latter three authors have once more taken up the objects and purpose of a Marxist criminology in their essay 'Critical Criminology in Britain: review and prospects'.[75] Significantly there is a shift in emphasis in this essay compared with the paradigm developed in *The New Criminology*. Firstly, the interactionist-oriented dimensions they wished to see retained and incorporated are notable by their absence. It is not so much that the notion of consciousness disappears from their analytical framework, but that it takes on a more explicitly Marxist, not interactionist, articulation. In the interactionist perspective consciousness is free-flowing and given. On the other hand, for Marxism, consciousness is not given but originates from, and is contained within, the material production of society. Secondly, the balance achieved in *The New Criminology* in terms of paying equal attention to deviancy and social control at both social and psychological levels of explanation is replaced by a Marxist analysis of social control only – more specifically, by an analysis of law. The object of study becomes the relationship between law, its creation and application, the state, and the material base of society. The deviant actor, either individually or collectively, as constituted within the interactionist perspective, disappears from the analysis. Finally, the very purpose of a Marxist criminology becomes much more fully articulated in 'Critical Criminology in Britain', particularly in terms of its relevance for practical political action.

The question, then, remains: how would a study of vagrancy and alcoholism differ from that offered above, given the debates surrounding attempts to develop a Marxist criminology? The answer to a large extent is determined by the use of concepts and objects of analysis specified by a Marxist criminology, assuming that such a criminology is possible. Evidently greater attention would be given to the social, political and economic forces behind the creation and implementation of laws on vagrancy and drunkenness, the development of social policy directed at homelessness and destitution, and the material and ideological reproduction of a class of permanently property-less, powerless, and unemployed men. The role of the welfare state in meeting problems of vagrancy and destitution would be more central to the analysis. Conversely, the detailed attention to the everyday practices of vagrants and social control agents, demanded by the interactionist stance, would not constitute an important component of the analysis, although the relationship between subcultural formations and class formations would need to be explored. The empirical object of analysis – vagrancy and alcoholism – would be informed by a materialist method, one stressing the necessity to define the relationship between the dominant mode of production, the state, and ideology.

A Marxist criminology would seek to explain why capitalism generates vagrancy and alcoholism and how it attempts to come to terms with it. It is difficult to specify with any certainty what questions a criminologist aspiring to a Marxist position would focus on, given a particular area of deviancy. But the groundwork has been laid to explore a Marxist problematic as a potentially fruitful theoretical and methodological framework transcending the radically chic concerns of interactionist deviancy theory.

Notes and References

Chapter 1

1. D. Matza, 'The Disreputable Poor', in R. Bendix and S. M. Lipset (eds), *Class, Status and Power* (London: Routledge & Kegan Paul, 1953) pp. 289–302.
2. In his essay Matza does not refer specifically to skid row but tends to focus on disreputable poverty among families. However, the dimensions by which he identifies disreputable poverty are clearly applicable to the skid row phenomenon. Indeed, in writing about Irish immigration to Britain and the USA and the process of recruitment to disreputable poverty he comes very close to focusing on skid row poverty.
3. Peterson and Maxwell write: 'Even though the term Skid Row is widely used, it is derived from Skid Road, a term which originated in Seattle, Washington, where a homeless man area developed alongside a prominent skid road – a logging skid – in early Seattle days'. W. J. Peterson and M. A. Maxwell, 'The Skid Road Wino', *Social Problems*, no. 5, 1958, footnote on p. 308. Wallace also specifies this origin of the name. See Samuel E. Wallace, *Skid Row as a Way of Life* (Totowa, N.J.: Bedminster Press, 1958) p. 18. Bahr has a somewhat different account: '. . . skid row is an American invention. It is one century old, and its place of birth is clearly recorded. Jerry McAuley . . . began his Water Street Mission in New York City in October 1872. A year later the Reverend John Dooley opened his first cheap Bowery lodging house. With the appearance of these two dominant institutions, the gospel mission and the lodging house, skid row was born.' H. M. Bahr, *Skid Row: an*

Introduction to Disaffiliation (New York: Oxford University Press, 1973) pp. 31–2.

4. Wallace, *Skid Row as a Way of Life*, p. 13.
5. G. Edwards, A. Hawker, V. Williamson and C. Hensman, 'London's Skid Row', *The Lancet*, 29 January 1966, p. 249.
6. D. Matza, *Becoming Deviant* (Englewood Cliffs, N. J.: Prentice Hall, 1969) p. 26.
7. K. Allsop, *Hard Travellin'* (Harmondsworth: Penguin, 1973) p. 6.
8. Wallace, *Skid Row as a Way of Life*, p. 143.
9. Agencies concerned with less visible forms of alcoholism – alcoholics who retain a permanent address, steady employment, and close contacts with their families – are often at pains to defuse the public stereotype of the alcoholic as a 'vagrant drunk'.
10. It is notoriously difficult to assess accurately the total homeless single population. All surveys, whether official or unofficial, are open to criticism as to the criteria employed to include or exclude certain categories and institutions in census counts. For a trenchant critique of an unofficial single homeless person survey carried out by a voluntary agency see P. Beresford, 'Without a Home', *New Society*, no. 564, 26 July 1973, pp. 212–13. The 1965 official National Assistance Board Survey has been criticised for excluding hospitals and, in particular, prisons from its survey, and for failing to assess adequately the extent of the most difficult category to enumerate, namely persons sleeping rough. NAB, *Homeless Single Persons* (London: HMSO, 1966). The Home Office, in its report *Habitual Drunken Offenders*, attempted to assess the extent of the skid row alcoholic problem while at the same time being aware of the gaps and deficiencies in the material available. The report tentatively accepted that there are close on 350,000 alcoholics in England and Wales, 13,500 single homeless persons on skid row, and that habitual drunken offenders total no more than 5000 individuals. Home Office Report, *Homeless Single Persons*, p. 29, but in particular see Chapter 4, pp. 21–31, as to how these figures were arrived at.
11. There are numerous surveys on skid row men. For a comprehensive bibliography see H. M. Bahr (ed.), *Disaffiliated Man: Essays and Bibliography on Skid Row, Vagrancy, and Outsiders* (University of Toronto Press, 1970).
12. In her incisive study on the treatment of American skid row

alcoholics Wiseman noted that the terms 'chronic drunken offender', 'problem drinker', and 'alcoholic' are applied interchangeably by both laymen and professionals despite the very real differences in each of the definitions. J. P. Wiseman, *Stations of the Lost: the treatment of the Skid Row Alcoholics* (Englewood Cliffs, N.J.: Prentice Hall, 1971) p. xvii. In the present study 'skid row alcoholic', 'habitual drunken offender', 'vagrant alcoholic', 'public inebriate', 'homeless alcoholic' and 'alcoholic dosser' are used synonymously.

13. B. Harrison, *Drink and the Victorians: the Temperance Question in England, 1815–1872* (London: Faber & Faber, 1971) pp. 21–2.
14. G. S. Jones, *Outcast London* (London: Oxford University Press, 1971) p. 11.
15. General W. Booth, *In Darkest England and The Way Out* (London: Salvation Army, 1890) p. 24.
16. Booth, ibid., p. 93, cited in Jones, *Outcast London* footnote 20, p. 311.
17. Harrison, *Drink and the Victorians*, p. 327.
18. Two reformatories under the state, and thirteen under local authorities or in conjunction with voluntary bodies, were established as a result of this Act.
19. H. Levy, *Drink: An Economic and Social Study* (London: Routledge & Kegan Paul, 1951) p. 156.
20. However, with social workers and psychiatrists working in the field, the fact that a man is drunk, or is seen drinking on skid row, is often automatically taken to be evidence that he is an alcoholic.
21. P. Halmos, *The Faith of the Counsellors* (London: Constable, 1965) p. 2.
22. Home Office Working Party Report, *Habitual Drunken Offenders* (London: HMSO, 1971).
23. Ibid., especially Chapters 10, 12, 14, 15 and 18.
24. Ibid., p. 192.
25. Ibid., p. 187.
26. Ibid., pp. 188–9.
27. Matza, *Becoming Deviant*, p. 289.

Chapter 2

1. Drunkenness is probably as old as mankind. But the term

'habitual drunkard' is only found for the first time in English law in what is a relatively recent statute, the Habitual Drunkards Act of 1879.

2. There are, of course, a number of literary and journalistic accounts of homelessness among single persons. See, for example, Philip O'Connor, *Britain in the Sixties: Vagrancy* (Harmondsworth: Penguin, 1965); Jeremy Sandford, *Down and Out in Britain* (London: Peter Owen, 1971); Robin Page, *Down Among the Dossers* (London: Dennis Poynter, 1973); Jeremy Sandford in his *Edna, the Inebriate Woman* (London: Pan, 1971) writes specifically about an alcoholic vagrant.

3. NAB, *Homeless Single Persons* (London: HMSO, 1966) pp. 175–7.

4. Home Office Working Party Report, *Habitual Drunken Offenders* (London: HMSO, 1971) p. 39.

5. However, programmes promised on this strategy have only been successful in shifting the problem to other locales; new skid row pockets emerge as more traditional areas are razed to the ground. Presumably this trend may eventually produce a situation similar to that in Britain, where no clearly identifiable skid row areas exist. But, as I have argued above, this does not mean the disappearance of skid row.

6. Donald J. Bogue, *Skid Row in American Cities* (University of Chicago Press, 1963) pp. 404–5.

7. Ibid., p. 406.

8. David J. Pittman and C. Wayne Gordon, *The Revolving Door: a Study of the Chronic Police Case Inebriate* (Glencoe: Free Press, 1958). The authors write: 'By undersocialisation we mean that the person is characterised by limited participation in the primary groups which are necessary to personality formation, by minimum participation in social activities, and by inadequate opportunities for sharing experiences with others. His life history is one that has been and continues to be deficient in membership in those associations of sharing that are found in the family of orientation and procreation, in the peer groups that stretch from pre-adolescence to old age, and in community activities' (p. 10). Fundamentally the image presented by Pittman and Gordon is of the skid row alcoholic as socially isolated and inadequate, not only before he arrives on skid row, but also once he is on it. Furthermore the alcoholic is portrayed as the passive victim of

socio-psychological forces beyond his control. As I argue in Chapters 3 to 6, an inside view of the social organisation of skid row reveals otherwise.

9. See, in particular, Robert Straus, 'Alcohol and the Homeless Man', *Quarterly Journal of Studies on Alcohol*, vol. 7, December 1946, pp. 360–404; Howard M. Bahr, 'Homelessness, disaffiliation, and retreatism', in Bahr, *Disaffiliated Man: Essays and Bibliography on Skid Row, Vagrancy, and Outsiders* (University of Toronto Press, 1970); Robert K. Merton, *Social Theory and Social Structure*, (New York: Free Press, 1965) pp. 121–94.

10. See especially, Nels Anderson, *The Hobo: the Sociology of the Homeless Man* (University of Chicago Press, 1923); Samuel E. Wallace, *Skid Row as a Way of Life* (Totowa, N.J: Bedminster Press, 1958); and James P. Spradley, *You Owe Yourself a Drunk: an Ethnography of Urban Nomads*, (Boston: Little Brown, 1970).

11. The limited literature on American skid row bottle gangs and tavern culture makes this point. For example, see James F. Rooney, 'Group Processes among Skid Row Winos', *Quarterly Journal of Studies on Alcohol*, vol. 22, September 1961, pp. 444–60; Joan K. Jackson and Ralph Connor, 'The Skid Road Alcoholic', *Quarterly Journal of Studies on Alcohol*, vol. 14, September 1953, pp. 468–86; W. Jack Peterson and Milton A. Maxwell, 'The Skid Row Wino', *Social Problems*, no. 5, 1958, pp. 308–16; Earl Rubington, 'The Bottle Gang', *Quarterly Journal of Studies on Alcohol*, vol. 29, December 1968, pp. 943–55; and Peter Archard, 'Bottle Gangs and Drinking Schools: the Social Organisations of Drinking on Skid Row', unpublished paper delivered to the 15th National Deviancy Conference, York, Summer 1973, for accounts of street drinking. Matthew P. Dumont, 'Tavern Culture, the Sustenance of Homeless Men', *American Journal of Orthopsychiatry*, vol. 37, October 1967, pp. 938–45, illustrates the point where bar drinking is concerned.

12. Raymond T. Nimmer, *Two Million Unnecessary Arrests: Removing a Social Service Concern from the Criminal Justice System* (Chicago: American Bar Foundation, 1971); Jacqueline P. Wiseman, *Stations of the Lost: the Treatment of the Skid Row Alcoholics* (Englewood Cliffs, N.J.: Prentice Hall, 1971).

13. Nimmer, *Two Million Unnecessary Arrests*, p. 6.

14. Ibid., p. 154.

15. For an exposition of the concept of social margin in Wiseman see *Stations of the Lost*, pp. 223–6.

16. Ibid., p. 226.

17. In reality definitions of homelessness and alcoholism as a social problem and typifications of homeless alcoholics are closely intermeshed. However, for analytical purposes the two may be separated.

18. The 'crisis' of accommodation is seasonal. The immediate issue is most apparent during the winter months when hostels and common lodging houses are filled to capacity and the dangers of exposure to cold nights are highest for those sleeping rough. Thus, not atypically, the organisation 'Crisis at Christmas' seeks to provide crash emergency shelter and food by opening disused churches.

19. All the quotations used in this report that are not acknowledged in the notes were collected by the author during fieldwork. Other quotations, including those taken from original documents, are acknowledged.

20. Letter issued by CHAR (Campaign for the Homeless and Rootless), an umbrella charity, to some of its constituent members, on 25 October 1973.

21. Howard M. Bahr, *Skid Row: an introduction to Disaffiliation*, (New York: Oxford University Press, 1973) p. 41.

22. Part of a letter entitled ' "Cesspit of Human Decay" Worsens' in *South London Press*, 1 June 1973, p. 14. See also 'Drinkers drive out old folk', *South London Press*, 13 October 1972, p. 12.

23. See, for example, 'Tramps in park campaign begins', *South London Press*, 6 October 1972, p. 4; 'Empty flats a draw for meths gangs', *Evening Standard*, 1 May 1971, p. 12; 'Publican in protest over down-and-outs', *South London Press*, 12 January 1973, p. 7.

24. Wiseman, *Stations of the Lost*, p. xvi.

25. P. Willis, 'Popular Music and Youth Cultures in Birmingham', unpublished PhD Thesis, Centre for Contemporary Cultural Studies, University of Birmingham, 1973, pp. 273–4.

26. Ibid., p. 309.

27. See pp. 64–6 and note 8 on p. 249 for status differences among different types of drinkers on skid row.

28. Statistically, there are very few women alcoholics in relation to the male population on skid row. Skid row is almost exclusively a male phenomenon. The few female alcoholics that are homeless

drink alone or join male drinking groups. However, the presence of a woman among men drinking on skid row is universally criticised by them, usually along the lines that they cause trouble and fail to participate fully in drinking schools by 'working' (i.e. begging, thieving) for their share of drink.

Chapter 3

1. As I have already argued in Chapter 1, the meanings and definitions attached to skid row by homeless alcoholics can only be properly understood from a sociological standpoint by contrasting them with the ideology and control practices of professionals.
2. Samuel T. Wallace, *Skid Row as a Way of Life* (Totowa, N.J.: Bedminster Press, 1958) pp. 156–60.
3. Food, clothing and sexual relationships are the other basic needs human beings find necessary to satisfy. Both food and clothes are often provided free to homeless men by charitable hand-out organisations. Food is bought from cheap cafés, fish and chip shops, streetside food stalls, or in common lodging house canteens. Some men scavenge for food from litter bins or manage to pick up left-overs at railway station cafeterias and tea-stalls. If the clothing of an homeless man is in an unsalvageable condition when he arrives in prison, then he will be kitted out on discharge. As to sexual relationships, since skid row is almost exclusively a male domain heterosexual union is rare, although not entirely unknown. This raises the question of the incidence of homosexuality among homeless alcoholics. Informants pointed out that it is rare for alcoholics to establish active homosexual relationships, although once again they are not unknown. In fact, alcohol consumed in large quantities acts as a depressant and diminishes sexual drive.
4. J. P. Wiseman, *Stations of the Lost: the Treatment of the Skid Row Alcoholics* (Englewood Cliffs, N.J.: Prentice Hall, 1971) p. 27.
5. The relationship between specific survival strategies and the manipulation of the environment is to some degree dependent on which institutions are created by broad social developments in particular societies. Thus, for example, the development of

privatised medical care in the United States is exploited by skid row alcoholics insofar as they are able to sell their blood to private blood banks. In many American skid row areas 'walk-in' donors are attracted by advertisements announcing that they will be paid $5 per pint of blood. This opportunity, of course, is not available to homeless men in Britain. See Richard M. Titmuss, *The Gift Relationship* (London: George Allen & Unwin, 1970) pp. 113–18.

6. Some street drinkers are heavily criticised for their apparent unwillingness to do any work for their drink. These men tend to be dependent on others for alcohol and are regarded (by men who, when not actually drinking, are constantly 'on the move' for the next bottle) as not being 'real alcoholics'.

7. Wiseman, *Stations of the Lost*, p. 31. Among the statements by informants she quotes to illustrate this assertion are the following: 'I always try to get a man with a woman. Men hate to look like cheapskates to a woman companion'; 'I catch them coming up from the commuter stations. They are in a hurry and often give me something to get away from me'; Women alone are good bets. They get so nervous' (p. 31).

8. An exception to this general rule is found in a begging technique that does provide a service, namely busking. Some derelict alcoholics earn their drinking money by singing or playing an easily portable musical instrument, such as an harmonica.

9. Four of Titmuss' propositions, numbers 3, 8, 9 and 10, cannot be strictly adapted to the begging situation. See Titmuss, *The Gift Relationship*, p. 74.

10. However, one informant explained: 'A good beggar does not ask for the price of a cup of tea – he knows he'll only get a few coppers. Instead he will ask for the price of a drink and get three bob.'

11. A variety of reasons were offered by men admitting to being unable to beg. Either they have not the patience or skill, cannot tolerate the frequent refusals inherent in begging from strangers, or claim the whole process to be below their pride and dignity.

12. On 19 September 1973 *The Guardian* reported that a man had been sentenced to a month's imprisonment for begging a cigarette from another man. The magistrate ruled that a cigarette came under the legal definition of 'alms'. Of course, it was not the asking for a cigarette that led to arrest and conviction so much as

the fact that the defendant was a skid row man well known to the police and court.

13. Titmuss, *The Gift Relationship*, p. 210.

14. A group of alcoholics interviewed in prison confirmed that it was possible to do this but added that it was rare for men to carry this plan out and then it was only confined to alcoholics who drank near the prison. The proximity of the prison made it an easy journey for the man effecting the release of his drinking companion.

15. A strikingly similar account of face-to-face encounters between homeless men and beneficiaries in an American skid row institution appears in Stanley K. Henshaw, *Camp La Guardia: a Voluntary Total Institution for Homeless Men* (New York Bureau of Applied Social Research, Columbia University, 1968) pp. 153–9. Henshaw states: 'Frequently the interview assumes the tone of a cross-examination in which the client tries to justify himself and the interviewer attempts to force some kind of admission or catch him in a contradiction. Relations . . . are abrasive and sometimes hostile.' Quoted in H. M. Bahr, *Skid Row: an Introduction to Disaffiliation* (New York: Oxford University Press, 1973) p. 48.

16. I am heavily indebted to Gareth Stedman Jones' brilliant study of London's casual labour problem and the reaction to it during the last four decades of the nineteenth century for the brief introduction to casual work in this report. Gareth Stedman Jones, *Outcast London* (London: Oxford University Press, 1971).

17. A methodological error might be inbuilt into my statement that 'casual work [today] is taken up by single homeless men'. Obviously this conclusion would be arrived at if a study were made of the occupations taken up by men in common lodging houses, etc. Should the total structure and extent of casual and seasonal work be the departing point for any enquiry, whether it be in London or nationwide, the social composition of the labour force would probably include a greater proportion of home-based family men. I am unaware of the existence of any such study.

18. Stedman Jones, *Outcast London*, Chapter 4, especially pp. 87–91.

19. One of the institutions that features prominently in some studies of American skid rows is the 'spot-job' labour exchange. In

London casual workers for the hotel industry and for demolition or construction sites can also be obtained through employment agencies catering for single homeless men, but generally speaking in these occupations, and in market work, knowledge of these jobs is obtained through word-of-mouth, by turning up at places where 'gangs' of casual labourers are picked up and transported to construction sites, or by hanging around busy markets. Furthermore, during fieldwork I witnessed 'gangers' actively recruiting casual labourers in both a lodging house and in a skid row pub. For a dissertation on casual work in a central London market see Peter Phillimore, 'A Dosser's World: a Study of Casual Workers in Spitalfields', unpublished MA thesis, Dept of Anthropology, University of Edinburgh, 1972.

20. Treatment strategies towards the skid row alcoholic are dealt with at greater length in Chapters 4–6.
21. James P. Spradley, *You Owe Yourself a Drunk: an Ethnography of Urban Nomads* (Boston: Little Brown, 1970) p. 106.
22. The bed occupancy rates in common lodging houses, cheap commercial hotels, reception centres and rehabilitation hostels rise to the maximum possible during the winter months, but inevitably a proportion of men remain sleeping out. This shortage of beds cannot be exclusively attributed to inclement weather. During the autumn and winter months migrant workers return to London after having worked in seasonal occupations, helping to staff seaside holiday camps and facilities or after harvesting fruit and vegetables. The closure of lodging house has also created greater pressure on the remaining skid row establishments.
23. Common lodging houses may be owned and run either by the Salvation Army, Church Army, local public authority, or private enterprise. In official terms the first two organisations are in the rehabilitation business but since there is very little evidence of any organised attempt to rehabilitate alcoholics resident in common lodging houses, then it is fair to categorise these facilities as merely providing shelter. Public authority and private enterprise owned facilities do not pretend to offer a treatment service to the alcoholic.
24. NAB, *Homeless Single Persons* (London: HMSO, 1966) p. 17.
25. Bahr, *Skid Row: an Introduction to Disaffiliation*, p. 123. It is not

always the case that cubicles are covered with wire netting to protect residents from being robbed.

26. Ibid., p. 127. For a full description of a British common lodging house and its inmates see M. Turner, *Forgotten Men* (London: National Council of Social Service, 1960).

27. Government reception centres are compelled by the National Assistance Act, 1948, Section 17(1), 'to make provision whereby persons without a settled way of living may be influenced to lead more settled lives' and to 'provide and maintain centres . . . for the temporary board and lodging of such persons'. London's Camberwell Reception Centre, the largest in Britain, has over 900 beds. The centre is divided into two parts. The first houses persons who book in daily and is known as Casual; unless destitute, men are not officially allowed to book in here. The second, known as Residence, is for men who mostly live and work in the centre; the orientation in this department is towards rehabilitation. The views expressed in this report almost entirely refer to the conditions in Casual.

Chapter 4

1. Neil Kessel and Henry Walton, *Alcoholism* (Harmondsworth: Penguin, 1965).

2. The social reaction to drinking and drunkenness is, of course, applied differentially according to who is doing the drinking and who is defining it as normal or deviant. Some of the variables which determine how drinking is defined are the time and place of consumption; the status of the drinker in terms of his age, class, occupational status and religion; and, finally, the moral, social and economic status and authority of the person or institution imposing the sanctions.

3. London County Council, 'Report on Crude Spirit Drinking', unpublished, London 1965, pp. 3 and 5.

4. Donald J. Bogue, *Skid Row in American Cities* (University of Chicago Press, 1963) p. 230.

5. W. J. Peterson and M. A. Maxwell, 'The Skid Row Wino', *Social Problems*, no. 5, 1958; and Joan K. Jackson and Ralph Connor, 'The Skid Road Alcoholic', *Quarterly Journal of Studies on Alcohol*, vol. 14, September 1953, pp. 468–86.

6. Jackson and Connor, 'The Skid Road Alcoholic', p. 473.
7. Indigenous term applied to methylated spirits and surgical spirits.
8. As we have noted, the status network alcoholics on skid row construct is not exclusively confined to drinking patterns (see pp. 64–5 above). The skid row institutions men make use of and the survival skills they develop constitute a basis by which homeless men judge their own behaviour and that of others. Nels Anderson also remarked on the status antagonisms existing on skid row and how different activities are viewed as justification for holding others in low esteem. He writes: 'The antagonisms between beggars and peddlers are very keen. The man who carries a permit to peddle has no respect for the individual who merely begs. Nevertheless, some peddlers, when business is slow, themselves turn beggars. On the other hand, the man who begs professes to consider himself far more respectable than the peddler who uses his licence as an excuse to get money . . . These antagonisms are evidence of a struggle for status. When a peddler denounces the beggars he is trying to justify himself. His philosophy . . . is an attempt to justify his vocation. The same is true of plain beggars. Most of them are able to justify their means of "getting by".' Nels Anderson, *The Hobo*, (University of Chicago Press, 1923) p. 50.
9. Peterson and Maxwell, 'The Skid Row Wino', p. 316.
10. James F. Rooney, 'Group Processes among Skid Row Winos', *Quarterly Journal of Studies on Alcohol*, vol. 22, September 1961, pp. 444–60.
11. Ibid., p. 454.
12. Earl Rubington, 'The Bottle Gang', *Quarterly Journal of Studies on Alcohol*, vol. 29, December 1968, pp. 943–55.
13. Ibid., p. 944.
14. Parks, streets and open spaces are the most obvious places where drinking schools congregate. Other locales used for drinking during fieldwork were tube stations, derelict buildings, public toilets, betting shops and social security offices, in soup kitchens and emergency shelters, and in different parts of common lodging houses. In addition, the following places were reported by informants: in reception centres, car parks, cemeteries and in pedestrian subways. Police surveillance is most intense in places like parks and streets.

15. The failure of one alcoholic to return to the drinking school I participated in resulted in the remaining three members discussing the matter for over an hour, during which the act was roundly condemned and the infractor threatened with violence should he ever again make an appearance.

16. H. M. Bahr, *Skid Row: an Introduction to Disaffiliation*, (New York: Oxford University Press, 1973) p. 156.

17. Ibid., p. 158.

18. During fieldwork some alcoholics were heard to remark 'He's a good man – he's a townie of mine'. Friendship among drinking school members is made evident in numerous ways. For example, chronically debilitated members are not expected to beg, work for their drink, or make runs to the off-licence, but are 'carried' by those who are more able and stronger, and are sometimes taken to hospitals or shelters if their debility warrants it. Knowledge of good 'skippers' is shared among friends but is denied to strangers. Moreover friendships developed on skid row are maintained by men who find themselves in correctional and rehabilitation institutions.

19. As far as I can establish there is no reported research on the structure and behaviour of drinking schools and bottle gangs that organise their drinking around non-ethyl alcohol. The material reported here is derived from three main sources: informal interviews with a veteran but recovered methylated spirits drinker, interviews with two recovered cheap wine drinkers, and on comments and observations recorded during fieldwork.

20. 'Jake' or 'jack' refers both to methylated spirits and surgical spirits. On the whole jake drinkers will drink either type of spirit but some men are said to prefer surgical spirits to meths because it is stronger and cleaner. Surgical spirit is referred to as 'surge' or 'clear'; methylated spirit as 'meths' or 'bluey'. Other terms by which alcoholics refer to methylated and surgical spirits are 'queer stuff' and 'the hard stuff'.

21. Occasional drinkers of jake often complain that 'boxed up' (mixed) wine and crude spirits offered them by seasoned jake drinkers is 'too heavy' (too strong).

22. Some crude spirit drinkers are 'loners', but these tend to be the exception.

23. The use of methylated spirits is often perceived as a symptom of

individuals having reached a stage of chronic alcoholism characterised by physical and mental breakdown. See Kessel and Walton, *Alcoholism*, Chapter 8, pp. 92–106.

24. As has been already pointed out skid row alcoholics sometimes congregate in gangs and drink in places where they manage to escape the gaze of police patrols. However, this does not mean that they totally avoid the authority of other skid row social control agents. Informants explained that they drank with others in common lodging houses as part of a strategy to avoid police detection but pointed out that they were often barred from the premises by porters and other personnel. During fieldwork in a common lodging house I observed a seven-man drinking school being ejected from the dining-room by a staff member with the assistance of three police officers. On this occasion none of the men were drinking or drunk, although on a number of previous occasions I observed this school pool its resources and drink on the premises.

25. A. Stinchcombe, 'Institutions of Privacy in the Determination of Police Administrative Practice', *American Journal of Sociology*, vol. 69, 1963, pp. 151–2.

26. The most frequently reported threat is one where police inform an individual that his continued presence in a particular area will result in his arrest and prosecution on a charge of begging or 'sus', viz., being a suspected person. Harassment usually consists of simply moving men on but occasionally this is coupled by patrolmen emptying the contents of bottles over the ground. All skid row men at some time have been arrested on a charge of drunkenness without being drunk or even having had a drink, especially during concerted drives by the police to clear parks, etc., of vagrants, drunks and other undesirables. As to police violence, this is much less frequent. During 15 months' fieldwork not one incident of violence was observed. Derelict alcoholics, particularly men who have been on skid row for years, generally accept arrest passively. The police are aware that habitual drunken offenders are on the whole not aggressive men. Consequently the arrest procedure is marked by a sense of inevitability and familiarity. Often the police and alcoholic know each other, and may even be on first name terms. This does not mean there is an absence of antipathy between the police and homeless alcoholic; the latter hold little, if any, respect for

officers of the law. Indeed, some men report being kicked, punched and generally manhandled by police officers.

27. Rubington, 'The Bottle Gang', p. 948.

28. Bogue, *Skid Row in American Cities*, p. 169–70. Bogue concludes that '. . . *any conception of Skid Row as a tightly knit, well-integrated and organised community where most of the residents interact freely and have a common "subculture" and tradition is a complete myth*' (Bogue's emphasis, p. 169).

Chapter 5

1. Spradley, in his anthropological study of the skid row drunk, constructs his explanation of the phenomenon around the thesis that repeated arrest, trial and jailing provides the opportunity for public drunks to learn how to survive and that consequently their deviant identity essentially derives from the never-ending process of legal control. See J. P. Spradley, *You Owe Yourself a Drunk: an Ethnography of Urban Nomads* (Boston: Little Brown, 1970).

2. The number of habitual drunken offenders who are detained in prison either as a consequence of a direct sentence or for failure to pay a fine is small relative to the total number of drunkenness offenders being found guilty in court.

3. B. C. Hollister, 'Alcoholics and Public Drunkenness: the Emerging Retreat from Punishment', *Crime and Delinquency*, 16 July 1970, p. 242, quoted in H. M. Bahr, *Skid Row: an Introduction to Disaffiliation* (New York: Oxford University Press, 1973) pp. 226–7.

4. Some of these issues are touched upon in Chapter 1 (see p. 11). For a detailed historical account of the passing of the 1872 Licencing Act see B. Harrison, *Drink and the Victorians: the Temperance Question in England, 1815–1872* (London: Faber & Faber, 1971) pp. 271–6 especially.

5. Home Office Working Party Report, *Habtual Drunken Offenders* (London: HMSO, 1971) p. 20.

6. Ibid., pp. 125–33.

7. Ibid., pp. 16–18.

8. E. Bittner, 'The Police on Skid Row: a Study of Peace-Keeping', *American Sociological Review*, vol. 32, no. 5, 1967, pp. 699–715.

9. Ibid., p. 713.

10. It is interesting to note that the arrests of vagrants and drunks are officially regarded as 'non-quality' arrests by the police in St Louis, Missouri, while those of serious offenders against the law, i.e. major criminals, are defined as 'quality' arrests. See R. T. Nimmer, 'St. Louis Diagnostic and Detoxification Centre: an Experiment in Non-Criminal Processing of Public Intoxicants', *Washington University Law Quarterly*, no. 1, 1970.

11. My arrival in one skid row area in London for the purpose of carrying out fieldwork was almost immediately checked out by the local police. I was stopped by a patrol car and interviewed by three policemen. My identity, occupation and address were asked of me. Pointing out that I was both homeless and jobless, the police proceeded to frisk me. A large bunch of office keys I had accidentally brought with me forced me to reveal my true identity. On accepting the purpose of my presence in the area, the police informed me that as a matter of routine they checked out on any new faces in the area who did not appear to be going about some kind of legitimate business.

12. On one occasion I was arrested together with five other members of a drinking school as a result of a sudden police swoop on a park frequented by skid row alcoholics. Only one alcoholic among us could be said to have been drunk to any degree.

13. It is, of course, notoriously difficult to confirm that skid row men are assaulted by the police, although all seasoned down-and-out alcoholics will recount occasions when they actually experienced or witnessed incidents of this nature. However, during fieldwork in one police station, a sergeant replied when asked directly whether drunks were physically abused: 'You remember that young drunk that several of my men were holding down on the floor? Well, if you hadn't been around in the station more than likely one of the men would have smacked him one. You've got to do it, if not they'll hit you first.' At a later stage in my conversation with the same sergeant he admitted that earlier in his career, when he was a patrolman in another area frequented by down-and-outs, he took part in harassing homeless men. The sergeant put it this way: 'From time to time we'd go out on the beat and have fun and games with the "methers" [methylated spirit drinkers].'

14. However, just as the police build up a body of knowledge about individuals frequenting the area they patrol, so veteran alco-

holics come to know specific policemen sufficiently well to be able to predict the particular stance the policeman will take towards them.

15. The number of offences of drunkenness proved in England and Wales between 1969 and 1973 were as follows:

Year	Offences of drunkenness proved
1969	80,502
1970	82,374
1971	86,735
1972	90,198
1973	99,274

16. 'Habitual' is usually taken to mean three or more offences in one year. See Home Office Working Party Report, *Habitual Drunken Offenders*, pp. 24–6, especially paragraph 4.17.

17. Ibid., pp. 24–6.

18. J. P. Wiseman, *Stations of the Lost: the Treatment of Skid Row Alcoholics* (Englewood Cliffs, N.J.: Prentice Hall, 1971) pp. 86–100.

19. Of the total number of persons found guilty for drunkenness offences each year, only about 4 per cent receive terms of imprisonment. Of this proportion, most receptions into prison arise out of non-payment of fines. A smaller number are jailed directly without the option of a fine, i.e. for being 'drunk and disorderly' or 'drunk and indecent'.

20. See, for example, *The Magistrate* (London: Magistrates' Association, December 1973) and the *Annual Report of the London Magistrates' Association, 1971* (London Magistrates' Association) pp. 3–4.

21. One magistrate put it this way: 'I think we have to accept the reality of the situation as it is and administer justice within the limitations of the present system. Prison offers the man a place to clean up and dry out – it might not be the right place but it is the logical conclusion to arrive at if there are no alternative facilities within the community.'

22. Drunkenness offences are only misdemeanours, which the authorities consider of minor importance. At the police station checks are made with the central Criminal Records Office as to whether

the person arrested has a criminal record and whether he is wanted for any outstanding charges. However, drunkenness offences are not recorded at the Criminal Records Office. Consequently drunken offenders with outstanding drunk charges incurred in a police and court area other than in the one they are being held at are not likely to be detained on the basis of such charges.

23. E. Goffman, *Asylums* (Harmondsworth: Penguin, 1968) pp. 139–40.

24. R. F. Sparks, *Local Prisons: the Crisis of the English Penal System* (London: Heinemann, 1971) p. 90.

25. A reflection of the type of inmate with which Pentonville is identified was symbolically represented in a roughly sketched coat-of-arms cellotaped on a wall in the Reception showers. A prison key, a cigarette butt, and an unkempt looking prisoner looking through the bars of his cell window were graphically illustrated on the coat-of-arms, while underneath were written the words, 'PENTONVILLE – THE DOSSERS RETREAT'.

26. Sometimes men may even spend less than 7 days in prison, either because someone on the outside will pay their outstanding fine or, more likely, because the limited cash an inmate may have on entry into prison is automatically taken in lieu of the outstanding proportion of an unpaid fine. For example, an inmate sentenced to a fine of £10 or 14 days, but who has £5 on him when he arrives in prison, will be discharged at the end of his first week.

27. An aerosol spray for sweetening the air is kept handy for use by the Officers in Reception.

28. The fact that skid row alcoholics are occupationally unskilled, physically unfit, and are in for periods too short to do semi-skilled work, means that Reception allocates them to jobs which make no demands on their physical and intellectual capabilities. Thus for the most part homeless men work in the 'Rag Room' (officially known as Light Textiles, where old rags are sorted out) or are alloted menial work, such as cleaning.

29. A. Arnold, 'Alcoholism in Prison: Pentonville' in T. Cook, D. Gath and C. Hensman (eds), *The Drunkenness Offence* (London: Pergamon, 1969) pp. 151–2.

30. A. Arnold, 'Alcoholism in Prison: Pentonville', pp. 152–5.

31. Men completing sentences of between 3 and 12 months are not handled by this department but are referred to a welfare depart-

ment, which enquires in greater depth into the manual and technical skills inmates possess, their recreational and educational interests, their home backgrounds and their plans for after-care. In addition the social-work trained staff of the Probation and After Care Service direct their expertise only towards the longer term prisoner. Any formal attention to alcoholics completing short sentences is universally regarded by the Service as a waste of energy and limited resources.

32. See, for example, D. Clemmer, *The Prison Community* (New York: Holt, Rinehart & Winston, 1961); J. Irwin and D. Cressey, 'Thieves, Convicts and the Inmate Culture', *Social Problems*, Fall 1962, pp. 152–5; S. Cohen and L. Taylor, *Psychological Survival: the Experience of Long-Term Imprisonment* (Harmondsworth: Penguin, 1972).

33. Significantly alcoholics never identify themselves as 'cons' in prison or as 'ex-cons' when they leave. Neither do other inmates view them as 'cons'. At all times the men remain dossers.

Chapter 6

1. An account of the rehabilitation network would not be complete without an analysis of the role that mental hospitals and their staffs play in the treatment of skid row alcoholics. However, no such account is included in this report. Statistically the proportion of skid row alcoholics admitted to alcoholism units in mental hospitals is very small. Most hospitals explicitly or implicitly pursue a policy of not admitting alcoholics from skid row. Furthermore, as yet, no detoxification centres operate in Britain. The information gathered during fieldwork on the medical and psychiatric treatment of skid row alcoholics does not warrant a section being written on it.

2. Home Office Working Party Report, *Habitual Drunken Offenders* (London: HMSO, 1971), especially p. 87 (paragraphs 9.3 and 9.4), pp. 135–43; and p. 183 (paragraph 18.2, section 10).

3. Ibid., p. 120.

4. The inclusion of a hospital-based alcoholism unit in the structure of a rehabilitation network does not mean that rehabilitation agencies administer and control the unit's operation, but that some street level contact services find it occasionally necessary to

refer men for medical treatment if they feel the client is suffering from acute withdrawal symptoms or is in need of immediate medical attention. Those hospitals that accept alcoholics from skid row for treatment usually do so on the understanding that the referring agency takes responsibility for the patient on his discharge by ensuring that a bed is available in a residential facility – usually a half-way house.

5. Since many street-level facilities offer hand-outs to homeless men – in particular food and clothing – such facilities are frequently defined by their clientele as primarily institutions to be used in their struggle to survive on skid row. Soup kitchens, day centres and shop-front offices are also viewed as convenient 'off-the-street' day-time retreats. Any rehabilitation services offered thus take on a somewhat peripheral meaning from the viewpoint of many homeless men.

6. Some agencies also use other settings where contact with homeless men is made, especially magistrate's courts and local prisons, where men are interviewed as candidates for residence in a rehabilitation facility.

7. St. Mungo Community Trust, 'Guidelines on the Running of the Community', unpublished mimeo., 1973 p. 4.

8. Home Office Working Party Report, *Habitual Drunken Offenders*, p. 170.

9. For a full account of the work of this agency see T. Cook, *Vagrant Alcoholics* (London: Routledge & Kegan Paul, 1975).

10. The views and opinions of shop-front workers quoted in this section are drawn from personnel manning three separate shop-front offices. I have attempted to present a composite picture of a shop-front office in my use of sources.

11. J. Walley, 'The Kennington Office, 1971', unpublished mimeo, Alcoholics Recovery Project, 1971, p. 2.

12. Ibid., p. 2.

13. S. England and T. Padden, 'Shop-Fronts', *Social Work Today*, vol. 5, no. 6, 13 June 1974, p. 170.

14. F. Finney, 'St. Giles Crypt – Third Year Review', unpublished mimeo, Alcoholics Recovery Project, 1972, p. 3.

15. Ibid., p. 1.

16. Ibid., p. 3.

17. All rehabilitation agencies, however, have short-lists of alcoholics who are blacklisted on the grounds of repeated mis-

behaviour, viewed as disruptive to hostel life.

18. F. Finney, 'St. Giles Crypt – Third Year Review', p. 2.
19. P. Roberts and D. Warke, 'Chapter House Crypt, London Bridge', in *Alcoholics RecoveryProject, Second Annual Report, 1970–71* (London: ARP, 1971) p. 16.
20. E. Rubington, 'The Half-way House for the Alcoholic', *Mental Hygiene*, vol. 51, no. 4, October 1967, p. 557.
21. A common argument advanced by agency personnel states that rehabilitation can only be achieved by offering skid row men different strategies of recovery. Thus the diversity of recovery settings is justified. In fact, in addition to the two operational ideologies described here, two other approaches to homeless men (one economic and the other quasi-religious) exist. The four broad types of residential facilities, then, consist of:

(a) *Communities*: emphasise non-structured group living in which homeless men and workers share the facility. No programmed rehabilitation takes place and relationships are premised on friendship rather than on a client-social worker basis. Established by Christian Action, Simon Community, Cyrenian Community, and St. Mungo's Community.

(b) *Hostels*: stress rehabilitation with a view to eventually returning the skid row alcoholic to the wider society. May or may not have residential social workers. Relationships are officially based on a social worker/client understanding. The original impetus behind these hostels may have come from persons with a religious or psychiatric orientation to the problem, but there is little, if any, evidence of either in the day-to-day running of the establishment. Established by the Alcoholics Recovery Project, West and East London Missions, Helping Hand, and the Royal London Prisoners Aid Society.

(c) *Employment hostels*: underline the need for sheltered employment for men defined officially as 'unemployable'. The stress is on work schemes such as office cleaning, carpentry, and printing. Established by the Peter Bedford Project.

(d) *Crypts and hostels*: there is little emphasis on rehabilitation although residents are encouraged to obtain outside employment. Founded on a quasi-religious basis by the Church Army. Religious services play a part in the crypt and hostel

life but there is no overt religious instruction. Full recuperation, however, is premised on the alcoholic's belief
and commitment to God and Jesus Christ.

22. Alcoholics Recovery Project, *Third Annual Report, 1973*, (London: ARP, 1973) pp. 8–9. Other accounts of Rathcoole appear in
T. Cook, 'The Rathcoole Experiment: The First Three years,
1966–69', Home Office Working Party Report, *Habitual Drunken Offenders*, pp. 229–37; T. Cook and B. Pollak, *In Place of
Skid Row*, (London: NACRO, Reprint no. 4, February 1970);
G. Phillips, 'Rathcoole House', *Social Work Today*, vol. 5, no. 7,
June 1974, pp. 199–200; T. Cook, *Vagrant Alcoholics*.
23. E. Rubington, 'The Half-way House for the Alcoholic'.
24. There has been no detailed and independent survey of the length
of time men stay in Rathcoole and the reasons for their discharge.
Phillips states: 'Whereas in the first two years of running
[Rathcoole] only one in 20 residents stayed longer than six
months, we've seen during the last two years [1972–74] at least a
quarter of the men staying over six months.' G. Phillips,
'Rathcoole House', p. 200.
25. T. Cook, 'Seminar on Rathcoole House', unpublished document, Alcoholics Recovery Project, 1974.
26. J. P. Wisemen, *Stations of the Lost: the Treatment of Skid
Row Alcoholics* (Englewood Cliffs, N. J.: Prentice Hall, (1971)
Chapter 6, pp. 129–66.
27. Rubington has attempted to spell out the transition from the
'dry' to the 'sober' state: 'In the "dry" state, most problem
drinkers re-experience the kinds of personal discomfort for which
only drinking gave relief. Once inner distress becomes unbear-
able, they "break out", and relapse into uncontrolled drinking. In
the "sober" state, the problem drinker experiences as much
personal discomfort, often a great deal more: the difference lies in
acceptance of the proposition that drinking will only add to,
rather than subtract from, the burden of discomfort.' See E.
Rubington, 'Relapse and the Chronic Drunkenness Offender',
Connecticut Review on Alcoholism, The Connecticut Commission
on Alcoholism, vol. 12, no. 3, November 1960, p. 9.
28. An important contribution as to how alcoholics organise their
sober time is provided in J. P. Wiseman, 'Sober Time: the
Neglected Variable in the Recidivism of Alcoholic Persons',

paper presented at the Seond Annual Alcoholism Conference of the National Institute on Alcohol Abuse and Alcoholism, Washington DC, June 1972.

29. For example, see E. Rubington, 'Grady "Breaks Out": a Case Study of an Alcoholic's Relapse', *Social Problems*, no. 11, Spring 1964, pp. 372–80.

30. Often residents do not return once drinking recommences, except to collect their personal belongings or outstanding welfare payments.

31. The classic statement on the meaning of total institutions is to be found in E. Goffman, 'On the Characteristics of Total Institutions', in *Asylums* (Harmondsworth: Peguin, 1968).

32. One of the functions that a short-stay assessment house or period of hospitalisation fulfils as a tier between the shop-front and Rathcoole as a half-way house is that it reduces the incidence of relapses on or soon after admission to Rathcoole. In other words, the critical first two or three weeks of abstinence are transferred to the hospital or short-stay house. Consequently men admitted to Rathcoole may have behind them a number of weeks of sobriety. But even the very process of referral from one rehabilitation facility to the next can produce in skid row alcoholics crises leading to relapse.

33. Significantly one worker responsible for Rathcoole, engaged in the selection of new residents, pointed out that he prefers to accept men who are known to drink in a drinking school as opposed to being loners on skid row. He explained that loners sometimes tend to isolate themselves in the house, whereas men who drink in a team are more likely to participate collectively in house activities.

34. J. P. Wiseman, 'Sober Time', p. 2.

Chapter 7

1. Home Office Working Party Report, *Habitual Drunken Offenders* (London: HMSO, 1971).

2. Ibid., pp. 192–3.

3. D. J. Pittman and C. W. Gordon, *The Revolving Door: a Study of the Chronic Police Inebriate* (Glencoe: Free Press, 1958).

4. W. K. Jordan, *Philanthropy in England* (London: George Allen & Unwin, 1959) p. 78.

5. J. F. Rooney, 'Societal Forces and the Unattached Male: an Historical Review', in H. M. Bahr (ed.), *Disaffiliated Man: Essays and Bibliography on Skid Row, Vagrancy and Outsiders* (University of Toronto Press, 1970) pp. 28–9.

6. NAB, *Homeless Single Persons* (London: HMSO, 1966).

7. Ibid., p. 1.

8. Ibid., p. 176.

9. H. R. Rollin, *The Mentally Abnormal Offender and the Law* (London: Pergamon, 1969) pp. 118–19.

10. In a detailed study of the Camberwell Reception Centre population Tidmarsh and Wood discovered that, of the men who had previously used the Centre, the mentally ill had spent 1.7 months in a mental hospital and 0.6 months in prison in the 12 months' period prior to being interviewed. Alcoholics, on the other hand, had spent 0.3 months in a mental hospital and 1.5 months in prison. D. Tidmarsh and S. Wood, 'Report on Research at Camberwell Reception Centre', unpublished, Institute of Psychiatry, University of London, 1972, Appendix 1.

11. The voluntary organisations that served on the survey's Advisory Committee were the Church Army, the Consultative Committee for the Homeless Poor in London, the National Council of Social Service, the Salvation Army, the Simon Community Trust, the Standing Conference of Organisations of Social Workers, and the Voluntary Hostels Conference. NAB, *Homeless Single Persons*, p. 2.

12. The Southwark Forum, 'Homelessness and Single People in Southwark' (Camberwell Council on Alcoholism, November 1973) pp. 1–3.

13. The Campaign for the Homeless and Rootless (CHAR), 'The Rights and Needs of Single Homeless People' (London: CHAR, 1973) pp. 10–11.

14. See, in particular, P. Beresford and G. Diamond, 'The Crux of the Problem', *C.C.A. Journal on Alcoholism*, vol. 3, no. 2, October 1973 (Camberwell Council on Alcoholism) pp. 27–32.

15. One possible causal factor that has not been explored in regard to this issue has been the relationship between unemployment figures and the number of men using skid row hostels and other cheap accommodation.

16. For an application of the term moral panic in relation to society's response to social problems see S. Cohen, *Folk Devils and Moral*

Panics: the Creation of Mods and Rockers (London: MacGibbon & Kee, 1972).

17. W. J. Chambliss, 'A Sociological Analysis of the Law of Vagrancy', *Social Problems*, no. 12, Summer 1964, pp. 67–77. This account demonstrates the relationship between vagrancy laws and the social setting in which they emerged between 1349 and 1743, noting a shift in the definition of vagrants and the purpose of the laws.

18. Campaign for the Homeless and Rootless, 'Campaign Charter', pamphlet published in 1973, p. 2 (CHAR's emphasis).

19. This section pays attention to government social policy in relation to single homeless persons deemed to be in need of specialist care and rehabilitation, such as the mentally ill and alcoholic. Government policy has also focused on the housing needs of the single homeless. See, in particular, the Joint Circular, Department of the Environment (18/74) and Department of Health and Social Security (4/74), 'Homelessness' (London: HMSO, 1974).

20. Department of Health and Social Security, London Boroughs Association, Final Report of the Joint Working Party on 'Homelessness in London' (London: DHSS, June 1972, p. 29).

21. See the report by the Campaign for the Homeless and Rootless (CHAR), *Drunken Neglect – the failure to provide alternatives to prison for the homeless alcoholic* (London: CHAR, July 1974).

22. DHSS, 'Homeless Single Persons in Need of Care and Support', Circular 37/72, September 1972, p. 3.

23. Ibid., p. 1.

24. Ibid., p. 4.

25. DHSS, 'Community Services for Alcoholics', Circular 21/73, May 1973.

26. Ibid., p. 6.

27. See DHSS, 'Homeless Single Persons in Need of Care and Support', p. 3 and 'Community Services for Alcoholics', p. 2.

28. D. Matza, 'The Disreputable Poor', in R. Bendix and S. M. Lipset (eds), *Class, Status and Power* (London: Routledge & Kegan Paul, 1953) pp. 289–302.

29. D. Moore, A. W. Simpson and R. Smith, 'Homeless Men in East London', East End Mission, Men's Care Unit, Mimeo, June 1968, p. 5).

30. Formal distinction between the idle and labouring poor goes

back at least to the Elizabethan Poor Law of 1576. See J. Pound, *Poverty and Vagrancy in Tudor England* (London: Longmans, 1971).

31. C. Woodward, 'The Charity Organisation Society and its Place in History – a Review Article', *Social Work*, vol. 18, no. 4, October 1961, p. 14.

32. D. J. Pittman, 'Public Intoxication and the Alcoholic Offender in American Society', in The President's Commission on Law Enforcement and Administration of Justice, *Task Force Report: Drunkenness* (Washington DC: US Government Printing Office, 1967) p. 17. A similar point on the lack of one government department to tackle the problem of single homelessness is made in the NAB Report, *Homeless Single Persons*, p. 176.

33. CHAR, 'Drunken Neglect', p. 5.

34. Ibid., p. 10.

Chapter 8

1. The perspective that has guided this research exercise is formally known as symbolic interaction. For the most lucid and concise exposition of this approach to social phenomena see H. Blumer, *Symbolic Interactionism: Perspective and Method* (Englewood Cliffs, N.J.: Prentice Hall, 1969) in particular his first essay in the volume, entitled 'The Methodological Position of Symbolic Interactionism', pp. 1–60.

2. For an exposition on these concepts see H. Blumer, *Symbolic Interactionism*, and N. Denzin, *The Research Act: a Theoretical Introduction to Sociological Methods* (Chicago: Aldine Publishing Co., 1970).

3. E. Rubington and M. Weinberg in a preface to a section on subcultures in E. Rubington and M. Weinberg (eds), *Deviance: the Interactionist Perspective* (London: Macmillan, 1968) p. 205.

4. A. K. Cohen, 'Delinquent Gangs', in Rubington and Weinberg (eds), *Deviance*, pp. 210–11.

5. The research technique employed throughout this study, of particular value to the study of subcultural organisation, has been that of participant observation. In Chapter 9 I expand on participant observation as part of the research methodology used for obtaining and analysing my research data.

6. A. Brittan, *Meanings and Situations* (London: Routledge & Kegan Paul, 1973) p. 147.
7. Ibid., pp. 152–5.
8. See J. Young, *The Drugtakers: the Social Meaning of Drug Use* (London: Paladin, 1971) chapter 5, especially pp. 95–100.
9. A. K. Cohen, 'The Sociology of the Deviant Act: Anomie Theory and Beyond', *American Sociological Review*, vol. 30, no. 1, 1965, pp. 5–14, quoted in Young, *The Drugtakers*, p. 95.
10. E. M. Schur, *Crimes Without Victims*, Englewood Cliffs, N.J.: Prentice Hall, 1965.
11. Young, *The Drugtakers*, pp. 99–100.
12. H. M. Bahr, *Skid Row: an Introduction to Disaffiliation*, (New York: Oxford University Press, 1973) p. 286.
13. A. Brittan, *Meanings and Situations* p. 156.
14. J. P. Wiseman, *Stations of the Lost: the Treatment of the Skid Row Alcoholics* (Englewood Cliffs, N.J.: Prentice Hall, 1971) pp. 240–1.
15. Young, *The Drugtakers*, p. 89 (my emphasis).
16. Ibid., p. 89.
17. I have not exclusively focused on the everyday life of alcoholics and professionals in interaction at the expense of totally ignoring some of the wider issues that help to shape the problem. Both Chapters 1 and 7 attempt to cover aspects of skid row which go beyond understanding how alcoholics and their guardians each handle their predicament. But, clearly, a full account of the skid row phenomenon would need to explain historical, structural and socio-psychological factors other than those explored in this study. For instance, the following questions need to be answered. (i) What role does the social structure of our society play in generating the values and opportunities that lead to deviant drinking, homelessness and chronic poverty? (ii) What social processes intervene between the social structure and the alcoholic? (iii) What social and structural forces lie behind the creation of (a) vagrancy and drunkenness laws, (b) social policy towards homeless alcoholics, and (c) a class of propertyless, powerless and unemployed men? The perspective of symbolic interactionism lacks the scope to include questions of this order within its framework. See, for example, R. Lichtman, 'Symbolic Interactionism and Social Reality: Some Marxist Queries', *Berkeley Journal of Sociology*, vol. 15, 1970, pp. 75–93, for the

perspective's lack of scope and I. Taylor, P. Walton and J. Young, *The New Criminology* (London: Routledge & Kegan Paul, 1973) for an attempt to formulate a theory of deviance that would allow the type of questions asked above to be answered.
18. H. M. Bahr, *Skid Row*, p. 287.

Chapter 9

1. H. Blumer *Symbolic Interactionism: Perspective and Method* (Englewood Cliffs, N.J.: Prentice Hall, 1969). See note 1, Chapter 8, p. 263.
2. I am indebted to D. Martindale for his interpretation of the intellectual roots of symbolic interactionism in *The Nature and Types of Sociological Theory* (London: Routledge & Kegan Paul, 1961) pp. 299–302 and 339–59.
3. W. I. Thomas and F. Znaniecki, *The Polish Peasant in Europe and America*, 2 vol. edition (New York: Dover Publications, 1958).
4. W. I. Thomas, *The Unadjusted Girl* (Boston: Little Brown, 1923).
5. Thomas, *The Unadjusted Girl*, p. 42, quoted in Martindale, *The Nature and Types of Sociological Theory*, p. 348.
6. Thomas, *Unadjusted Girl*, p. 42, quoted in Martindale, *The Nature and Types of Sociological Theory*, p. 348.
7. Martindale, *The Nature and Types of Sociological Theory*, p. 351.
8. G. H. Mead, *Mind, Self and Society*, edited by C. W. Morris (University of Chicago Press, 1934) p. 154, quoted in Martindale, *The Nature and Types of Sociological Theory*, p. 358.
9. Mead, *Mind, Self and Society*, pp. 260–62, quoted in Martindale, *The Nature and Types of Sociological Theory*, p. 358.
10. H. Blumer, 'The Methodological Position of Symbolic Interactionism', in Blumer, *Symbolic Interactionism*, pp. 2–6.
11. See R. K. Merton, *Social Theory and Social Structure*, revised and enlarged edition (New York: *Free Press*, 1957); and, especially, A. K. Cohen, *Delinquent Boys: the Culture of the Gang* (Chicago: Free Press, 1955) and R. Cloward and L. Ohlin, *Delinquency and Opportunity: a Theory of Delinquent Gangs* (Chicago: Free Press, 1960).
12. H. Becker, *Outsiders: Studies in the Sociology of Deviance* (London: Macmillan, 1963) p. 9.

13. E. Lemert, *Social Pathology* (London: McGraw-Hill, 1951) and *Human Deviance, Social Problems and Social Control*, second edition (Englewood Cliffs, N.J.: Prentice Hall, 1967).
14. S. Cohen, 'Criminology and the Sociology of Deviance in Britain: a recent history and current report', in P. Rock and M. McIntosh (eds), *Deviance and Social Control* (London: Tavistock Publications, 1974).
15. S. Box, 'Review of Matza's *Becoming Deviant*', *Sociology*, vol. 4, 1971, pp. 403–4.
16. See Becker, *Outsiders*, and Lemert, *Social Pathology*.
17. K. Plummer, *Sexual Stigma: an Interactionist Account* (London: Routledge & Kegan Paul, 1975) p. 21.
18. I. Taylor, P. Walton and J. Young, *The New Criminology: for a Social Theory of Deviance* (London: Routledge & Kegan Paul, 1973) p. 172.
19. D. Matza, *Becoming Deviant* (Englewood Cliffs, N.J.: Prentice Hall, 1969).
20. Ibid., p. 15.
21. N. Polsky, 'Research Method, Morality and Criminology' in *Hustlers, Beats and Others* (Harmondsworth: Penguin, 1971) p. 115.
22. Matza, *Becoming Deviant*, p. 26.
23. Plummer, *Sexual Stigma*, pp. 24–5.
24. C. E. Reasons, 'The Politicizing of Crime, the Criminal and the Criminologist', *The Journal of Criminal Law and Criminology*, vol. 64, no. 4, 1973, pp. 471–7.
25. H. Becker, 'Whose Side Are We On?', *Social Problems*, vol. 14, no. 3., 1967, pp. 239–47.
26. H. Blumer, 'Foreword' to S. T. Bruyn, *The Human Perspective in Sociology: the Methodology of Participant Observation* (Englewood Cliffs, N.J.: Prentice Hall, 1966, pp. iii–vii.
27. Bruyn, *The Human Perspective in Sociology*.
28. Blumer, 'Foreword' to Bruyn, *The Human Perspective in Sociology*, p. vi.
29. Bruyn, *The Human Perspective in Sociology*, p. 9.
30. H. Blumer, 'Society as Symbolic Interaction', in A. Rose (ed.), *Human Behaviour and Social Processes: an Interactionist Approach* (Boston: Houghton Mifflin, 1962) p. 188.
31. Bruyn, *The Human Perspective in Sociology*, pp. 13–22.
32. P. Archard, 'The Alcoholic Dosser: Some Problems of Research

for the Participant Observer', unpublished paper delivered to the 10th National Deviancy Conference, York, April 1972.

33. A. Strauss, L. Schatzman, R. Bucher, D. Ehrlich, and M. Sabshin, *Psychiatric Ideologies and Institutions* (New York: Free Press, 1964) quoted in G. J. McCall and J. L. Simmons (eds), *Issues in Participant Observation: a Text and Reader* (London: Addison-Wesley, 1969) p. 25.

34. Polsky, 'Research Method, Morality and Criminology', p. 117.

35. This erroneous imputation as to my purpose in hanging around with skid row alcoholics became apparent within a few days of my commencing full-time fieldwork when an alcoholic requested my assistance in facilitating his admission to a rehabilitation hostel.

36. One of the main complaints directed at social control agents by homeless inebriates is the lack of appreciation they have as to the struggle to survive alcoholics face in view of their addiction, poverty, homelessness, and institutionalisation.

37. A characteristic feature of the skid row culture is the almost total lack of any explanations or justifications offered by skid row alcoholics as to how they came to be on skid row. One's credentials for gaining admission to a drinking school are not in any way based on biographical details in advance of accommodating to the skid row culture, but rather on one's performance on skid row and observance of the sophisticated rules and norms that determine appropriate behaviour on the row. Evidence that I had been accepted into the company of the drinking school was reflected in me being described as 'a good man' by alcoholics who knew of my true research identity but who needed to introduce me to men who were strangers to me. Thus I was able to avoid explaining my research purpose to everyone whom I came into contact with on the row. Further evidence of my incorporation and acceptance into skid row became apparent when I was invited to sleep rough in a derelict house – a skipper – since frequently convenient derelict houses are kept a closely guarded secret, even from other alcoholics, in order to avoid too many men making use of them and thereby drawing the attention of the public and police to the fact that derelict properties are being used as shelters.

38. Polsky, 'Research Method, Morality and Criminology', p. 129. Actually Polsky uses the term 'snowballing' to refer to the

process by which the investigator has his original fieldwork contact introduce him to other members of the deviant culture. Nevertheless, the 'snowballing' concept can also be applied in terms of informants guiding and introducing the investigator to other appropriate research locales and institutions.

39. For a rewarding analysis of the different roles adopted by the participant observer in the field – the complete participant, the participant-as-observer, the observer-as-participant, and the complete observer – see R. L. Gold, 'Roles in Sociological Field Observations', *Social Forces*, no. 36, 1958, pp. 217–23, reprinted in McCall and Simmons (eds), *Issues in Participant Observation*, pp. 30–9.

40. See J. P. Dean, R. L. Eichhorn and L. R. Dean, 'Establishing Field Relations', in J. T. Doby (ed.) *An Introduction to Social Research* (New York: Appleton-Century-Crofts, 1967) pp. 281–3, reprinted in McCall and Simmons (eds), *Issues in Participant Observation*, pp. 68–70.

41. For some of the issues raised in the debate between objective and subjective research, particularly with reference to problems surrounding the validity and reliability of concepts and raw data, see M. Zelditch, 'Some Methodological Problems of Field Studies', *American Journal of Sociology*, vol. 67, 1962, pp. 566–76; G. J. McCall, 'The Problem of Indicators in Participant Observation Research', in McCall and Simmons (eds), *Issues in Participant Observation*, pp. 230–7; H. S. Becker and B. Geer, 'Participant Observation and Interviewing: a Comparison', *Human Organization*, vol. 16, no. 3, 1957, pp. 28–32; M. Trow's 'Comment' on Becker and Geer's paper, *Human Organization*, vol. 16, no. 3, 1957, pp. 33–5; Becker and Geer's 'Rejoinder' to Trow's 'Comment', *Human Organization*, vol. 17, no. 2, 1958, pp. 39–40; and Bruyn, *The Human Perspective in Sociology*, pp. 55–70.

42. A. V. Cicourel, *Method and Measurement in Sociology* (New York: Free Press, 1964) p. 18.

43. Advocates of qualitative research methods employing the perspective of symbolic interactionism stress the importance of monitoring the impact that fieldwork has on the researcher's awareness of his role as investigator. See, for instance, N. Denzin, *The Research Act: a Theoretical Introduction to Sociological Methods* (Chicago: Aldine, 1970); Bruyn, *The Human*

Perspective in Sociology; H. S. Becker, *Sociological Work* (London: Allen Lane, Penguin Press, 1971); B. G. Glaser and A. Strauss, *The Discovery of Grounded Theory: Strategies for Qualitative Research* (London: Weidenfeld & Nicolson, 1967); A. V. Cicourel, *Method and Measurement in Sociology*. These works constitute an important contribution to the relationship between interactionism as a perspective and the methodology of qualitative research in general.

44. Bruyn, *The Human Perspective in Sociology*, p. 15.
45. Ibid., p. 18.
46. Ibid., p. 214.
47. Ibid., p. 217.
48. The fieldwork notes included 159 entries on technical problems encountered while carrying out participant observation among alcoholics on skid row and its satellite institutions, and 23 entries on technical problems in relation to fieldwork among social control agents.
49. For an analysis of role tensions in participant observation see Gold, 'Roles in Sociological Field Observations'.
50. See for instance Chapter 5, note 12, p. 253 above.
51. For a discussion of the problem of "going native" see Gold, 'Roles in Sociological Field Observations', pp. 35–7; S. M. Miller, 'The Participant Observer and "Over-Rapport"', *American Sociological Review*, vol. 17, 1952, pp. 97–9, reprinted in McCall and Simmons (eds), *Issues in Particpant Observation*, pp. 87–9; G. J. McCall, 'Data Quality Control in Participant Observation', in McCall and Simmons (eds), *Issues in Participant Observation*, pp. 132–3.
52. There were two exceptions to this general rule. On the occasion when I was arrested for public drunkenness with a number of alcoholics I did not divulge my research identity to the police authorities. Consequently I was processed through the police station and magistrate's court. Undergoing the process confirmed much of what I had been told by alcoholics about the police and lower courts. It also served the purpose of raising my credibility as a researcher among alcoholics who knew of my research role. The second occasion consisted of presenting myself at an out-patients psychiatric unit as an homeless alcoholic. The central criticism of medically staffed psychiatric units was also confirmed, namely that when it comes to homeless alcoholics

psychiatrists are unable to offer any substantial assistance, merely referring patients to the government Reception Centre, an institution which itself is viewed with scepticism by alcoholics.

53. R. Lichtman, 'Symbolic Interactionism and Social Reality: Some Marxist Queries', *Berkeley Journal of Sociology*, vol. 15, 1970, pp. 75–94.

54. Lichtman, 'Symbolic Interactionism and Social Reality', p. 77.

55. Taylor, Walton, and Young, *The New Criminology*, p. 173.

56. Blumer, *Symbolic Interactionism*, pp. 1–60.

57. Ibid., pp. 59–60.

58. See, for example, L. Goldmann, *The Human Sciences and Philosophy* (London: Cape, 1969) especially Chapter 1, entitled 'Historical Thought and its Object'. It is worth quoting Goldmann at some length on the artificial distinction made between history and sociology: 'Every social fact is a historical fact and vice versa. It follows that history and sociology *study the same phenomena* and that each of them grasps some real aspects of these phenomena; but the image which each discipline gives of them will necessarily be partial and abstract in so far as it is not completed and qualified by the findings of the other . . . It is not, then, a matter of combining the findings of sociology and history but of abandoning all abstract sociology and all abstract history in order to achieve a concrete science of human reality, which can only be a historical sociology or a sociological history' (p. 23 – Goldmann's emphasis).

59. For an analysis of the phenomenological concept of typification see P. Berger and T. Luckmann, *The Social Construction of Reality: a Treatise in the Sociology of Knowledge* (London: Allen Lane, Penguin Press, 1967).

60. Lichtman, 'Symbolic Interactionism and Social Reality' p. 79 (Lichtman's emphasis).

61. Ibid., p. 83.

62. Ibid., p. 89.

63. Blumer, 'Sociological Implications of the Thought of George Herbert Mead' in *Symbolic Interactionism*, pp. 61–77.

64. Ibid., p. 61.

65. Goldmann, *The Human Sciences and Philosophy*, Chapter 3, pp. 85–111.

66. Ibid., p. 92.

67. Taylor, Walton, and Young, *The New Criminology*, p. 143.

68. Goldmann, *The Human Sciences and Philosophy*, pp. 118–19.
69. A. Gouldner has drawn attention to this criticism in relation to one of the foremost proponents of the new deviancy theory – Howard Becker – in his 'The Sociologist as Partisan: Sociology and the Welfare State', in A. Gouldner, *For Sociology: Renewal and Critique in Sociology Today* (Harmondsworth: Penguin, 1973) pp. 27–81.
70. Examples of the work produced within the National Deviancy Conference are to be found in S. Cohen (ed.), *Images of Deviancy*, (Harmondsworth: Penguin, 1971) and I. Taylor and L. Taylor (eds), *Politics and Deviance* (Harmondsworth: Penguin, 1973). See also Cohen, 'Criminology and the Sociology of Deviance in Britain'.
71. See, for example, Taylor, Walton and Young, *The New Criminology*; A. Liazos, 'The Poverty of the Sociology of Deviance: Nuts, Sluts and Perverts', *Social Problems*, vol. 20, 1972, pp. 102–20; S. Spitzer, 'Towards a Marxian Theory of Deviance', *Social Problems*, vol. 22, 1975, pp. 638–51; and all the papers collected in I. Taylor, P. Walton and J. Young (eds), *Critical Criminology* (London: Routledge & Kegan Paul, 1975).
72. P. Hirst, 'Marx and Engels on law, crime and morality'; I. Taylor and P. Walton, 'Radical Deviancy Theory and Marxism: a reply to Paul Q. Hirst's "Marx and Engels on law, crime and morality"'; and P. Hirst, 'Radical Deviancy Theory and Marxism, a reply to Taylor and Walton'; all in Taylor, Walton and Young (eds), *Critical Criminology*.
73. Hirst, 'Marx and Engels on law, crime and morality'.
74. Taylor, Walton and Young, *The New Criminology*, p. 221.
75. I. Taylor, P. Walton and J. Young, 'Critical Criminology in Britain: review and prospects', in Taylor, Walton and Young, *Critical Criminology*.

Bibliography

Alcoholics Recovery Project, *Second Annual Report, 1970–71* (London: ARP, 1971).

Alcoholics Recovery Project, *Third Annual Report, 1973* (London: ARP, 1973).

Allsop, K., *Hard Travelling*, (Harmondsworth: Penguin, 1973).

Anderson, N., *The Hobo: the Sociology of the Homeless Man* (University of Chicago Press, 1923).

Archard, P., 'The Alcoholic Dosser: Some Problems of Research for the Participant Observer', unpublished paper delivered to the 10th National Deviancy Conference, York, April 1972.

Archard, P., 'Bottle Gangs and Drinking Schools: the Social Organisation of Drinking on Skid Row', unpublished paper delivered to the 15th National Deviancy Conference, York, 1973.

Archard, P., 'Sad, Bad or Mad: Society's Confused Response to the Skid Row Alcoholic', in Bailey, R., and Young, J. (eds), *Contemporary Social Problems in Britain* (Farnborough: D. C. Heath, 1973).

Arnold, A., 'Alcoholism in Prison: Pentonville', in Cook, T., Gath, D., and Hensman, C. (eds), *The Drunkenness Offence* (London: Pergamon, 1969).

Bahr, H. M. (ed), *Disaffiliated Man: Essays and Bibliography on Skid Row, Vagrancy and Outsiders* (University of Toronto Press, 1970).

Bahr, H. M., *Skid Row: an Introduction to Disaffiliation* (New York: Oxford University Press, 1973).

Becker, H. S., *Outsiders: Studies in the Sociology of Deviance* (London: Macmillan, 1963).

Becker, H. S., *Sociological Work* (London: Allen Lane, Penguin Press, 1971).

Becker, H. S., 'Whose Side are We On', *Social Problems*, vol. 14, no. 3, 1967.

Becker, H. S., and Geer, B., 'Participant Observation and Interviewing: a Comparison', *Human Organisation*, vol. 16, no. 3, 1957.

Becker, H. S., and Geer, B., 'Rejoinder to Trow's Comments', *Human Organisation*, vol. 7, no. 2, 1958.

Beresford, P., 'Without a Home', *New Society*, no. 564, 26 July 1973.

Beresford, P., and Diamond, G., 'The Crux of the Problem', *Journal on Alcoholism*, Camberwell Council on Alcoholism, vol. 3, no. 2, London, October 1973.

Berger, P., and Luckmann, T., *The Social Construction of Reality: a Treatise in the Sociology of Knowledge* (London: Allen Lane, Penguin Press, 1967).

Bittner, E., 'The Police on Skid Row: a Study of Peace Keeping', *American Sociological Review*, vol. 32, no. 5, 1967.

Box, S., 'Review of Matza's *Becoming Deviant*', *Sociology*, vol. 4, 1971.

Blumer, H., 'Foreword' in Bruyn, S., *The Human Perspective in Sociology: the Methodology of Participant Observation* (Englewood Cliffs, N.J.: Prentice Hall, 1966).

Blumer, H., 'The Methodological Position of Symbolic Interactionism', in Blumer, H., *Symbolic Interactionism: Perspective and Method* (Englewood Cliffs, N.J.: Prentice Hall, 1969).

Blumer, H., 'Society as Symbolic Interaction', in Rose, A. (ed.), *Human Behaviour of Social Processes: an Interactionist Approach* (Boston: Houghton Mifflin, 1962).

Blumer, H., 'Sociological Implications of the Thought of George Herbert Mead', in Blumer, H., *Symbolic Interactionism: Perspective and Method* (Englewood Cliffs, N.J.: Prentice Hall, 1969).

Blumer, H., *Symbolic Interactionism: Perspective and Method* (Englewood Cliffs, N.J.: Prentice Hall, 1969).

Bogue, D. J., *Skid Row in American Cities* (University of Chicago Press, 1963).

Booth, General W., *In Darkest England and the Way Out* (London: Salvation Army, 1890).

Brittan, A., *Meanings and Situations* (London: Routledge & Kegan Paul, 1973).

Bruyn, S. T., *The Human Perspective in Sociology: the Methodology of Participant Observation* (Englewood Cliffs, N. J.: Prentice Hall, 1966).

Campaign for the Homeless and Rootless, *Campaign Charter* (London: CHAR, 1973).

Campaign for the Homeless and Rootless, *Drunken Neglect: the Failure to Provide Alternatives to Prison for the Homeless Alcoholic* (London: CHAR, July 1974).

Campaign for the Homeless and Rootless, *The Rights and Needs of Single Homeless People* (London: CHAR, 1973).

Chambliss, W. J., 'A Sociological Analysis of the Law on Vagrancy', *Social Problems*, vol. 12, Summer 1974.

Cicourel, A. V., *The Social Organisation of Juvenile Justice* (New York: John Wiley, 1968).

Clemmer, D., *The Prison Community* (New York: Holt, Rinehart & Winston, 1961).

Cloward, R., and Ohlin, L., *Delinquency and Opportunity: a Theory of Delinquent Gangs* (Chicago: Free Press, 1960).

Cohen, A. K., *Delinquent Boys: the Culture of the Gang* (Chicago: Free Press, 1955).

Cohen, A. K., 'The Sociology of the Deviant Act: Anomie Theory and Beyond', *American Sociological Review*, vol. 30, no. 1, 1965.

Cohen, S., 'Criminology and the Sociology of Deviance: a recent history and current report', in Rock., P., and McIntosh, M., (eds), *Deviance and Social Control* (London: Tavistock, 1974).

Cohen, S., *Folk Devils and Moral Panics: the Creation of Mods and Rockers* (London: MacGibbon & Kee, 1972).

Cohen, S. (ed.), *Images of Deviance* (Harmondsworth: Penguin, 1971).

Cook, T., 'Seminar on Rathcoole House', unpublished document (London: Alcoholics Recovery Project, 1974).

Cook, T., *Vagrant Alcoholics* (London: Routledge & Kegan Paul, 1975).

Cook, T., and Pollak, B., *In Place of Skid Row* (London: National Association for the Care and Rehabilitation of Offenders, Reprint Report no. 4, February 1970).

Dean, J. P., Eichhorn, R. L., and Dean L. R., 'Establishing Field Relations', in Toby, J. T. (ed.), *An Introduction to Social Research* (New York: Appleton-Century-Crofts, 1967).

Department of Environment and Department of Health and Social Security, *Homelessness*, Joint Circular 18/74 and 4/74 (London: HMSO, 1975).

Department of Health and Social Security, *Community Services for*

Alcoholics, Circular 21/73 (London: HMSO, May 1973).

Department of Health and Social Security, *Homeless Single Persons in Need of Care and Support*, Circular 37/72 (London: HMSO, September 1972).

Department of Health and Social Security, London Boroughs Association, *Final Report on the Joint Working Party on Homelessness in London* (London: DHSS, June 1972).

Denzin, N., *The Research Act: a Theoretical Introduction to Sociological Methods* (Chicago: Aldine Publishing Co., 1970).

Dumont, M. P., 'Tavern Culture, the Sustenance of Homeless Men', *American Journal of Orthopsychiatry*, vol. 37, 1967.

Edwards, G., Hawker, A., Williamson, V., and Hensman, C., 'London's Skid Row', *The Lancet*, January 1966.

England, S. and Padden, T., 'Shop-Fronts', *Social Work Today*, vol. 5, no. 6, 13 June 1974.

Evening Standard, 'Empty Flats – a Draw for Meths Gangs', 1 May 1971.

Finney, F., 'St. Giles Crypt – 3rd Year Review', mimeo (London: Alcoholics Recovery Project, 1972).

Glaser, B. G., and Strauss, A., *The Discovery of Grounded Theory: Strategies for Qualitative Research* (London: Weidenfeld & Nicolson, 1967).

Goffman, E., *Asylums: Essays on the Social Situation of Mental Patients and Other Inmates* (Harmondsworth: Penguin, 1968).

Gold, R. L., 'Roles in Sociological Field Observations', *Social Forces*, no. 36, 1958.

Goldmann, L., *The Human Sciences and Philosophy* (London: Jonathan Cape, 1969).

Gouldner, A., 'The Sociologist as Partisan: Sociology and the Welfare State', in Gouldner, A., *For Sociology: Renewal & Critique in Sociology Today* (Harmondsworth: Penguin, 1973).

Halmos, P., *The Faith of the Counsellors* (London: Constable, 1965).

Harrison, B., *Drink and the Victorians: the Temperance Question in England, 1815–1872* (London: Faber and Faber, 1974).

Henshaw, S. K., *Camp La Guardia: a Voluntary Total Institution for Homeless Men* (New York Bureau of Applied Social Research, Columbia University, 1968).

Hirst, P. 'Marx and Engels on law, crime and morality', in Taylor, I., Walton, P. and Young, J. (eds), *Critical Criminology* (London: Routledge & Kegan Paul, 1975).

Hirst, P., 'Radical Deviancy Theory and Marxism: a reply to Taylor and Walton', in Taylor, I., Walton, P., and Young, J., (eds), *Critical Criminology* (London: Routledge & Kegan Paul, 1975).

Hollister, B. C., 'Alcoholics and Public Drunkenness: the Emerging Retreat from Punishment', *Crime and Delinquency*, 16 July 1970.

Home Office Working Party Report, *Habitual Drunken Offenders* (London: HMSO, 1971).

Irwin, J. and Cressey, D., 'Thieves, Convicts and the Inmate Culture', *Social Problems*, Fall 1962.

Jackson, J. K. and Connor, R., 'The Skid Road Alcoholic', *Quarterly Journal of Studies on Alcohol*, vol. 14, September 1953.

Jones, G. S., *Outcast London* (London: Oxford University Press, 1971).

Jordan, W. K., *Philanthropy in England* (London: George Allen & Unwin, 1959).

Kessel, N., and Walton, H., *Alcoholism* (Harmondsworth: Penguin, 1965).

Lemert, E., *Human Deviance, Social Problems and Social Control* (Englewood Cliffs, N.J.: Prentice Hall, 1967).

Lemert, E., *Social Pathology* (New York: McGraw-Hill, 1951).

Levy, H., *Drink: an Economic and Social Study* (London: Routledge & Kegan Paul, 1951).

Lichtman, R., 'Symbolic Interactionism and Social Reality: Some Marxist Queries', *Berkeley Journal of Sociology*, vol. 15, 1970.

London County Council, 'Report on Crude Spirit Drinking', mimeo, 1965.

London Magistrates' Association, *Annual Report of the London Magistrates' Association, 1971* (London Magistrates' Association, 1971).

McCall, G. J., 'Data Quality Control in Participant Observation', in McCall, G. J., and Simmons, J. L. (eds), *Issues in Participant Observation: a Text and Reader* (London: Addison-Wesley, 1969).

McCall, G. J., 'The Problem of Indicators in Participant Observation Records', in McCall, G. J., and Simmons, J. L. (eds), *Issues in Participant Observation: a Text and Reader* (London: Addison-Wesley, 1969).

McCall, G. J., and Simmons, J. L. (eds), *Issues in Participant Observation: a Text and Reader* (London: Addison-Wesley, 1969).

Magistrates' Association, *The Magistrate* (London: December 1973).

Martindale, D., *The Nature and Types of Sociological Theory* (London: Routledge & Kegan Paul, 1961).

Matza, D., *Becoming Deviant* (Englewood Cliffs, N.J.: Prentice Hall, 1969).

Matza, D., 'The Disreputable Poor', in Bendix, R., and Lipset, S. M. (eds), *Class, Status and Power* (London: Routledge & Kegan Paul, 1953).

Mead, G. H., *Mind, Self and Society*, edited by C. W. Morris (University of Chicago Press, 1934).

Merton, R. K., *Social Theory and Social Structure* (New York: Free Press, 1965).

Miller, S. M., 'The Participant Observer and "Over-Rapport"', *American Sociological Review*, vol. 17, 1972.

Moore, D., Simpson, A. W. and Smith, R., *Homeless Men in East London*, mimeo (London: East End Mission, Men's Care Unit, June 1968).

National Assistance Board, *Homeless Single Persons* (London: HMSO, 1966).

Nimmer, R. T., 'St. Louis Diagnostic and Detoxification Centre: an Experiment in Non-criminal Processing of Public Intoxicants', *Washington University Law Quarterly*, no. 1, 1970.

Nimmer, R. T., *Two Million Unnecessary Arrests: Removing a Social Service Concern from the Criminal Justice System* (Chicago: American Bar Foundation, 1971).

O'Connor, P., *Britain in the Sixties: Vagrancy* (Harmondsworth: Penguin, 1963).

Page, R., *Down Among the Dossers* (London: Dennis Poynter, 1973).

Peterson, W. J. and Maxwell, M. A. 'The Skid Road Wino', *Social Problems*, no. 5, 1958.

Phillimore, P., 'A Dosser's World: a Study of Casual Workers in Spitalfields Market', unpublished MA thesis, University of Edinburgh, 1972.

Phillips, G., 'Rathcoole House', *Social Work Today*, vol. 5, no. 7, June 1974.

Pittman, D. J., 'Public intoxication and the Alcoholic Offender in American Society', in the President's Commission on Law Enforcement and the Administration of Justice, *Task Force Report: Drunkenness* (Washington DC: US Government Printing Office, 1967).

Pittman, D. J., and Wayne Gordon, C., *The Revolving Door: a Study of the Chronic Police Case Inebriate* (Glencoe: Free Press, 1958).

Plummer, K., *Sexual Stigma: an Interactionist Account* (London: Routledge & Kegan Paul, 1975).

Polsky, N., 'Research Method, Morality and Criminology', in *Hustlers, Beats and Others* (Harmondsworth: Penguin, 1971).

Pound, J., *Poverty and Vagrancy in Tudor England* (London: Longmans, 1971).

Reasons, C. E., 'The Politicizing of Crime, the Criminal and the Criminologist', *The Journal of Criminal Law and Criminology*, vol. 64, no. 4, 1973.

Roberts, P., and Warke, D., 'Chapter House Crypt: London Bridge', in *Alcoholics Recovery Project: Second Annual Report, 1970–71* (London: ARP, 1971).

Rollin, H. R., *The Mentally Abnormal Offender and the Law* (London: Pergamon, 1969).

Rooney, J. F., 'Group Processes Among Skid Row Winos', *Quarterly Journal of Studies on Alcohol*, vol. 22, September 1961.

Rubington, E., 'The Bottle Gang', *Quarterly Journal of Studies on Alcohol*, vol. 29, December 1968.

Rubington, E., 'Grady "Breaks out": a Case Study of an Alcoholic's Relapse', in *Social Problems*, no. 11, Spring 1964.

Rubington, E., 'The Half-Way House for the Alcoholic', *Mental Hygiene*, vol. 51, no. 4, October 1967.

Rubington, E., 'Relapse and the Chronic Drunkenness Offender', *Connecticut Review on Alcoholism*, The Connecticut Commission on Alcoholism, vol. 12, no. 2, November 1960.

Rubington, E., and Weinberg, M., (eds), *Deviance: the Interactionist Perspective* (New York: Macmillan, 1968).

Sandford, J., *Down and Out in Britain* (London: Peter Owen, 1971).

Sandford, J., *Edna, the Inebriate Woman* (London: Pan, 1971).

Schur, E. M., *Crimes without Victims* (Englewood Cliffs, N.J.: Prentice Hall, 1965).

South London Press, 'Cesspit of Human Decay Worsens' (reader's letter), 1 June 1973.

South London Press, 'Drinkers Drive Out Old Folk', 13 October 1972.

South London Press, 'Publicans in Protest over Down and Outs', 12 January 1973.

South London Press, '"Tramps in Park" Campaign Begins', 6 October 1973.

Southwark Forum, *Homelessness and Single People in Southwark* (London: Camberwell Council on Alcoholism, November 1973).

Sparks, R. F., *Local Prisons; the Crisis of the English Penal System* (London: Heinemann, 1970).

Spitzer, S., 'Toward a Marxian Theory of Deviance', *Social Problems*, vol. 22, no. 5, 1975.

Spradley, J. P., *You Owe Yourself a Drunk: an Ethnology of Urban Nomads* (Boston: Little Brown, 1970).

St. Mungo Community Trust, 'Guidelines on the Running of the Community', mimeo, London, 1973.

Stedman Jones, G., *Outcast London* (London: Oxford University Press, 1971).

Stinchcombe, A., 'Institutions of Privacy in the Determination of Police Administrative Practice', *American Journal of Sociology*, vol. 69, 1963.

Strauss, A., Schatzman, L., Bucher, R., Ehrlich, D. and Sabshin, M., *Psychiatric Ideologies and Institutions* (New York: Free Press, 1964).

Strauss, R., 'Alcohol and the Homeless Man', *Quarterly Journal of Studies on Alcohol*, vol. 7, December 1946.

Taylor, I., and Taylor, L. (eds), *Politics and Deviance*, (Harmondsworth: Penguin, 1973).

Taylor, I., and Walton, P., 'Radical Deviancy Theory and Marxism: a reply to Paul Hirst's "Marx and Engels on law, crime and morality"', in Taylor I., Walton, P., and Young, J., *Critical Criminology* (London: Routledge & Kegan Paul, 1975).

Taylor, I., Walton, P. and Young, J., *The New Criminology: for a Social Theory of Deviance* (London: Routledge & Kegan Paul, 1973).

Taylor, I., Walton, P. and Young, J., (eds), *Critical Criminology* (London: Routledge & Kegan Paul, 1975).

Taylor, I., Walton, P. and Young, J., 'Critical Criminology in Britain: review and prospects', in Taylor, I., Walton, P. and Young, J., (eds), *Critical Criminology* (London: Routledge & Kegan Paul, 1975).

Thomas, W. I., *The Unadjusted Girl* (Boston: Little Brown, 1923).

Thomas, W. I., and Znaniecki, F., *The Polish Peasant in Europe and America*, 2 vol. edition (New York: Dover Publications, 1958).

Tidmarsh, D. and Wood, S., *Report on Research at Camberwell*

280 Bibliography

Reception Centre, unpublished, Institute of Psychiatry, University of London, 1972.

Titmuss, R. M., *The Gift Relationship* (London: George Allen & Unwin, 1970).

Trow, M., 'Comment', on Becker, H., and Geer, B., 'Participant Observation and Interviewing: a Comparison', *Human Organisation*, vol. 16, no. 3, 1957.

Turner, M., *Forgotten Men* (London: The National Council of Social Service, 1960).

Wallace, S. E., *Skid Row as a Way of Life* (Totowa, N.J.: Bedminster Press, 1958).

Walley, J., 'The Kennington Office, 1971', mimeo (London: Alcoholics Recovery Project, 1971).

Willis, P., 'Popular Music and Youth Cultures in Birmingham', unpublished PhD thesis, University of Birmingham, 1973.

Wiseman, J. P., 'Sober Time: the Neglected Variable in the Recidivism of Alcoholic Persons', paper presented at the 2nd Annual Alcoholism Conference of the National Institute on Alcohol Abuse and Alcoholism, Washington DC, June, 1972.

Wiseman, J. P., *Stations of the Lost: the Treatment of Skid Row Alcoholics* (Englewood Cliffs, N.J.: Prentice Hall, 1971).

Woodward, C., 'The Charity Organisation Society and its place in History – a Review Article' *Social Work*, vol. 18, no. 4, October 1961.

Young, J., *The Drugtakers: the Social Meaning of Drug Use* (London: Paladin, 1971).

Zelditch, M., 'Some Methodological Problems of Field Studies', *American Journal of Sociology*, vol. 67, 1962.

Index